Collectively Yours

Collectively Yours

Tales From The Borderline

by

David Merron

COUNTRY BOOKS

Published by: Country Books
Courtyard Cottage, Little Longstone, Bakewell, Derbyshire DE45 1NN

ISBN 1 898941 30 0

© 1999 David Merron

British Library Cataloguing in Publication Data:
a catalogue record for this book is available from the British Library.

Typesetting and production by:
Dick Richardson, Country Books, Little Longstone, Derbyshire DE45 1NN

Cover design by:
HAHA Graphics, PO Box20648, London NW6 1FG

Printed in England by:
MFP Design & Print, Stretford, Manchester M32 0JT

Acknowledgements

I wish to thank all those who helped to bring this project to fruition, first and foremost to Rob Sved for editing the manuscript and providing invaluable prompts for clarifications, to my son Yaron for the graphic design work, to my wife Ann for her patience, to various members of kibbutz and to friends who encouraged me to bring these stories to print.

The cartoon illustrations are by Shmuel Katz of the kibbutz Artzi and Dan of the kibbutz Meuchad, and are reproduced by permission.

Contents

	page
Foreword	ix
The border	1
Tamar	7
The intellectual peasant	14
Culture	18
No laughter tomorrow	26
The choir	30
The carpet	34
On guard	42
A clash of principles	50
The village pump	65
Shula and the baby	72
Whose hand on the plough?	82
A matter of trust	94
Dining out	103
Come the revolution . . .	113
Visitors and volunteers	124
To Mount Sinai	134
Work and more work	145
Too bright a flame	155
Festivals and holidays	158
High finance	167
Frost on borderline	178
One man's war	184
The one who knew	191
Old enemies	199
Shimshon and the staircase	205
Past and present	216
A friendship	226
Felafel in Gaza	236
Looking back	241
Glossary	245

Note: kh is pronounced like <u>ch</u> in the Scots word loch

Foreword

On a hostile border and surrounded by sand dunes we were building a future, convinced that our small, isolated community embodied the future for all of civilised society.

We were by no means the first to establish a communal settlement, nor were those who founded the first kibbutzim in the twenties. Throughout history, various groups with similar ideals of equality, collective ownership and co-operation had tried. And mostly failed. For us, the kibbutz was not an end in itself. After two thousand years of being divorced from the land, our commune would be part of the rebirth of the Jewish people, farmers on our own land who would also be politically aware and educated. Equally, as socialists, despite the isolation, our kibbutz would be an integral part of the national and worldwide struggle for freedom and social justice. Our personal fulfilment was in the realisation of those ideals, rather than some egoistic navel-watching to 'find oneself'.

In our enthusiasm however, we tended to forget that the kibbutz, like any other society, was made up of ordinary human beings with all their foibles and weaknesses as well as strengths.

Although based on similar principles, each kibbutz was distinct by virtue of its geographical, economic and security situation, but above all through the composition of its members. Our unique mix — the politically intense founder members from war torn Romania, our idealistic group from England and the *Sabras*, pragmatic, native Israelis, created the vibrancy as well as the contradictions which have provided the raw material for these stories.

The fifties and sixties were a critical period for the kibbutzim in Israel. Previously, they had been the darlings of the Jewish community in Palestine, epitomising the return to the soil and the spirit of co-operation, making the desert bloom and manning the borders of the embryo state. Now, for the first time, despite a sneaking regard for its principles and achievements, the kibbutz began to experience antagonism from state institutions, and indifference from the majority of the population. Being mostly left-of-centre, they became the targets of political sniping from the growing right-wing and chauvinist press.

Above all, it was a time when, as a result of all these pressures, there was a weariness from within. Amidst a search for a new function, doubts were surfacing, seriously fraying the ideological fabric of the kibbutz and penetrating every aspect of its specific way of life.

Today, the kibbutz movement still has over two hundred settlements, many with a vibrant economy and tens of thousands of members. But within, it has greatly changed and its future form is far from certain.

Through short story, impression and personal anecdote, COLLECTIVELY YOURS strives to capture the atmosphere and spirit of one young kibbutz during those heady days. It was the autumn of a heroic period, a time when we still felt that we were the future.

The border

Finding us on the map was simple: tucked into a corner where the Gaza border met the sea. The border. Coming out from the dining hall or returning from work we couldn't miss it, the crest of the high sand dunes on the far side of the *wadi Assi*, a broad, dry river-bed of winter floodwater sediments brought from far inland. And however much everyday matters occupied our minds, the border regularly reminded us of its presence. From the very first year.

Hannah was crossing the courtyard when a muffled explosion came from the direction of the wadi. On the far side of the young orange groves, a thin plume of smoke rose into the still, morning air. And hobbling away from the bushes was Avrameleh, the white stallion.

'It's Arieh,' she shouted, running into the kitchens, 'It must be. His horse, Avremeleh. He's limping!' Arieh, the head of the garage was also the security chief in the kibbutz. He'd been setting trip-wire mines for the army along the banks of the wadi. One too many.

Amos sped out in the jeep with Shoshannah, the nurse, but Arieh died on the way back. The first casualty of our border. But not the last.

The border stretched, unmarked, across the sand dunes to the south. We could see neither where it began somewhere east of the coast road, the ancient Via Maris, nor where it ended, as it plunged down the last barren dune into the sea. But everyone on both sides knew it was there and crossed it at their peril. With the border came the vast silence of the barren dunes, the lush green of the wadi — and our own stretch of Mediterranean seashore, to which no one else dared to come. It was some consolation for the constant tension, the recurrent guard duties and occasional ambushes. But it never made up for the permanent anxiety for the safety of the children and the dangers of night work in the fields. Above all, the border separated us from those on the other side, who probably feared us just as much as we feared them, but with whom we would have to share a common future.

Like many others settled after the War of Independence, our kibbutz had been positioned intentionally along the borders of the State. There was no way the army could patrol the hundreds of miles, delineated by the United Nations, that twisted between us and the five surrounding, hostile Arab countries. Our own borderlands started from the far side of the wadi. Dammed by an ancient shoreline ridge of sandstone, the floodwaters had carved a deep narrow gorge out to the sea. And this bottleneck was the convenient strategic crossing point. In both directions.

We rarely ventured across the wadi and never alone or without weapons. Yet the fact that it was "beyond the pale", together with its very desolation, was a constant mystery and a source of temptation. For those of us who were amateur archaeologists, it was hard to resist visiting the small "Tel", an ancient buried settlement known to have been a Roman trading post. The other attraction was a site of Neolithic stone tools scattered over the dunes, bringing new finds of flint arrowheads and scrapers after every sandstorm or winter's rain.

Like the rest of the nearby coastline, the area had once been a fertile plain, dotted with farms and villages between the towns of Ashkelon to the north and Gaza to the south. But it had also been the main highway between the mighty empires of antiquity; Assyrians, Hitites, Persians, Greeks and Romans, all followed this route on their way south to do battle with the Pharaohs of the Nile valley. The devastation of century after century of invading armies had allowed the dunes, thrown up from the sea, to encroach ever further inland, smothering everything beneath fine white sand, often thirty or forty feet deep.

And across these dunes, we looked and tried to imagine life on 'the other side' — the distant water tower outside Gaza and nearer, about two miles away, the mud huts and bushes of Beit Lehiya, a small village nestling in one of the hollows. From the lookout post atop our water tower, we attempted to make out more. But apart from the odd herd of goats and a few lone camels, there seemed to be nothing. Could they see us? Did they wonder who we were, or what we did? Had they ever heard of kibbutz? Did they believe that we wished to live in peace with them?

While by day, we neither saw nor heard anything, by night it all changed. Between Gaza and Beit Lehiya, lay the huge Palestinian refugee camp of Jabaliya. On the shore, at Shaati, there was another and to the east, by Beit Hanun, yet another. In addition there were many desperately poor people in Gaza and the surrounding villages. It was this desperation to feed and clothe their families, that tragically drove some to risk their lives and become infiltrators.

At first, we noticed the odd sack of grain missing from the fields, or bales of hay. Once, they stripped off all the binder twine from recently baled hay. Bunches of bananas were cut down and taken away by camel; the tracks were clearly visible across the wadi, up the dunes and away to the south. We set guards in the fields but caught no one. These were people who knew how to find their way around silently in the dark. We were convinced they had a sixth sense that alerted them to our presence, even from fifty yards away. And we couldn't keep it up. We all had to get up for work the next day!

That was the first stage. The second was more serious. Lengths of aluminium irrigation pipes would vanish overnight from the fields and orchards. And if the pipes were too difficult to move, all the sprinklers would be unscrewed and taken away — sold to merchants in Cyprus, we were told. And all this done without a sound. It was a Tom and Jerry act with the Jerry winning all the time. But unlike the cartoons, it wasn't funny. Having to purchase replacements was making huge holes in our already overstretched budgets.

The army couldn't afford manpower, so they laid trip-wire mines along the banks of the wadi. Every few nights, we would hear an explosion from the south. Next morning, by the wire lay a dead donkey, or bloodstains. Or nothing. The situation became more serious when the Egyptian army decided to use the border as a training ground for its officers. Rumour had it that they had to bring back a trip mine, intact, as proof of their valour and competence. The idea of Egyptian army personnel wandering through our fields at night, a hundred yards from the kibbutz was less than comforting. One group tried to enter the kibbutz after blowing up a fence light post; another actually succeeded, but fled before doing any damage, leaving huge footprints in someone's garden.

But the real tension came after Ahmed Shukheiri started to organise the *Fedayeen*: Palestinian units, in the refugee camps. These specially trained fighters were not out to steal, but to kill. They set mines on the farm tracks. Tractors left out in the fields were blown up, trucks were ambushed on lonely roads and, worst of all, civilian targets within range of the border were indiscriminately attacked. Intense debates raged throughout the whole country as to how to deal with these incursions. Massive reprisal raids were launched into the Gaza strip against Egyptian army bases suspected of aiding the Fedayeen. But the incursions continued.

Night after night, we had to go down to the bank of the wadi to lie in ambush. It strained our manpower to the limits, creating general weariness and lethargy after work. And the ambush itself was no fun either, lying motionless and silent hour after hour, often freezing stiff in the process. Occasionally, there would be a sudden footfall in the dark followed by shouts and challenges, shooting at unseen targets. At other times, we had to dive behind a drift of sand as a hail of bullets came back from the darkness.

For a short while in '56, after the Suez crisis, the border disappeared. We harnessed our mules, "Consumptive" and "Crazy", to the four-wheeled cart and trotted along the hard sand by the seashore, down to the strand at Gaza and up into the town. For the first time, we met our neighbours. We also saw at first hand, the terrible conditions of the refugee camps, which added fuel to the political arguments taking place in the kibbutz. But within a few months, the border was back, this time with a United Nations peacekeeping force. Opposite us, one post was on the seashore and another by Beit Lehiya. For the very first time, vehicles crossed the dunes on a roughly constructed road to the sea.

That winter, as the rainstorms blew in from the sea, we pitied the Scandinavian UN soldiers out there in their tin huts. Occasionally, we took a tractor and brought them a box of oranges and biscuits. And at Passover, we decided to invite them over for the festivities. Officially, they were confined to the Gaza side and forbidden to have contact with Israelis. But when we invited a few to join us for Passover celebrations their commander turned a blind eye and at dusk, four of them made their way to our side of the wadi, where Shimon met them in the jeep.

To this day, I can only conjecture what impression they gained, these four shy, blond Danes, after six months away from home and having been subjected to anti-Israeli propaganda ever since arriving on the border. Suddenly they were in our brightly-lit dining hall: decorations on the walls, tables covered with white cloths and heaped with fruit and cakes for the Seder Night celebrations; the choir, community singing, dancing, the children's mimes — and sitting next to attractive girls. As faithful scions of the Vikings, they took good advantage of the beer and wine and when they rose to go, piled high with tins of food and bottles and fruit for their comrades, we wondered whether they would make it back that night to their outpost on the dunes.

We were glad they had come. After the Israeli collusion with the Anglo-French invasion of Suez, those were difficult political times for Israel. We hoped that, in our small way, we had given those neutral observers a different perspective and in passing, had also fulfilled the age old Passover custom of welcoming all those who are in need.

Not another security alert . . . ?

The cease-fire after Suez never became a real peace. The Palestinian question became even more acute and attacks from across the border were renewed. Once again, those who lived on the other side were unseen and regarded only as enemies. The barbed wire perimeter fence was strengthened, the Uzi sub-machine-gun replaced the rifle on guard duty and the army took over the ambushes in the wadi. The border and its dangers had returned to become a permanent feature of our daily life. And it stayed like that until the Six Day War.

A small marble plaque marks the eucalyptus grove that we planted in memory of Arieh. Shortly after he died, his wife and baby left the kibbutz and we lost contact. Avremeleh, still hobbling, survived into old age. Now, he too has gone. The border though, is still there and now seems permanent.

Tamar

Tamar loved Yeremi. She could have had anyone, but she didn't want anyone. She wanted Yeremi. Yeremi was married, or as good as, sharing a room with Tzipi who loved him fiercely, possessively. And she was not letting him go for anything.

Tamar was tall and slim, with long blonde hair, honey-tan skin and wide grey eyes. She had a brilliant mind too, read widely and spoke a beautiful clipped Hebrew.

Apart from her passion for Yeremi, Tamar seemed the ultimate puritan. She never flirted and blushed when the boys tried to, wincing at their bawdy humour. The "vestal virgin", they called her. She wore her hair in a long plait down the centre of her back. Many of the teenage girls had plaits in those days, but after their army service, they would coil them tight on their heads or adopt more sophisticated hair styles. Not Tamar. She left hers long and loose looking every inch like a young 'Pioneer' presenting red roses to the visiting Party leader.

Tamar worked in the babies' house. She loved babies and had a wonderful way of soothing even the most fractious infant. In the heat of summer when she wore shorts at work, her long sculptured legs attracted lecherous glances from the boys as they came in from the fields. In the evening, she would change into a skirt, always dark blue, always with a neatly folded white handkerchief tucked into its waistband.

As far as anyone knew, she'd never had a boyfriend. Perhaps she was waiting for some modern knight to come galloping across the sand dunes and carry her away to his castle. But it was Yeremi she pined for and Yeremi, with his stocky build, mop of unruly black hair and an infectious grin, seemed completely oblivious to her passion. Nothing ever ruffled Yeremi. The eternal optimist. Everything would be fine; no one need have enemies. A committed Socialist, convinced that understanding and friendship would win over the Arabs to a peaceful co-existence. Just give it time. Time and patience, he would say.

Tzipi was from a family of the early Jewish pioneers, colourful Tolstoyan figures from southern Russia who settled in Palestine at the end of the last century. With wiry bodies and brilliant minds, they survived the backbreaking work in a hostile land as well as the intrigues of the local Turkish pashas. Living rough amongst the peasants, they spoke Arabic and learnt to fight, but never to kill or seriously injure, knowing that it would start a blood feud. In the sultry evenings, they lay with the dusky village girls who later bore hulking, blond babies — but it bothered no one. Eventually they prospered and built large stone houses amidst their orange groves. Now, a hundred years later, they were the nearest thing to an Israeli landed aristocracy.

Born to all that, Tzipi had an iron will, and despite his sharp brain and stubborn personality, Yeremi was like putty in her hands but it never seemed to bother him. He had a lot going on in his own life: head of the dairy herd and an ace on the volleyball court — one thump and the ball was in the far corner, way out of reach of the opposing team. Yet in the room, or the dining hall, he was all Tzipi's as she voiced righteous indignation over this issue or that with a fierce gypsy-like beauty, her black eyes darting fury at any who disagreed.

It was on festive evenings and at parties that Yeremi really came into his own, fingers rippling over the accordion keys or dancing the *horra* with boundless energy. Tamar would dance too, on the far side of the circle where she could see him and discreetly try to catch his eye, her supple body swaying to the rhythm, skirt swinging this way then that and her smooth calves shining in the lamplight.

After an hour, maybe two, the *horra* would run its course to exhaustion. As the less strenuous, couples' dances began, Tamar would withdraw into a corner, watching and listening and thinking and rarely taking part. She would smile, gently refusing offers from all the boys who approached her. Except Yeremi. In full flow, he would suddenly break away from Tzipi or another girl and reach out his hand and abruptly her whole demeanour was transformed. As his strong hands grasped her waist, swinging her round and round, leaning back she would laugh, tiny white teeth gleaming, her plait flowing and spinning and at times unravelling, whilst she held one hand against her skirt lest it indiscreetly fly up and billow out. For those few, brief minutes, Tamar became life itself, face glowing, eyes shining, hands holding loosely round the back of his neck whilst Yeremi, grinning and joking as his feet kicked and spun, seemed completely unaware of her ecstasy. Could anyone be so blind?

Tzipi, sure and confident, would watch from the side, eyes half-closed and observing them both. Yeremi was hers — hers alone and always would be. Then, at some point before the end of the evening, unnoticed, Tamar would glide softly out and back to her room whilst Yeremi continued dancing, or playing the accordion until the end, before walking out into the night with his arm around Tzipi.

Tamar shared a room with Leah, short and dark, a daughter of the ancient religious community of Safed, home of the Kaballah and its mysteries, the two so completely different characters living in complete harmony, their room impeccably tidy and coming up to eat together every evening whilst talking softly over the day's events. Like sisters. Did they ever talk about Yeremi?

Yeremi and Tamar actually met quite frequently. Both were on the members' social committee. Apart from a small amount of petty cash, we received all our material and cultural needs in kind: food, clothing, books, trips to the theatre, furniture. Everything. Since budgets were always tight, it was the task of the members' committee to see that it was shared fairly and equally. One evening, the committee decided that instead of people "borrowing" mugs and cutlery from the kitchen, it was about time that every room had cups and saucers and spoons to make coffee. But it was to be a surprise. Tamar made the calculations and lists, Joe buttered up Reubek, the treasurer, to release the money whilst Yeremi worked out the logistics.

Late one moonless night, the three crept from veranda to veranda, depositing the crockery outside each door, trying not to make a sound and all the while Tamar kept close to Yeremi, talking softly about which room was next as though it were an assignation. And he answering in grunts, matter-of-factly. Could anyone be so insensible and oblivious? Or was it a deliberate defence mechanism?

Around midnight the deed was done. Not wanting to play gooseberry, Joe said goodnight and was about to go when suddenly, silently, out of the darkness, Tzipi materialised, all smiles, congratulating them on their good deed. Tamar smiled back, murmured a hurried goodnight and melted away into the night. Joe was choked.

Yeremi and Tzipi had their own problems and their relationship didn't always run smoothly. Tzipi wanted to leave the kibbutz; Yeremi, a staunch member, would not. One evening, after a furious row which echoed all around the courtyard, Yeremi slammed his door and went to sleep in a spare room in one of the old huts. He'd had enough of being controlled, he confided later to Dudu, his fellow dairyman. Like a shot, Tamar streaked from her room and across the lawn. For two hours they talked, he pouring out his frustrations and she sitting opposite, listening, nodding in sympathy at every sentence, love shining from her eyes and admiration issuing from every pore in her lovely skin.

She waited, hoping, yet not daring to make the first move while he, almost in tears but gradually regaining his self control, thanked her again and again, not understanding that it wasn't thanks she wanted, but love. His love. Then, well after midnight, he said that he was weary and wanted time to think, to be alone and to sleep.

The moon lit her way as Tamar walked slowly back to her room, body aching, mind numb and unable to comprehend. Why? Why didn't he want her to stay the night? To stay forever? With her he would grow, reach his full potential. With her, he would be so free, so happy. She would never domineer him like Tzipi had done. Never. And all that night, Leah heard her sobbing quietly into her pillow.

Tamar rose for work the next morning and went to work red-eyed and saying nothing. Later that day, Yeremi moved back in with Tzipi.

Winter came and with it, the rains. Then one day, Tamar announced that she was leaving. She was devoted to the kibbutz and to its way of life, but now nothing we said could change her mind. At Tu B'shvat, the New Year of the Trees, she planted one last pine sapling in the new grove by the laundry, and left. It was a terrible loss. The babies weren't the only ones crying that day.

Yeremi and Tzipi continued much as before, but the strain told as the arguments became more frequent. That autumn, they decided to separate for a while. It happened to be the time of general elections and Yeremi was sent to canvass for the Party in Jerusalem. Tamar was now a student at the university, studying biology. One free afternoon, Yeremi went to the faculty and there in the department he found her, a few lines around her mouth, the grey eyes a little less sparkling, but still the same slim, intelligent, beautiful Tamar.

They walked and talked through the silent, tree-lined streets of the once wealthy Arab quarter of Talbieh and on into the dusk. Streetlights came on and from the ancient walls of the Old City glowing softly in the darkness, Jordanian sentries peered across the divide. Perhaps then, for the first time, Yeremi felt the tenderness and the romance. At the door to her lodgings they stood and talked, he waiting, she hesitant, her moral scruples preventing any precipitous move. And when they finally said goodnight, Tamar went in. Alone. Yeremi, head bent, strolled back through the empty streets, past the old ramparts now shrouded in darkness.

The elections came and went. Yeremi returned and as though compelled by some magnetic force beyond his control, moved in againwith Tzipi. They married, then had a child, Eynat. But the arguments soon brought them to the brink again. Tzipi blamed it on kibbutz life and said she was stifled. Brought out the old chestnut of wanting to keep the baby in her room instead of the babies' house. Eventually, she announced that she was leaving — to save the marriage, she said. Yeremi went too; he doted on that kid. So we lost them both: Tamar and Yeremi. What they would have only contributed to the kibbutz had they got it together and stayed. But it was not to be.

Yeremi met Tamar just once more. Many years later. She had been to the States and back, and was now a lecturer at the Tel Aviv University. He was a journalist and had come to the campus to research an article. Her study was neat and pristine as he would have expected. The lines on her face were deeper, the hair lighter and coiled tightly on her head, the cheeks slightly plumper, but still, as ever, Tamar.

'You know, Yeremi,' she said after a while, 'It was only much later that I heard that you were alone — that you had broken up, that time you came to Jerusalem.' Yeremi sat back, eyes wide, hands trembling.

'You . . You didn't know?'

'No,' she said, 'and you didn't tell me.' Yeremi's face flushed deep red. He lowered his hands.

'But everyone knew, Tamar. I thought everyone ...' They sat for a full minute, silent, looking at each other across the polished teak desk.

'No,' said Tamar, almost inaudible, 'I didn't know, Yeremi. Anyway,' she said, sitting up. 'How's Eynat?'

'Oh, fine. She's fine.'

Tamar stood up and held out her hand.

'Nice of you to come, Yeremi. Look after yourself.'

'You too.' He took her hand and held it, until she drew it away, 'See you again sometime?'

'Maybe.' Tamar shrugged, 'I'm taking a sabbatical at the University of California. Might extend to a three year post.' Yeremi stood up, his eyes smarting.

'Tamar. It . . I .' Her face was set, unmoving, 'Shalom, Tamar. I wish you all the best.'

'You too. Shalom Yeremi.'

At the door Yeremi turned, raised his hand and tried to smile, then walked away, his feet dragging on the marble tiles. Tamar watched him go, then sat down and buried her head in her arms on the desk.

The intellectual peasant

It was the morning break and we were talking about work —
much easier. Long rows of banana palms marched away like
gigantic leeks to merge into the shadows. Huge green leaves hung
listless in the damp heat. We leaned back against the smooth, silky
trunks, shirts sodden, muscles aching from humping twenty and
thirty kilo bunches of bananas to the trailers. And drawing breath,
we continued our endless discussions about principles, ideals,
politics and the frailties of human nature. This time it was about
the boring, repetitive, manual labour that agriculture entailed.

In the espresso bars of London we'd talked revolution and
ranted on about the liberating value of physical work, even
though most of us hadn't wielded anything heavier than a pen or
paintbrush. It would be a glorious ideal to live by the sweat of
one's brow, enjoying the fruits of our own two hands without
exploiting others. Most importantly, we wished to abolish the
artificial division between mental and physical labour.

When we came out to the kibbutz, we continued to argue and
discuss late into the nights as we had always done. But rising at

five each morning made those nights end earlier and earlier. Now sheer fatigue had blunted our enthusiasm and in the blistering heat of the fields and orchards, this ideal of manual labour was fast evaporating. Day after day the baking sun tested our commitment. There were mornings when we prayed for rain so that the fields would be too muddy to work in. And all the time, at the back of our minds, was the knowledge that any of us could chuck it in and return to join the academics and professionals in England. Forget the whole damn thing, just as some soon did.

Now, as we chatted, the first morning breeze began to ruffle the banana leaves, opening up wedges of brilliant blue sky. But not a breath of wind reached us below in the foetid shade, where Eliezar, an old timer was reading his morning paper. He seemed oblivious to the argument, having probably heard it a dozen or more times before, but we continued slugging it out. Could a brain surgeon hoe cabbages and still retain the skill of his fingers? Was Mao right to send professors to work the land for part of the year? And, more relevant, could active and creative minds gain any real satisfaction from repetitive, mind-numbing agricultural work?

'Well?' Geoff turned to him. 'Can they?'

Eliezar folded his newspaper and tucked it into his back pocket.

'Look.' He smiled as he spoke, revealing his gold tooth. 'It's as old as civilisation, this division between manual and mental labour. The literate became the ruling classes, the priesthood, the scribes and the officials. The illiterate laboured in the fields. Nowadays,' he flicked a fly from his face, 'although most people are literate, the old stigmas still apply to the manual labourer.'

Eliezar stood six feet two in his sandals. A long, sharp, ascetic face with a prominent, bony nose. His blue eyes were deep set, a legacy of his childhood in wartime Romania where he almost starved to death. Yet, without formal schooling, he had gained a breadth and depth of knowledge beyond that which any of us had encountered. And quite apart from a fine, literary Hebrew he also read and spoke French and English. And as for music ...

He leaned forward, pointing with one finger.

'For us,' he said, 'physical work has an extra dimension.' He raised his two hands, showing his calloused palms. 'Look. For two thousand years, Jews were not allowed to own land, couldn't be farmers nor join the guilds and become craftsmen. So,' he tapped the side of his head, 'we lived off our wits. Became merchants, moneylenders and traders. Then with emancipation, we entered the free professions and finance and all that, and looked down on manual labour as demeaning.' He smiled. 'Fit only for the *Goyim*. But here,' he continued, 'in our own land. We are the *"Goyim"*. We have to be the workers and farmers; no one else will do it for us.' He waved his hand around the small clearing in the trees. 'Most countries have to educate semi-illiterate peasants and workers. Here, in Israel, it's the opposite. We have to create workers!'

A tractor puttered along the road and, still out of sight, changed gear and began to grind up the track towards us. Eliezar glanced at his watch then back to us.

'And on the kibbutz, we have a unique opportunity to create educated workers — a "working intelligentsia" if you will — where all work is considered equal. So,' he smiled at Yehuda, 'it may not be as glorious as the barricades. But that is our revolution!'

Raising his lanky figure, he picked up an earthenware jar and poured water straight from the spout into his open mouth, Arab felakh style.

'*Davai!*' he grinned as we pulled ourselves up, our aching joints creaking. 'To the barricades!'

Eliezar became our mentor, sustaining those of us who stuck it out and remained. For even after a gruelling day's work, he still had the energy to argue over the supper table on the relative merits of Gounod's or Berlioz's "Faust" and with equal vehemence, fought his corner at the work rota every evening. He would apply as intense an analysis to his irrigation schedule on the new plantation, as to expounding on Engels' definition of Freedom: 'Not, "the recognition of necessity",' he would smile. 'The correct translation should be: "the appreciation of necessity".'

And when working in the fields, he would be halfway down a row thinning onions, before the rest of us had barely started. A real intellectual — and a real peasant.

The tractor pulled up alongside us on the muddy path. Once again we followed the cutters down the rows, humping the huge, green bunches to the trailers. And at the end of the day, having loaded about ten tons of bananas we rode back on the end of the rear trailer, feet dangling over the sides and eyes half-closed with fatigue.

Back in the kibbutz, as we staggered up the hill to the showers, feeling that it was like climbing the north face of the Eiger, Eliezar strode past in ten league boots.

'*Davai*,' he grinned, slapping us on the back, 'It will be easier tomorrow!'

Culture — with a capital 'K'

The play was *Hedda Gabler*. The language as dramatic and gripping as though Ibsen had written in Hebrew. The audience were hushed and spellbound as Hedda took out the pistol and raised it to her head. Watched her finger curl around the trigger, waiting for the shot in a silence so thick you could cut it.

At that very moment, the sound of a muffled explosion came from the no-man's-land by the wadi. Someone had tripped a mine. Hedda heard it too. She paused until the echo had died away, then pulled the trigger. At the enthusiastic applause on the final curtain, we remembered only the play. Border incidents were an everyday occurrence.

Going out to the theatre was popular during the summer when the local amphitheatre was in use. And when, a few days later, a new list went up in the dining hall lobby, it rapidly filled up.

'Got a pen?' Rina called across as we came out of the dining hall. I threw her a *Globus*.

'What's it for?'

'*A View from the Bridge*', she said. 'Arthur Miller.'

'Quick. Put my name down too,' I said, 'and Yona's.' Three nights later, the list came down. There were no more tickets allotted or too many people for the lorry. Usually the first — our GMC truck seemed to have elastic sides.

Cultural activities were mainly of our own making. It was the pre-television era and the cultural committee was always in session: organising festivals, the choir, sing-songs in the dining hall, amateur dramatics, study groups and Israeli folk dancing. We also invited speakers and groups from outside: audiovisual presentations from remote regions or cultures of the world, the odd magician or juggler, a piano recital, visiting ethnic ensembles and so on.

There was also the fortnightly film show with our 18mm projector. The screen was a clean sheet from the clothes' store and the films, hired from a film club in Tel Aviv, were always the obligatory black and white. Technicolour was extra and our budget didn't run to it, but there was always a scramble for the best seats.

With the Israeli film industry being non-existent, all the films came from abroad, which posed the problem of translation. The 35mm films shown in the cinemas in town had Hebrew subtitles, but apparently it wasn't economical to subtitle 18mm films. So together with each film came a transparent acetate roll, on which the gist of the dialogue was written in Hebrew — handwritten.

We used a magic lantern to project the words alongside the film, but to synchronise with the dialogue it had to be operated by hand. So as soon the words were spoken, our translator had to turn the handle, hoping that the sentences could coincide. This meant that he or she had not only to be conversant with the original language, but also understand the finer points of colloquial Hebrew, which was where the fun began.

For British and American films, we had no shortage of English speakers but at the time, only a few of us had the necessary mastery of Hebrew even to read the handwritten translation script quickly enough, let alone decipher it. For eastern European films, many of the Romanians had a smattering of Russian and Slavic

languages and somehow muddled through. Benji, an Egyptian
and Eliezar, were the only ones sufficiently fluent in French but
even they lacked the post-war slang and the nuances of the New
Wave films. And when either was on guard or away, there were
great problems. Italian films relied on Shutzeh who still remembered a little from his wartime imprisonment in Modena.
'Capisco. Capisco,' he would grin, but it was still touch and go
with a Fellini film. And of course no one at all spoke Swedish. We
just felt eternally grateful to Ingmar Bergman for those long, long
silences.

Whenever a scene grew tense or passionate, the translator often
became too engrossed to turn the spool, only to be brought back
into action by furious shouts and whistling. At other times, some
great joke or humorous play of words was completely lost by the
time the translation appeared. And in rapid repartee, the translation of one character often appeared alongside the speech of
another, turning the whole scene into a farce. Occasionally, the
poor translator became completely lost. The Hebrew script would
flash too far forward to try and catch up, then, ending up way
ahead, began to frantically reverse back too far. In a desperate
effort to find the right place, amidst an increasing cacophany of
catcalls and whistles, the script ran back and forth faster and
faster until eventually, someone became sufficiently exasperated
to switch on the lights. The projector would stop, the two were re-
synchronised and, with the lights off again, everyone tried to pick
up where it had left off.

The translator's lot was a thankless one. Having to concentrate
on the dialogue and read the Hebrew at the same time took a lot
of the enjoyment out of the film. So after a while, no one wanted
to translate. And those who were best at it, deliberately came up
late or even hid round the back of the kitchen until the film show
had started and some other less competent soul had been roped
in, often with disastrous results.

Westerns were always popular.

'Hey. We've got an Agricultural Film tonight.' Elisha would
yell across the courtyard, explaining to the sceptics that it was all

A slight technical hitch . . .

about cattle breeding. The English loved the British comedies, infuriating the rest by laughing at the jokes before the translation had been revealed. It didn't help that the translation scriptwriter in Tel Aviv often hadn't understood them either. The one advantage we did have however, was an opportunity to see the pick of world cinema: fantastic films from Russia, Japan and from all over Europe, that never reached the screens in the Hollywood-dominated cinemas of the West.

A night at the theatre, however, proved the most popular, despite the effort required to travel out after a hard day's work. Perhaps it was an urge for a different atmosphere, even an unconscious desire for escapism from the daily routine and stress. Occasionally, we travelled to the Habimah national theatre in Tel Aviv, but usually it was local. The settlements in the area had clubbed together to build an open-air amphitheatre, a large concrete stage with proscenium arch and curtains and tiers of wooden benches rising up a graded earth slope. Dressing rooms were of bare block walls and pretty cramped. But it was ours, all ours and all for a local population of just a couple of thousand people. 'Getting our priorities right!' Issy maintained.

On the appointed day, the truck inevitably arrived late. In addition, it was invariably fully loaded with fodder meal for the dairy, or phosphates for the corn crops. Or even worse, fish meal for the poultry.

'Bloody peasant,' Geoff would mutter alluding to Giora, the driver, who preferred cowboy films. 'Bet he does it on purpose.' Either way, the four people listed on that evening's rota could never unload and wash down the truck in time. So all the men going to the theatre, often already showered and changed, would run to help unload, so that the smell of fish meal or fertiliser emanated from their shirts throughout the performance.

Invariably leaving late, the truck would speed down the track towards the main road. With the high-sided ladders tied across with ropes swaying like palms in a storm, we bumped and swerved around the pot holes, everyone clinging on for dear life to the sides or strap hanging from the ropes. For the men, informality was the word — light shirts and blue zip-up sweaters, some still wearing the ubiquitous carpet slippers in which we slouched about in every evening or, in the height of summer, even barefooted. The women however, took advantage of the night out to wear something special, making the hassle of climbing up and down the improvised steps of orange boxes onto the back of the truck, theatre in itself, especially after the Israeli version of the mini-skirt became the fashion.

The journey however, wasn't always so humorous. On most occasions, at least half a dozen of us carried loaded weapons. It was inevitably dark by the time we'd taken the kids back to the children's houses for supper, before getting away. On top of which, there was always the return journey around midnight. Once we had left the fence lights behind us, we were in infiltrators' territory. There was no knowing when or where the next ambush might be. But generally, we managed to forget our anxieties as we sped along the dark road under a star-studded sky above and the raucous strains of popular songs echoing away behind us into the night.

We had to buy the theatre tickets out of our annual, meagre personal cash allowance, but some of thè boys recently demobbed from the army couldn't kick the habit of sneaking into everything for free. So as soon as the truck stopped on the dusty parking lot, they jumped from the sides to wriggle through holes in the tattered wire netting fence at dark corners. It wasn't much to pay and in vain we argued with them that the amphitheatre was ours — we had helped to build it and the ticket receipts financed its running costs — that they were only stealing from themselves and from ourselves! But they still regarded any authority as "them". It was an attitude that sneaked into our lives more than just at the theatre.

The outing was also a chance to buy ice cream and cans of drink we didn't have on the kibbutz, sold by an enterprising shopkeeper from Ashkelon. Nearly everyone took their seats sucking an ice lolly or choc-ice. But quietly.

During the fifties and early sixties, the kibbutz was still held in high regard throughout the country, the border kibbutzim even more so. Mainstream theatrical companies and musical ensembles willingly trouped up to the mountains of Galilee or down to the Negev desert to perform. The Tel Aviv Chamber Theatre brought us Shakespeare and Ibsen, Miller, Albee and Chekhov. Marvellous productions that sounded as though they had been written in Hebrew and so full-blooded after our experience of the effete pre-fifties London theatre. Under the open skies, Malvolio strutted across the stage in his crossed garters and Sir Andrew Aguecheek pranced and fawned as if the Bard had written in the Holy tongue, a language that conveyed equally the claustrophobic drama of *A Doll's House* or the sniping farce of Molière.

Comedy came with veteran actor Margalit whose *Good Soldier Schweik* had us rolling about in the sand. It was also the era of satirical groups like *'Spring Onions'*. Spawning stars of the future like Topol and Almagor, they lampooned the bourgeoning government bureaucracy, the nouvelle riche in the towns and the growing religious bigotry and protectionism. We also played host to international folk groups like The Weavers and Pete Seeger.

During the performance, we sat transfixed to the hard wooden benches, oblivious to the darkness and the border and to the isolation around. Above, stars shone in the velvet sky, distant fence lights twinkled across the fields and nearby, during dramatic pauses, came the tck-tck-tck of irrigation sprinklers. And even when early rains fell during a September performance we sat through it all, well soaked till the end. We could never remain completely oblivious to where we were, however. In the deathly silence after that kiss in *A View from the Bridge*, which, for most of the audience was their first ever confrontation with overt homosexuality, automatic gunfire sounded nearby. The actors heard it too, making the silence even longer.

Every performance was followed by a furious and hearty final applause. We appreciated the players coming out into the border at night when they could have stayed in Tel Aviv or Haifa. They certainly couldn't have done it for the money. But if the applause was enthusiastic, it was always brief. Within a few minutes, everyone was making a dive for their transport, wanting to load up quickly and be out of the parking lot first, to be quickly home and in bed. For most, it was up again for work in six hours and for the cowmen and early kitchen staff, even less, theatre night out or no.

The track down to the main road was narrow and winding. Going home from the amphitheatre created the only known traffic jam in the area, as a long convoy of trucks, vans, buses, pickups and even mule carts headed down the hill. Behind us, the lights of the amphitheatre went out one by one, leaving the fence lights of nearby kibbutz, Gvar Am, growing steadily fainter until at the main road, the trucks and buses peeled away one by one, each heading for a different destination and swallowed up by the night.

The journey home was usually a more solemn affair, everyone with their own thoughts and emotions aroused by the evening's performance. Or thinking about the following day. Once into our own road, the headlight beams danced along the hedgerows and prickly pear cactus, with the cool night air rushing through the open truck. We gripped the weapons and scanned the dark fields on either side, looking for suspicious movements. And wondering what we would do if there were.

As our own fence lights grew brighter ahead, the day's work weariness began to tell, creating an intense desire to be home and tucked up in bed, hoping that one of the guards, having heard the engine in the night's silence, would already be waiting to open the large steel gates. Praying that we would not lose precious minutes having to hoot and then wait for him to come down.

Tomorrow would be just another ordinary working day. But for tonight, we had been aroused by a fresh experience, stimulated to feel and think in a different way about universal human problems and relationships. To relate them to our own lives and own experience. As Issy always said:

'Culture, mate. With a capital K!' And that felt good.

The kibbutz goes to the theatre

No laughter tomorrow

They found only one piece of Eli: his right hip. The rest lay scattered over the hillside. More remained of Zvikeh and Amitai, but they had gone too. The last thing the platoon heard was the tap-tap of the mattock as the three set an anti-tank mine. It must have missed. Just once. A flash of yellow in the moonless night; the snap and crump. Then the terrible silence.

We leaned on the pick handles and stared at each other across the mounds of sand. No word, no sound, save the hiss of the breeze through the casuarina trees and the pulse of the waves on the shore. Three days ago, the men were all home on leave. There was a party on the lawn outside Yael's room, Zvikeh still in his boots and denims, beret perched on his unruly straw mop. He'd stopped off on the way home to visit his sick mother and hadn't bothered to change. Zvikeh cared about her. Cared about everything: his family, the kibbutz, his country, his ideals, but was always playing the fool. Hiding his concerns under a jester's cap.

And when one of the group had to join a sapper's course, Zvikeh volunteered. Someone had to go.

After the party, at around midnight, everyone crowded into the dining hall. A few notes on Asher's flute, a wheeze from Khagai's accordion and we swept into a wild *horra*: feet stamping, hands gripping shoulders and heads thrown back, shouting and singing. Round and round, faster and faster, Zvikeh's legs dangling as if with a will of their own and Eli's handsome head bobbing above the rest. Eli, the quiet one, tall and olive-skinned with thick black hair. He was most at home on the basketball court and also a wonderful dancer with supple body and strong hands, and the girls watching and waiting. Waiting for him to grab them by the waist and whirl them into a frenzied *krakoviak*.

Amitai didn't go up to dance. He stayed down on the lawn with a small group to continue the argument. Amitai, short and stocky, dark hair falling over his thick lensed glasses and forever splitting dialectically materialistic hairs, carried the world's problems on his shoulders. Out there, on another planet, the world was 'Rocking around the Clock'. Here, hate and resentment spilled across the borders, sowing mines along country roads and shooting up farms. Public anger and frustration mounted, demanding action. The government's response was massive reprisal raids and Amitai was incensed: 'Like taking a sledgehammer to swat mosquitoes,' he snapped. 'There is no military solution. We need to negotiate — to have a policy for peace.'

The next day, they had to go back to camp. Orders had already been posted: a night raid on the Jordanian barracks at Husan. It was before the army had issued rubber-soled boots, and hobnails clattered on the road. The Arab Legionnaires heard, waited and then fought like lions for three hours before it was over. 'Much good it would do,' muttered Amitai. Zvikeh always joked that a sapper had two lives: one he lost when he signed up, the other hung by a thread. At Husan, it snapped and Eli and Amitai went up with him.

By dawn everyone was back at base, the casualties on

stretchers. Eli didn't need one. All that morning we sat around the kibbutz in small groups, nodding and gesturing like Trappist monks. Khaya sat alone on her veranda and wept. Amitai had never requited her love, but in death he would be hers, for ever. That afternoon, five of us trudged up the hill to dig the graves. Silent, white dunes stretched to the horizon. We stood and stared down at the empty sea. A lone gull skimmed along the water's edge. At noon the next day there. would be a military funeral. Parents and families would be coming from town. All three were only sons. Moshe cursed: 'Who the hell needed the head chaplain and his damned prayers? The boys had been blown out of this world and there was nothing beyond. Nothing! No one need tell us how to mourn.' Itzik shrugged and marked out the plots.

Three holes, six feet deep. The chalky sandstone took the pick with a dull thud and yielded just a few grains. After two hours, small heaps of sand rose at each end but the pits had hardly deepened. The sun burned and sweat poured and our stomachs clenched and heaved. An hour later, we paused to rest, squatting on the sand and staring at the open graves. The sun dipped towards the sea and as the breeze freshened, the casuarina needles began to quiver and whisper, like voices from the dead.

A tingling sensation spread from my chest. I looked up. Itzik and Moshe sat opposite. Moshe's lips twitched. So did mine. I looked away as the tingling ran up my neck.

'Have to make that one wider at the bottom,' muttered Itzik. I looked up and our eyes met. His mouth twisted and he looked away. Uri lit a cigarette and tossed the match into one of the pits.

'One big hole, would have made it easier,' he muttered. Motke turned, eyes wide and half smirking.

'What? On top of one another?'

'No. One box he means,' said Moshe, shaking his head. His buck teeth gleamed in the sun. 'Inconsiderate, I call it. All three going together like that.' And all the time, the fluttering in my chest grew stronger.

'Too true. Too true,' muttered Uri, 'I mean, it's not as though poor Eli needs a whole box!' Drawing on his cigarette, he leaned sideways to tap ash into the pit. The cigarette slipped from his fingers. He snatched at it, lost his balance and, as if in slow motion, slid helplessly into the grave.

It was the trigger. One by one we began to grin, then laugh, hesitant at first, but very soon, uncontrollably. Tears streamed down our cheeks. Motke leaned over the side, his hand flapping like a lame wing.

'Hey. Wait your turn mate. It will come. It will come!' Moshe crawled across on all fours, face convulsed with laughter.

'Come out of there, you idiot. Get out! There's enough digging for three, as it is!' Uri struggled to his feet and tried to climb out, his face streaked with yellow finger marks. Itzik stared, then sitting back on his heels, raised one palm and grunted.

'How! Big chief rises from land of ancestors!' It was the final straw. We collapsed and rolled about in the sand, gasping and clutching at our sides, whilst shrieks of laughter rebounded from the casuarinas and echoed away across the dunes. Uri was slumped to the bottom of the grave, burbling like a baby.

I don't remember how long it lasted. The sun began to drop behind the trees. Shadows crept across the holes and we lay still. Then one by one we sat up, dangling our feet in the graves, our sweat-sodden clothes clinging, cold and clammy. To the east, the sky was darkening. Picking up the tools, we set to, thudding picks and scraping shovels. It took until nightfall.

A full moon rose over the Hebron mountains. The breeze died away and the casuarinas sighed their last breaths. We stood back, chests heaving, arms aching: silent. Between the mounds of moonlit sand, the dark graves: eyeless sockets gaping at the night sky. Behind us, the fence lights came on. Below, on the dark sea, fishermen put out from Gaza to spread their nets, boat lanterns lighting a roadway out into the void.

We shouldered the picks and shovels and turned away. Trudging in silent file down to the courtyard. I glanced at Moshe. He closed his eyes for a moment. There would be no laughter tomorrow.

The choir

The choir was something special. So was our conductor, Eldad, a brilliant student at the Tel Aviv Conservatoire. He played umpteen different instruments as well as composing. And despite being only in his mid-twenties, he had that kind of presence that demanded immediate attention the moment he raised his hands. And to conduct our unruly crew, he needed it.

Once a week, around half past eight, we would assemble in the dining hall after supper had been cleared from the tables. Rehearsals couldn't start any earlier; the two principal altos were children's nurses and had to put their charges to sleep. Sometimes we had to contend with the clatter of pots and cutlery from the kitchen. When it dragged on into rehearsal time, we would delegate one of the sopranos to silence them; evening kitchen rota was strictly a male province. At the other end of the dining hall, we often had to compete with vociferous arguments out on the porch over the next day's work roster. That was more difficult to dampen down.

Eventually, at around quarter to nine, with noises off now sufficiently unobtrusive, we could start rehearsals. None of us ever arrived late. If the conductor made the thirty odd miles from his own kibbutz on time, so could everyone else. Eldad hitch-hiked along country roads, all the way from Beth Gubrin. Only one bus served our kibbutz and that was at six in the morning. After that it was a four mile walk from the main road, unless you struck lucky with an army patrol going down to the wadi, or a tractor coming home from our fields at Beit Jirja. And hitching a lift along the main road wasn't easy either. It had once been part of the Cairo to Damascus highway. Now it was a dead end, cut short at Erez on the Gaza border and used only by the local settlements. And as if this wasn't enough, Eldad's kibbutz was beyond Faluja, on an equally dead end road that had once been the highway from Gaza to Hebron and now truncated at the Jordanian border.

There were days when Eldad would leave his own kibbutz shortly after lunch, if that was the only truck going out. Yet every Tuesday, without fail, there he was, snatching a hurried meal in our dining hall before warming up for the rehearsal.

The choir was remarkable through its rare combination of voices. Firstly, there were the Romanians, the girls with smooth, high-pitched, almost operatic, sopranos, but with a slight touch of Slav timbre that gave an extra resonance. Aliza, one of them, was the head cook and when she was in a good mood stirring the porridge before breakfast, you just had to stop and listen. Eliezer and Arieh were tenors, full-throated with more than a touch of the Russian steppes and Ephraim the bass, was well in the Chaliapin class.

Then there were the English: two extremely delicate and precise sopranos who would have sung a superb Gilbert and Sullivan, plus a barber shop quartet of mellow tenor cum baritones, depending upon the key of the piece.

To this heady mix, were added the *Sabras*, the 'natives' who, since they had all been allowed to scream their heads off ever since they'd learned to speak, sang with a somewhat raucous and rasping edge. Eldad had managed to soften it a little and they provided much power and confidence. Five girls made up the contraltos, whilst the boys were divided equally between tenor and bass. Their only drawback was their readiness to break into noisy banter immediately the piece was finished. Eldad, however, being a *Sabra* himself, had a neat way of silencing them with a short, sharp Arabic curse; then everyone was ready again.

We sang an interesting and mixed repertoire, ranging from French chansons through Bach and Lewandowski to Mozart, Black spirituals, Russian folk songs and modern Israeli works. Carefully, he would lead us through a part, then send each voice section away to a different corner of the hall to practise for a while, before calling everyone together again. And when we reassembled, however ragged the first few attempts, in next to no time it was musical magic.

Out on the porch, arguments might still be raging over the work lists. Down below, the compressors in the dairy hummed away into the night, and out there in the blackness, infiltrators might be stealing our irrigation pipes. But for those two hours, there was only music. Again and again working and re-working the phrasing, the balance, the pauses and the breathing. And getting it just how he wanted. How we wanted. For he inspired perfection.

During the rehearsal, every so often, someone had to pass through the dining hall. It might be a night guard to collect hot coffee, a cook to check something in the refrigerators or a dairy-man on evening milking snatching a late supper in the kitchen. All passed by on tiptoe, in silence and reverence. Once, as Shoshanna crept past in the middle of a French chanson, Yeremi dropped to one knee and stretched out his arms and in full throat sang out:

'One glance from your eyes has captured my heart,'
'One smile from your lips has imprisoned my soul . . !'

She smiled, ruffled his hair and carried on. Eldad frowned, but the song never faltered.

Whether on an improvised stage or, as in the Passover celebrations, scattered amongst the audience and interspersed with readings, the choir performed at all our festivals. We always sang in Hebrew but the songs were drawn from many lands, cultures and centuries. What seemed to make the choir so special was its camaraderie and the creation of something new and meaningful from a combination of our individual efforts, a metaphor for the kibbutz itself. It was an expression in song of our kinship, our hopes and our community, like the choirs of the Welsh valleys, the Maoris, the Russian choirs and the Mormons of Utah, each with its own songs, helping to make civilised, a harsh and often brutal world. In our own language and our own land, we felt part of that community of song.

The Sinai War came. We manned the trenches and many of the boys were called back to the army. When it was over, Eldad didn't return. Five members of his kibbutz had been killed in the fighting and with his community in deep shock, he didn't feel able to take the time off. We understood; three of our own had fallen in the reprisal raids shortly before.

The choir managed to get together again, with a new conductor, not quite as talented, but sufficient to keep us in good voice. And we continued what Eldad had started.

One of my fondest memories is of a warm summer's night. I was on guard duty and had to miss the rehearsal. The night was dark and moonless, the searchlight beam sweeping round and back and security lights shining on the perimeter fence. Eucalyptus leaves rustled in the night breeze and above, myriad stars studded a velvet black sky. Crossing the lawn to patrol round the children's houses, I stopped and listened. Through the brightly lit windows of the dining hall came the sound of the choir, practising the haunting tune of a Black Spiritual:

'Noo'ah rikhbi shakeit,'

'Noo'ah na habayta la'avor . . .': 'Swing low, sweet chariot, coming for to carry me home . . ,' the words and the music flowing over the damp grass and between the houses, echoing across the barbed wire into the darkness and onto the silent dunes. Along a borderline of war and hatred, came the sound of sanity and peace.

The carpet

It wasn't that large, nor at all plush — a simple wool weave you might hang on a wall or throw over as a bedspread. But a vital principle was at stake. The carpet was too big and it would have to go back. I knew it. Geoff knew it. So did his wife Leila. But there was no way she was going to let him return it and thought the whole fuss was ridiculous. Equality, she said, was an illusion anyway.

In the kibbutz movement if someone said: 'Oh, she's a dancer,' it denoted single-mindedness and temperament. And as well as being intelligent and forceful, Leila was a dancer. Geoff, in contrast, was laid-back, but he was a man of principles — kibbutz principles. And the principles in question were embodied in the concept of *shituf* — sharing equally.

'From each according to their ability, to each according to their needs,' was the fundamental principle by which a future egalitarian society would operate. It was the one that we tried to apply to our own daily life. And with the first part, the kibbutz had little difficulty. Everyone did give as much of themselves as they could

— in work, organising ability, cultural talent and so on. And every kind of work was considered to be of equal importance.

The two sides of the coin

The second part of the maxim was more problematic. Sure, a future communist society with unlimited resources could satisfy these needs — or so we thought then — but our resources were strictly limited. So, to adhere to the principle we added the proviso: 'to each equally — as far as our economy would allow', and *shituf* was the practical implementation of that principle. We were conscious that throughout the history of communal settlements, private property and the inequalities and materialism that came with it, had inevitably hastened their demise. This feeling of equality was the social cement that bound us together and affected much of our daily life. It helped us to survive through difficult times in the isolation along the border. Without it we felt we would become just another village and gradually decline.

Most needs were in fact provided equally as a matter of routine: housing, food, services, schooling, work clothing, personal cash and so on. But there remained areas which, although minor in comparison, were nevertheless very visible and thus became disproportionately important. For not only was everyone to be treated equally, it had to be demonstrated. But how to distribute equally without it becoming rigid, monochrome and boring? Everyone had equal status but people have different characters and priorities. One person may consider fashionable clothes their principal need, another a small refrigerator in their room, a third might plump for a record player, even if they had to stay in an old hut. So elements of choice had to be maintained and we set a budget for each sector as far as we could define it. Under "Housing", room size and furniture norms were set up for each stage: moving into a new room, getting married, having a baby and so on. For example: so many chairs, a certain standard for a settee, so many feet of bookshelf etc., each within the same financial limits but allowing choice of style and material to avoid creating identikits.

The system had its problems — and its critics — but it was fair. Above all, it was seen to be fair. It also satisfied another principle: to live off our own resources. We may have had little, but what we had was the result of our own labours and efforts and of that we were proud. In the early days of scarcity, the system worked reasonably well but it soon came under pressure, mainly from amongst the Sabras, who usually had parents and family in town.

Most kibbutzim had been founded by people from Europe who were firm idealists and wished to be independent. In addition, the war had since cut them off from their families, very many of whom had perished in the holocaust. Similarly, although settlers from England, USA etc. could still contact their families, we saw material gifts from them as debasing the very principles which had brought us here.

The nucleus of the Sabras was imbued with similar ideals and principles and later became the backbone of the kibbutz. At the time however, their group had a very large periphery of egoistic hangers-on, to whom the kibbutz was just a passing phase. Unfortunately, these often set the tone for the whole group and had no objection to receiving significant presents from outside. On top of this, parental pressure was relentless. Which mother, seeing her son or daughter living in an old hut out in the desert doesn't want to help them? And why shouldn't they give them a larger radio or tape recorder, curtains or a settee. It would help the kibbutz budget and the money saved could be given to others, they rationalised.

But in the early Sixties, as more and more "presents" began to make their appearance, it was obvious that we were approaching a crisis. Either the kibbutz took a stand to uphold its principles, or this trickle of presents would grow into a flood which would sweep away all that was special and cherished to our way of life.

It started with the camera. At the time, we had two old *Leica* cameras which circulated according to kids' birthdays or people's holidays and we managed happily. Film and developing could anyway eat up a large part of our personal cash allowances. Then, one day, Boaz flaunted a new *Pentax* his father brought for his birthday.

'What will you do,' he taunted, 'throw me out?' Which was precisely what some of us wanted to do. But with an ever-present shortage of manpower and the Sabras being a close-knit group, throwing people out wouldn't be easy, even if it were justified. Also, his wife was a children's nurse and much liked. So we tried to use the only form of discipline we had — public opinion. And amongst those most strongly condemning these breaches of principle at the general meetings was Geoff.

It so happened that shortly after the "affair of the camera", Geoff and Leila, having lived together for a year or so, decided to get married. They received the customary budget, and their room soon took on a more homely appearance. Leila however, came from a comfortable family in town. And a few weeks later she came in on the afternoon bus, bringing with her a large carpet, bought with help from her mother. It also happened to be the week following a particularly bitter general meeting about the flood of presents.

By supper time, the tom-toms of our bush telegraph had broadcast the news and Boaz and his band of "pragmatists" were parading outside the dining hall.

'See how the mighty are fallen,' they crowed, sarcastically quoting from the Great Book. 'If mighty cedars fall, what can the moss on the wall say?' Others joined in with more pithy, Arabic idioms and during the weeks that followed, it was as though a dam had burst. New radios suddenly blared from different corners, kids came back to the children's houses in expensive new clothes that grandma had just bought, Ruthie appeared in the dining hall with a new dress "her sister in town" didn't like, and so on. Again the matter came to the general meeting. Again the furious arguments. But Geoff was our Achilles heel. We knew it. He knew it. So did Leila. But she didn't care that much. So something had to be done and, being on the members' social committee, it fell to me.

Geoff and I were of the same generation. We'd been kids in the war, gone to the same grammar school in London and been shocked by the revelations of Belsen and Auschwitz. Politically, having started from the viewpoint of the then 'Statesman & Nation', we'd moved further to the Left, our perceptions sharpened by the street fights with Mosely's fascists in nearby Ridley Road. Many of our friends saw this as purely a political matter and joined the Young Communist League. But in the late '40's, the machinations of the British mandate to prevent the remnants of the holocaust from reaching Palestine, followed by the creation of the State of Israel in 1948, had awakened strong feelings of Jewish identity.

Along with many young Jews, Geoff and I found a social and ideological home in Zionist youth movements, in our case the *Hashomer Hatzair* group, which gave expression to our socialist ideals as well as our Jewish awareness. From then on, enthused by the spirit of the young state and especially of the kibbutzim, we had abandoned our studies and come out to join the kibbutz. Over and over again, under the lazily flapping leaves of the banana plantation, we picked over the bones of what was happening in the kibbutz. We hadn't left England to exchange one acquisitive, materialistic society for another. And he didn't deny the damage that "the carpet" was doing to our credibility. Without personal commitment, we agreed, there was no chance of succeeding in stemming the flood of presents and maintaining equality and self-sufficiency.

For many days however, I procrastinated in tackling him head on again, conscious that it would create a domestic crisis. Did I want to feel responsible for creating strain their marriage, to cause Leila to up and leave? But the issue of the carpet had to be resolved. It was symbolic of what was at stake now. So face it we had to. And soon.

It was turning dusk when I knocked on their door. Leila was sitting on the bed sewing a button on one of Geoff's shirts. Geoff was in his favourite position, leaning back in their one easy chair, an open book on his knees. Leila looked up and smiled.

'Coffee?' she asked, immediately adding, 'because the carpet is staying, whatever you say.' No subtlety there. *Dughri* — straight out, as was the Sabra way. Geoff half-smiled, more in helplessness than in joy and, folding down a page corner, he shut the book.

'I'll put on the *kum-kum*,' he said, going out to the veranda and plugging in the small kettle. I sat on the bed and waited. Perhaps it would be easier over a cup of coffee. Geoff hovered by the door as it began to simmer. I couldn't stand the tension.

'Look, Leila,' I began, 'you know it's not the carpet itself. It's a symbol. A flouting of principles that makes it impossible to confront Boaz and his mob. Soon . . ,' I continued, wanting to get it all out as quickly as possible, 'someone might turn up with a private car. Anything. There'd be nothing left . . ' Leila stopped sewing and leaned forward, her staccato colloquial Hebrew cutting like a scalpel.

'Boaz and the others will do what they like anyway. In the end, everyone will do what they like.' She sat back and finished the button. 'It's human nature. You're fighting a lost battle.' And with a sharp tug of her teeth she cut the cotton. Geoff came in with the coffee. Leila didn't want any. He and I sipped in silence. The cups weren't from the kibbutz budget either.

'*Nu*, Geoff,' I asked. 'What do you think?' It was unfair on him, but the matter had to be thrashed out sooner or later.

'Look,' he began, 'the carpet is hardly bigger than the usual ones. Much worse things are going on.'

'Sure,' I agreed, 'but not by people like us.' I reminded him that the whole matter was coming to the general meeting again that Saturday. 'It's a matter of credibility,' I pressed, 'like fighting with one hand tied behind our backs.' Geoff didn't answer, just nodded, glancing anxiously at Leila who was rubbing cream into her hands. We continued to talk, the discussion circling round and round but never reaching the crunch. I would have to tackle Geoff on his own again. Far too much was at stake.

Yehuda and I took the opportunity next morning at work as we sat for a short break. Yehuda favoured the blunt instrument. In his no-nonsense Yorkshire manner he looked Geoff straight in the eye.

'Look, mate. There comes a time when you have to stand up for your principles. It's easy when there's a choice. Now there isn't. You've got to persuade Leila,' he said, then added quietly, 'or you've just got to return it yourself.' He dug his machete point into the earth. 'If not, we can forget the whole bloody struggle and the kibbutz will go the way of Boaz and his crew. End up like the *Moshav* village down the road: private houses, inequality, hiring outside cheap labour, and all the rest.' Geoff listened, head down, picking at a stone in the brown soil. I added a few words, trying not to sound so harsh, preferring to think that it could somehow be resolved peacefully.

A few days later, Geoff made his decision. He felt as deeply as us about our principles and knew there was no way out. Above all, as he said afterwards, he had to live with himself. Geoff had done it on his own, taken the carpet back to the shop and returned with a smaller one of similar design and colour. The shopkeeper did a lot of business with kibbutzim and had made no problems.

Leila refused to spread it on the floor and threatened to take it back and change it again. She called down fire and brimstone on Geoff and his crazy friends and their stupid principles — on and off for about two hours. Everyone heard. Geoff came up for supper alone, his eyes bloodshot yet smouldering, almost accusing as we met him on the path. The "pragmatists" stared at him with a mixture of incredulity and wonder. But we were proud. We had shown them. We were people of principles!

Leila disappeared to mother and returned two days later, eyes

like slits. In the dining hall, she and Geoff hardly exchanged a
word as they sat together. Probably didn't speak much in their
room either. Bang to conjugal rights and all that, we supposed. But
in that week's general meeting there was an overwhelming vote to
ban outside presents. We had won the day and for a while, it did
indeed seem to work. Boaz and his cronies no longer crowed. We
felt that we were returning to our basic values. The kibbutz way of
life and its principles had received a boost.

It was only a reprieve, however. Despite the vote, as the
months passed, parental pressure and laissez-faire combined to
breach the walls again and again and the flow of "presents" and
private property began to grow. Renewed arguments at the
general meeting were inconclusive. Like water dripping on a
stone, we were gradually being worn down. We constantly had to
fight and argue. All they had to do was sit back and let the parents
do their natural thing. And with this came a painful realisation;
our principles of sharing and equality might be inevitably
doomed to founder on the rock of acquisitive human nature. And
we began to question whether we could ever live our way of life
as we wanted, and for which we had come out here.

We were all prone to a touch of cynicism now and again.
Saintliness and flagellation were not our strong points. But with
Geoff, the cynicism now had a bitter edge. His sacrifice looked to
have been in vain. Leila had never made it a secret that she did
not want to spend the rest of her life on a kibbutz. Geoff did. And
they would have had to resolve that one day. But the carpet had
brought it to a head much sooner. From that day, Geoff's will to
remain, seemed to weaken. A year later, without much argument,
they left.

On guard

It was Shimon's bad luck that Giora was on guard duty, taking his turn on the searchlight in the tiny tin hut perched up on the water tower. Giora the mischief maker. Not malicious, just seeking fun at anyone's expense.

To cover the full circle of the perimeter fence and beyond, the searchlight was turned round to the right until it clunked against a metal stop. Then it had to be turned all the way back round again. Before we put in the stop, Yankeleh had casually turned it round and round one way until, with a bright blue flash and a bang, the cables shorted out and everyone dived into the trenches.

That night, a warm summer night, Giora was turning the light back to the left again, when the beam shone over the huts, illuminating the haystack by the children's farm. He stopped to pick out a shadowy figure. Two in fact: Shimon with Shlomit, Barukh's wife. Barukh was down at evening milking. By noon the next day, the affair was common knowledge. To everyone except Barukh of course, with Giora repeating the finer details to anyone who would listen. But it was the only enlivening moment arising from the tedious two hour guard stint up on the searchlight that anyone could recall. And in the winter, it was absolutely freezing too.

Night guard duty, *shmira*, came round every few months for the men and, at first, for single women too. Mothers usually did their turn as night duty nurse. But as the number of children increased, more women were required as night nurses and the men had to carry on alone. It had the effect of making guard duty less interesting; many relationships took their first tentative steps in the dark no-man's-land between the children's houses and the cowsheds, or around the perimeter fence.

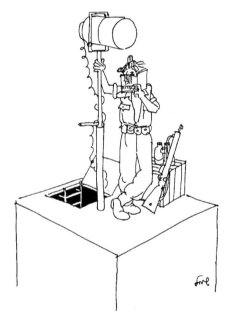

The duty was for a week at a time, in lieu of working during the day. Occasionally, a spell as night guard might come as a blessed relief, but at most times, it was a drag, coming either in the midst of a busy season or upsetting carefully laid plans at work. And whenever it came round, the first night was always the worst.

Ideally, you took a Shabbat day-off beforehand. But as the

pressure of work grew, most of us went straight from a day's work into the first night. The hours before midnight passed quickly — meeting people on the pathways, keeping the late shift company in the milking parlour, or looking in at a late coffee evening in one of the rooms. But after midnight, the time until dawn seemed to hang on a length of elastic, the hours dragging as if each were a day long. You fought to keep your eyes propped open, with every bush or clump of grass beyond the perimeter fence seeming to shimmer or move like an armed intruder. These were the hours to call in on the night nurse for a cup of black coffee in the lobby of the babies' house, eyes tormented by the fluorescent light whilst trying to make some kind of conversation. Never very successfully, since the brain, being kept torturously awake like in some KGB interrogation, was dying for sleep.

For the night duty nurse it was very much the same. The first two nights were an agony, with heavy eyelids and an almost irresistible urge to sleep. But there was no way she could relax, for if she wasn't giving a bottle to one of the infants or changing a baby that had woken up, there would be a mother to call to come and feed her infant. On top of that, she made regular rounds to the other children's houses and, once we had the intercom rigged up, answering calls from children in those houses. The night duty nurse always had more than a full day's work.

During security alerts, even that stimulating quick cup of coffee with the night nurse was denied as patrols were stretched to cover every sector. You peered across the fence, watching where the searchlight beam skidded and bumped over the sand dunes and scrub, imagining *Fedayeen* units drawing a bead on you as you became silhouetted against a porch light or the pathway lamps.

Even on "normal" nights the worst part was always the two hour stretch up on the searchlight. At least in patrolling around the fence or the cowsheds, the scene changed and you could keep moving. But the watchtower had just enough room to stand, or to perch on the high stool, peering along the white beam into the darkness until your eyes ached. Between bouts of searching, whilst sitting in the dark, tiredness gripped the eyes so tightly that it required superhuman efforts to stay awake. Many was the time the relief guard would find the searchlight man on his first two nights, sitting bolt upright on the stool, fast asleep.

The one consoling factor of guard duty was the midnight meal, taken any time between eleven thirty and two in the morning. For whatever the economic situation of the kibbutz and however hard the times, the kitchen staff always cared for the night guards. It was something of a tradition that we had no intention of discouraging. Above all, there were the chips.

In the mass catering of the kibbutz dining hall, fresh crispy chips were a rarity; it took too much labour to have someone frying for the whole two hours of lunch time. But on a small scale, it was a cheap D.I.Y. solution for the guards. So the first twenty minutes of midnight mealtime were spent peeling, cutting and frying gigantic quantities of chips. This left about ten minutes to scoff it all down. And with the chips, came the omelette, made from the cracked or misshapen eggs that could not be sent to market. And with a few thousand laying hens, these were plentiful. Omelettes of five or six eggs were commonplace, some mixing with chunks of ersatz salami, others preferring plain fried eggs — a nest of yellow yolks with the whites bubbling up like lace in the boiling oil. And when all this was washed down with huge mugs of jungle coffee, it was as good as any five star meal.

But with the kibbutz permanently short of labour, one way of saving precious hours was to use the guards for odd jobs that had to be done at night. One week there would be crates of broiler chickens to be loaded up for early market at Rechovot. In another, grapes from the cool room to reach town before the morning heat, or the irrigation pumps would need switching on after midnight. And, prior to the era of the bulk tanker, milk churns had to be loaded for early delivery to Tel Aviv. These tasks were usually performed in the hours just before dawn, when we knew that any infiltrators would already be making their way back over the border. Unfortunately, these were the very hours of the crisis period when body functions and responses were at their lowest, each crate of chickens or full churn feeling like a ton weight and made even more galling by the energy and dedication of the poultry worker or cowman who had slept the night and risen full of beans.

The final, and the most onerous task of the night was that of waking up the early risers. It was eased somewhat in the knowledge that it was almost the time to finish, and by the odd hilarity of finding people sleeping where they were not supposed to be. This early call procedure originated from the time when the kibbutz was too poor to buy every room an alarm clock. In addition, three or four people often slept in the same room and the strident ringing sent the others into paroxysms of anger. So the night guard's duties included gently waking up those who rose before six o'clock. Years later, even though alarm clocks were no longer a luxury and most people had their own rooms, the habit was taking a long time to die out.

Ostensibly, the system was simple. On a sheet of paper hung in the dining room porch, you wrote down your name, with the

4.15 Uri , Rina,
4.20 Eli -next to Yoske
4.30 Barukh, Ruth - new
                room
4.45 Yoske -in Avi's room

5.00 Avi -3rd door old
                huts.
5.15. Dan -knock loudly,
            Moshe, Orna
5.30 Natan - Dudi's old
                room
5.45 Simkha, Leah,
        Gila- Ruth's old room

Early morning call . . .

requested wake-up time alongside. After his midnight meal, the night guard would take the paper and then make the rounds before dawn, tapping on doors and calling out names. So far so good. During the evening however, someone in the dining hall would need a scrap of paper to jot down a telephone number — there was only one telephone in the kibbutz in those days. So they would tear a strip off the bottom of the waking-up sheet. Later, more strips might be removed for odd notes. And on the cramped remnant remaining, others would continue to jot down names and times as they came up to supper. If there was no ball-point pen — that too might have been "borrowed" — they would grab a blunt pencil and write with that, or with a kid's crayon left in their pocket from saying goodnight to the children.

As a result, the final waking up list bore more than a passing resemblance to a Braque drawing. So with the chances of mismatching the names and times rating quite high, the night guard usually sat in the babies' house lobby after his midnight meal, rewriting the entire list in chronological order. Not always succeeding very well.

It didn't end there. As the kibbutz expanded and the distance between the huts and houses increased, so the possibility of waking two people at the same requested time grew slimmer — and impossible when they lived at opposite ends of the kibbutz. So the guard would lump together all those living near one another, within fifteen minutes of their times written on the list.

This meant that some would be woken ten minutes early and others five minutes late — or the other way round. With sleep always at a premium, ten minutes lost of a morning because the night guard had the wrong time, or couldn't manage to get to the far houses and back, was serious business. And on the waking up list the next evening, a red note would warn of dire consequences if the exact time wasn't adhered to. After all, it might be the other way round when night duty changed next week.

Guard duty was also the time of secret liaisons. 'At night', the adage ran, 'all cats are black!' Most kibbutzim were quite puritan in outlook and in such a close community, the only time two "attached" people could legitimately be alone together, was on night duty. Discreet affairs would suddenly erupt between the most unlikely of people and remain unnoticed, until events such as Giora's searchlight, or one night guard discovering that his comrade had spent an inordinate amount of time accompanying the night nurse around the children's houses — or their being seen chatting quietly together the next day, whilst everyone else was out at work.

But most times, guard duty was a routine that just had to be endured for a week, then out of mind for another few months. It involved changing into warm working clothes at nine in the evening, when everyone else was preparing to relax or socialise after supper. It meant missing coffee evenings, the film you desperately wanted to see, or lively sing-songs where it seemed that everyone except you was having a great time. Then the kibbutz would gradually go to bed, leaving you alone with the night and the tension.

But at times, it really was tense. Even quite scary. For without rhyme or reason, suddenly the border would come alive. Shots echoed from the dunes and the ground would tremble as sharp explosions split the silent night. Groups of *Fedayeen* crossed over in the dark, laying mines on the tracks, firing into houses and blowing up wells or tractors left out in the fields. Twice, they blew up perimeter fence posts in the hope of putting out all our fence lights. Once we discovered a set of huge footprints by the outlying huts and a pair of rubber boots went missing, probably taken as proof of having penetrated into the settlement.

In such periods, the guards would be doubled. Sometimes, our machine gun nests were manned all night with ammunition belts loaded, people taking two hour shifts as well as working the next day. By the end of a fortnight, everyone was wandering around like zombies through lack of sleep. If only they had known, Egyptian intelligence in Gaza could have crippled the economies of all the border settlements had they kept it up. Mercifully, it would cease as suddenly as it began and life would return to normal. So would guard duty.

There were however, the odd moments of consolation: a chance to see the myriad stars of a summer's night, moonlit nights when the sand dunes glowed with an atmospheric, ghostly light almost as bright as day and setting the mind at ease because we knew that infiltrators would not risk it. Occasionally, sitting up in the searchlight tower, you could watch the fishing boats putting out from Gaza strand, stringing a row of yellow lamps across the sea, as though times were normal and peace had broken out.

Sometimes, near the end of the week, when your body clock managed to become reorientated, the nights passed as smoothly as a holiday. Then you would rise rested and refreshed just before noon, with warm sunlight and birds chirping outside the window. There was time to enjoy a quiet cup of coffee and biscuits in the shade of the veranda with a feeling of schadenfreud, that everyone else was out working, sweating in the fields. Then after seven days, the guard duty ended and it was back to work again. The body clock strove to reorientate itself to daylight hours and the midnight platefuls of chips and the tranquil late morning coffee receded into the distance. Until the next time.

Taking two or three — and sometimes four — people out of a work force of less than a hundred however, was a huge economic burden which we, along with all the other border kibbutzim, shouldered alone for many years. Eventually, in recognition of our contribution to security along the borders, the government agreed to part-subsidise the night guard duty and two Druze watchmen from a village in Galilee replaced two of our own members each night.

As for the searchlight, well from then on, the few that chanced liaisons in our tight-knit community were more careful. Eventually it was used only in heightened security situations and finally, phased out.

A clash of principles

Jane and John arrived one day out of the blue, on the afternoon bus, the only one at the time. It was January. We had just celebrated *Tu B'Shvat*, the new year of the trees and freshly planted pine and eucalyptus saplings tossed in the squalls of rain that swept in from the sea.

Celebrating the New Year of the Trees . . .

Eliezar and I bumped into them as they crossed the courtyard and when they introduced themselves as Jane and John, his literary mind immediately latched on to the similarity of the title of the previous evening's film show. He'd had to do the translating. It had been 'Jules et Jim', a French, New Wave film, with its haunting tune and tragic conclusion to an 'eternal triangle', as the woman drives herself and her lover into the river.

'Life coincidences,' said Eliezar, after we'd pointed them towards the secretary's office, 'are always stranger than fiction.'

'But not much Gallic passion about those two,' I joked. Jane and John seemed so very English. What neither of us could have dreamed, was that here too were the seeds of a triangle. One of conflicting principles instead of passions and though not as tragic as in the film, to our small community, quite devastating.

John was tall and spindly, as though at any moment, a strong breeze might well waft him over the border to Gaza. He had straight, fair hair and a long, pale face, with brown eyes peering through steel-rimmed spectacles. Dangling sleeves and faded, knee-length khaki shorts added to the stereotype of an ascetic. Jane was shorter, attractive in a bouncy sort of way with curly, fair hair and a ready smile. She had broad, flat hips and rounded legs which seemed well and truly planted on the ground. But the eyes, grey and wistful, betrayed a mind dwelling in higher spheres.

Jane worked with sharp, energetic movements. In the sugar beet, the weeds had no chance. With equal vigour, she sorted potatoes on the harvester or washed dishes, her hair always neatly tied in a red headscarf. John, however, struggled with physical work. God, how he tried — and what his body lacked, willpower compensated. He humped box after box of chicken manure into the banana groves, dragged mud-caked irrigation pipes through the dripping orange trees and even managed to acquire a faint tan as spring came. But there was always an anxiety that we might find him in a crumpled heap under a sack of barley after we had finished unloading a lorry.

At first they seemed just two more of the steady stream of volunteers that passed through. Labour was always short and the two of them were made very welcome. But being neither left wing, nor hippie, nor Jewish, Jane and John didn't fit into any of our pre-defined categories. In fact, they were deeply Christian, in the way that small groups in the West were rejecting existing churches and hierarchies, going back to basics and meeting in each other's houses. It was this spirituality, they said, that had attracted them to the kibbutz.

John and I were discussing religion as we loaded cattle-beet down by the wadi; huge, ten and fifteen kilogram, yellow monster beets. As we stretched our backs for a moment and chatted, instinctively, I scanned the crest of the sand dunes opposite — the border.

'No,' I said, 'we don't believe in God — ours or anyone else's,' adding, 'certainly not in original sin and all that. Only in Man itself.'

'Can't see where Man has demonstrated any innate goodness, without a guiding spirit. Without God.' John said, half-smiling as he adjusted his glasses. I agreed that history hadn't shown us in a very good light. But in a classless, non-materialistic society, Man's goodness would out.

'Anyway,' I added, 'religions have created more than their fair share of persecution and misery.'

'I can't deny that.' John nodded and flicked back his hair. 'But I also can't imagine life without God. He is everywhere. Especially here,' he said, wagging his finger, 'in the way you all live.' He paused, took off his glasses and wiped the sweat from his face. 'That was what made Jane and I come here.' The stuttering of a tractor came from the track beyond the well and we bent down to finish loading the trailer.

Passover came and went. The last rains fell and the sun grew hotter. Jane and John started to learn Hebrew and read books on Jewish history and they joined in our songs and dances. But they kept a lot to themselves. The boys in the garage gave them two months: 'Won't last the course,' grunted Omri. But they did.

Then, one morning, Jane didn't show up for work, which was most unusual. She said she felt sick. Rivka went to see if she wanted anything. Rivka, the wife of Yosef, the general secretary, was a large woman with jet black eyes and heavy features, straight out of Turgenev. It didn't take her long to note that Jane was pregnant and the news soon spread. In the garage, Omri's crew proclaimed the Immaculate Conception — John hadn't the energy to climb the hill after work, let alone . . . But then they would say that.

Jane's pregnancy was viewed seriously. Pregnant and nursing mothers worked less hours and received special food. Every baby was assured of a place in the nursery with cot, clothes, toys, nurse — everything. Kibbutz kids lacked nothing, even in the hardest times. And the times weren't easy. Aliza mooted that she had arrived pregnant. England was still in the pre-swinging fifties and abortions were illegal and costly.

'Why didn't anyone talk to them about contraception?' moaned Dan. No one had thought of it. John seemed a born ascetic. Yet to ask them to leave now was unthinkable.

Jane was soon put on lighter work in the clothing store where Rivka happened to be in charge. And as Jane's time grew near, despite the language difficulties, they became quite close. Imperceptibly, the angles of Eliezar's triangle were being drawn.

Jane and I chatted as I drew my weekly laundry from the store one Friday. She foresaw no problems. They'd intended to stay so the baby would grow up in the kibbutz anyway. It would be a boy, she said. She felt it. They even had a name, Gideon — the code-name of Orde Wingate of Chindits' fame, the pro-Zionist British officer who had helped create Jewish fighting units in Palestine. And, like him, they seemed imbued with a biblical fervour. She looked past me through the open doorway, staring at the mulberry tree in the courtyard, her eyes growing even more wistful.

'You know,' she said softly, as she turned back. 'We want to become full members of the kibbutz. John spoke to Yosef yesterday.'

Our clothing store was the intelligence centre of the kibbutz. A whisper there would be broadcast as quickly as a news item on

Kol Yisrael radio. This news too, spread rapidly. Becoming a member was a deep commitment — accepting our rules and standard of living, handing in all private money, taking full part in all the after hours work rotas and accepting our system of collective education for their child. But first, they had to be accepted as candidates for six months. Some were sceptical, but most of us gave them the benefit of the doubt and we waited for their application to come to the general meeting. A week passed. Two. Nothing. Until one Friday afternoon.

Gerry and Miriam had just joined us for a quiet cup of coffee after work, when Joe burst in, red-faced and hair all over the place.

'Yosef!' he snorted, 'Who the hell does he think he is? Refuses to discuss John and Jane's membership.' He plonked himself down on the bed. 'Bloody dictator!'

'Why not?' spluttered Miriam, half choking on a mouthful of coffee.

'Says that *goyim* can't be members. Just like that. He won't even put it on the agenda for the general meeting,' continued Joe, still fuming. 'Bloody Stalinist!' He glanced at Miriam. 'Here, I could murder a cup of coffee.'

Joe was a member of the secretariat, our highest committee. It met every Friday afternoon and Yosef was *mazkir*, the general secretary. But like all our committees and officers, the mazkir was still an elected, rotating position and subject to our open democracy. A member could bring any subject he wanted to the general meeting and we couldn't believe what Joe was saying. Apart from ignoring our kibbutz democracy, Yosef's stance negated everything we stood for: brotherhood of Man, socialism, equality.

'Who the hell is Yosef to decide anyway?' said Miriam.

'Used to getting his own way too much,' snorted Gerry. 'Too big for his damn boots.' He drained his coffee and stormed out to spread the news.

All that week the arguments raged — in the fields and orchards, at milking time in the dairy, over washing up in the kitchen and in the showers — especially the showers. Everywhere where Jane and John weren't around. Their command of Hebrew was still minimal and they didn't seem to pick up what was going on. The *vatikim*, the old timers from Romania, were less vocal, appearing to know more than the rest of us and when I brought the John Deere into the garage with a flat tyre one day, Meir nudged me.

'You shouldn't push it, you know. Yosef has his reasons.' Yehuda and I belted into him about principles and kibbutz democracy. Meir changed the tyre, lips pursed.

'Some things,' he muttered, 'you can't understand. Unless you've been through them.' He didn't say more and left us no wiser.

The week after Joe's outburst, Yosef again refused to discuss it at the secretariat. So we decided to force the issue by way of a question, at the end of that Saturday's general meeting.

It was a hot, sticky June night but the meeting was packed. Vatikim who hadn't attended for months, suddenly reappeared. Heads leaned in through the opened windows, including those of two of the sentries: 'We're keeping guard on the greatest concentration of people,' grinned Eli. The agenda dragged on: a vacancy on the education committee, increased living allowance for the party worker in town, a new milk cooler for the dairy to which Shlomo objected, maintaining that his new cultivator was more vital. All the time, Giora played the fool, strolling in and out with jugs of water.

'Just keeping things cool,' he joked. Everyone knew what was coming.

It was almost midnight when the main agenda was through. Yosef snapped his notebook closed and stood up to signal the end of the meeting. He was a short, burly figure with curly brown hair and prominent lips and, like most of the Romanians, spoke Hebrew with aspirate 'h's and rolling 'l's. Having made up for a lack of schooling with dogged perseverance, he was now a skilled mechanic who didn't suffer fools lightly, especially when they brought carelessly broken machinery into his workshop. As he turned to go, Gerry rose. Suddenly, the dining room fell silent. Eliezar even put down his crossword.

'Is it true,' asked Gerry calmly, glancing around the hall. 'That Jane and John have asked to become members?' Yosef remained standing.

'Yes. John did speak to me,' he began, his face muscles twitching, 'but I can't take it seriously.' The normally firm, strident voice trembled. 'It's nothing personal. You all know how Rivka is helping Jane.' His wife sitting opposite, fingered the small, red and blue cardigan on the table in front of her. Sarah always knitted throughout the meetings; tonight, she hadn't added a stitch. 'Look,' he continued, 'they can work here. Stay here. Even have their baby here. But they cannot become members of the kibbutz.' He paused again and looked around the hall. 'I repeat. It's nothing personal. They are good people.'

'Sure,' Gerry interjected, 'some of our best friends are Jews.' Yosef ignored him, looked down at his notebook, then carried on.

'For me, the kibbutz is Jewish. Part of the rebirth of the Jewish people in our own land. There could be thousands of Janes and Johns out there. And if they all came, where would it end?' He waved towards Gerry and Miriam and myself. 'Sure. I'm also a socialist. If they are socialists and idealists, let them go and build a kibbutz in England. Not here. Not in my home. And that's all I have to say.'

He sat down and aimlessly flicked over the pages of his notebook. Gerry's face flushed as he jumped up again.

'That's not the point, Yosef. You can think what you like. Even oppose their candidature. But as general secretary, you are duty bound to bring it to the secretariat and to the general meeting.' He glanced around the hall. 'There will be no Stalins or Zhdanovs here,' he continued, alluding to Yosef's habit of fighting his side of an argument as though right was automatically on his side. 'Only the kibbutz as a whole can decide. Not one person. Whoever he is!'

Yosef sat and listened, impassive. Rivka stared at the table, her face drawn and sad as a low hubbub spread around the hall.

Suddenly Meir stood up. Having been elected our military commander, a position of great trust, Meir was listened to carefully. Vital principles were involved, he agreed but if a founder member had such deep feelings over a particular matter, we should respect that and take these feelings into consideration.

'So,' he continued, 'I propose that in this case, the vote to accept Jane and John has to be unanimous.'

'There,' murmured Eliezar, 'speaks the military tactician.'

In the silence that followed, Giora, who had stopped playing the clown, raised his hand, seconding the motion. Uproar followed. On procedure, everyone was a barrack room lawyer. Eliezar returned to his crossword. 'Sweet sounding,' he murmured, 'Four letters. Gimel in the middle.' Gerry exploded.

'Listen. This is serious, Eliezar. Can't you put that damn thing down for a minute?' Eliezar tapped his pencil on the table.

'Calm down, friend. There will be no final decision tonight.'

The arguments around the hall carried on for a further ten minutes before Yosef abruptly snapped his notebook shut for the second time and stood up again. In the expectant silence came the sound of crickets chirruping in the bushes outside.

'Alright,' he began. 'I didn't want to say what I am going to. And it pains me to say it in public. But since so many people don't understand and don't trust me, I will.' And in low tones, almost without inflexion, he began to tell of his wartime childhood in Jassy and the slaughter of his family. 'No. Not by the Nazis,' his voice now firm again, 'but urged on by the fascist Iron Guard, by local people we all knew; people my father traded with. And we could do nothing. Nothing. Because we were treated like foreigners. Outcasts!' He glanced around the hall then leaned forward, 'So when the Red Army liberated us, I swore I would go and live in a Jewish homeland amongst my own people, where, if something like that happened again, I could take up my rifle and defend myself and my family.' Yosef looked around the hall and stared at Gerry. 'Sure, there were decent goyim. Some even risked their lives for Jews. But I never want to be at their mercy again. And if a large number of non-Jews came to live here, that feeling of security would completely disappear. And for me,' he ended, 'that too is a principle I cannot betray. Ever.' And he sat down and placed his hands together over the black notebook.

It was nearly one o'clock. Most of us had to be up for work in five hours, but no one moved. I felt humbled. What had we experienced that could compare? Even Gerry was silent. Beside me, Eliezar was doodling on the margins of his newspaper — triangles. Triangles interlocking and the words at each corner, Jane, John, Yosef. Suddenly, above the low conversation, came Yosef's voice.

'And if the kibbutz presses this to a vote, I shall resign as general secretary.'

Joe sprang to his feet shouting, 'Blackmail!' but the vatikim looked shocked. Rivka sat head down, Aliza was crying and Giora glared daggers at everyone as bedlam broke out with charge and countercharge flying across the hall. Eventually Reubek, making himself heard above the din, proposed an adjournment until the following Saturday. We were exhausted. Slowly, everyone dispersed.

Throughout the week, the arguments raged again. John happened to ask me when their candidature was being discussed. I lied that the secretariat was tied up with next year's budgets. It was, but not that tied up. He just smiled and said they were in no hurry. I felt rotten.

'Yosef's got himself into a right fix,' said Joe as we scooped mugs of cold milk from the refrigerated tank in the dairy. 'Like the little man who climbed to the top of a high tower and threatened to jump if no one took notice. And when they didn't, he wrung his hands, crying: 'How do I get down from here?' But Yosef wasn't that little man. During the week, he announced that he was resigning. The kibbutz could do what it liked, he said. And he wouldn't even attend the next general meeting.

The vatikim grew despondent. Yosef was a leading member of their group. Meir sighed when we met in the garage, with that, 'I told you so', look in his eyes. Eliezar became uncharacteristically monosyllabic at work. He had a kid in the same class as Yosef's youngest. Rivka had told him it wouldn't end there.

Reubek, the treasurer, chaired the next meeting. Speaking in his low, soft drawl, he emphasised the significance of the debate and the vote at the end. As if any of us needed reminding. Like Meir, he probably knew things we didn't. But we were too indignant to care. One man was holding the kibbutz to ransom and we had no intention of giving way.

There was no clowning from Giora this time. The heavy atmosphere could have been cut with a knife. No one wished to speak first. Suddenly Avrumcho, short and skinny with a mop of spiky black hair, stood up. He looked the eternal teenager, but his dark, deep set eyes betrayed a childhood living off his wits in the ruins of Bucharest. Avrumcho hated speaking in public and, strained and impassioned, his words came in short sentences like bursts of automatic gunfire as he pleaded that this should be considered as a special case.

'After all that happened in the war,' he ended, 'hasn't Yosef a right to peace of mind? After all, this is his home.'

When he finished, a low murmur swept up and down the hall. We began to have doubts again and knew that the vote could go either way. We knew that a lot depended on how the Sabras felt and at that moment, Yeremi rose to speak.

'Tireh,' he began. Everything with the Sabras started with a Tireh: look or a Shma: listen. 'It's easy to be swayed by Avrumcho's emotional appeal. Me too. But vital principles are at stake, both ideological, and procedural.' He turned to look along the rows of his friends, his square face taut and concerned. One of their group had been killed in the Sinai campaign and they had only recently been demobbed from the army.

Speaking softly and choosing his words carefully, he told of the arguments about treatment of Egyptian prisoners. How their group did not get carried away in the heat of battle.

'In the end,' he continued, 'it was because we kept to our principles. And here too, we have to decide on the basis of principles: equality and friendship between all peoples, as well as our kibbutz democracy. Otherwise,' he flicked his hand in the air, 'it's all

Ba blaat — just a load of hot air.' With the Sabras, as with us, the idea of one person holding the kibbutz to ransom, really rankled. And as he sat down, my own doubts evaporated. Whatever the outcome with Yosef, we had no alternative. And at half past eleven, Reubek shrugged, rose and put it to the vote: To bring John and Jane's candidature to the next meeting? Or not. Whilst Gerry and Giora counted, Aliza sat stony-faced. Rivka clenched the knitting in her hands, knuckles white. And, for once, the two men agreed; for candidature, there were fifty-eight votes. Twenty-one were against and there were nine abstentions. In spontaneous relief from the tension, we stood and cheered. I caught Yeremi's eye and we smiled across the hall to each other. Then he and Issy hurried out and down to the cowsheds. They'd come up to the meeting immediately after the evening milking and still had to wash down for the dawn shift.

I turned to speak to Eliezar, but he was already walking out of the door, arm around his wife, Anna. He had voted for acceptance. She'd abstained. On the table lay his newspaper, the crossword unfinished.

Outside in the darkness, silent brooding groups walked down the paths. The brightly-lit windows of the deserted dining hall glared across the courtyard, empty and drained. But Gerry, Miriam, Joe and a few others crowded into our room to celebrate. We brewed jungle coffee and finished off our ration of dry biscuits. Jokes flew in a mixture of Hebrew and English. We'd won. Upheld our principles.

'*Khamor gerem*: stubborn ass, old Yosef,' snapped Gerry. And it was nearly two o'clock by the time we broke up. Work in four hours. It didn't bear thinking about.

The bombshell landed during breakfast; Yosef was leaving. Rakhel cut her tomatoes into even smaller segments than usual. Eliezar seemed to stare at the same paragraph in the morning paper for the entire meal. Meir had hinted, but we were still stunned. Giora and Avrumcho sat at the next table with Aliza, her eyes red. They all glared at us and I knew what they were thinking. They were losing one of their family — Jassy, the war, the camps in Cyprus, the Gaza border and all they had come through together. Now Yosef was leaving, pushed out by these ivory tower idealists.

As we hurried out to the orchards, Aliza ran after Eliezar. 'Speak to him,' she pleaded. 'He respects you Eliezar. What will Rivka do? Be a housewife with three children? Speak to him.' Eliezar nodded and put his hand on her shoulder, then carried on.

That night, and for many after, people came and went to Yosef's room. Arguments and crying came through the closed shutters.

'Look, Yosef,' said Gerry as we brought some hoes into the workshop to be sharpened, 'don't be a shmock.' Gerry never minced words. 'You're leaving because the vote went against you. It's pride. Just injured pride and you know it.' Yosef picked up one hoe and pursed his lips.

'You think so?'

'I bloody know so, mate.'

Yosef adjusted his goggles, switched on the grinder and nodded.

'Well. You just carry on thinking that. Okay?' When we came back to collect the hoes, he had gone.

Succoth came. Yosef announced his leaving date: four weeks hence. The first rains fell, heavy drops thundering on the roofs and the kids jumping and splashing through the puddles in their rubber boots. And a week later, Jane gave birth to a boy — smiling round face, wisps of fair hair — a real kibbutznik. And they called him Gideon. We held a *kumsitz* in their room the day she came home from hospital, Jane blooming but John looking awkward, as though embarrassed by what he had done. We drank black malt beer and scoffed a gooey chocolate cake from the kitchen and joked and sang until Jane had to go to the babies' house to feed. The party broke up and as we went out, Jane held up a knitted, red and blue baby jacket. It was from Rivka. Strolling home in the starlight, we passed Yosef's room, dark and with its shutters closed. And we fell silent.

The evenings drew in. Around the orange groves, the last

yellow leaves fell from the Chilean poplar windbreaks. Our refreshing afternoon sea breeze became a biting wind and thick sweaters were taken down from top cupboards. Yosef travelled to town each day to find work and a flat, taking back the Shabbat days off owing to him. Jane made her four-hourly trips to the babies' house with John loping alongside, smiling more and now finding work much easier.

With the kibbutz reconciled to Yosef and Rivka going, everything seemed to be taking a gentle course for the winter when, a week before they were due to leave, Jane announced that she and John had changed their minds. They didn't want to become members and they were not staying. They deeply appreciated everything we had done for them and were truly sorry, but their decision was final.

'Jane didn't like the idea of the baby not sleeping at home,' said John as we unloaded hay bales later that day. It didn't fit. Not liking the baby house was a standard excuse when people wanted to leave the kibbutz and nearly always a cover for the real reason. But what was the real reason?

That same afternoon, Eliezar and Avrumcho pounced on Yosef when he got off the bus. All that evening and far into the night, friends crowded into their room, their voices mingling with the wind hissing through the pine trees. There was no reason for him to go now that Jane and John were leaving. Rivka pleaded too, but Yosef wouldn't change his mind. Yes. He knew he was being stubborn. But the kibbutz hadn't listened to him. Now it was too late. Yes, he was thinking of Rivka and the kids. But they would manage in town. Then he played his trump card.

'And if another John and Jane came in the future and wanted to stay,' he asked. 'What then?' To that, no one had an answer.

The truck left at midday on Tuesday with a double bed, two children's beds, a cot, a wardrobe and a table and four chairs, and two crates of clothing and odds. They were also given a small amount of cash. Not a lot for the years of sweat and tears along the border. Yosef got a job with the Settlement Agency. It came with a small flat in Beer Sheva. For Rivka, it would be like Siberia.

But then Yosef always made the decisions.

That Friday, I bumped into Jane as we collected our weekly laundry from the clothes store. Aliza sat by the ironing board, pouting and glaring as I told Jane how upset we all were. How unexpected. Jane heaved her bundle onto her hip and looked away. They were upset too, she said. Then, turning back, she looked straight at me.

'Why did no one tell us about Yosef and Rivka?' The grey eyes were hard and accusing. Thinking fast, I stepped back and put my laundry on the counter.

'How did you know?' Jane glanced at Aliza. We were speaking in English, but she could understand the drift.

'Oh. Vibrations,' she said, 'odd comments we half understood. And yesterday John asked Issy outright.' She half smiled. 'You know Issy. He can't flannel.'

'Look, Jane,' I said, 'it was a matter of principle. Basic principles of our life here. Nothing to do with you or John personally.' I touched her arm. 'It will be sad if you leave. As though all our struggle was for nothing. Won't you think again?' Jane looked past me, through the open doorway and out across the sand dunes. The wistful look had returned to her eyes.

'We're very sad too,' she said softly, 'but do you honestly think that we could live here, knowing that a whole family had left because of us?' She paused and looked at me again, a pained look. 'Because we were not Jewish?' Then, after a short pause she added, 'I don't know. Perhaps Yosef had a point.'

We went out together and down across the lawn. I tried to convince her to think again, feeling sure that it was she who had made their decision. She shook her head, thanking me and the kibbutz again for all we had done.

'John and I really enjoyed being here,' she added, 'but then, we too have principles.' She hurried away along the path, head down. And I knew she was crying.

We drove them to Haifa in the green Dodge pick-up. It was a Turkish ship: black hull and cream decks with a smoke-grimed, red funnel. All ports to Genoa, then rail to London. I didn't envy them the journey with the baby. Especially not in winter. They waved from the upper deck. Wet eyes all round. Then we had to leave. It was a long drive south and we had to get back before dark.   December was cold, but dry. The first frost had already scorched the edges of the huge banana leaves as we ate breakfast out in the plantation, Eliezar was slicing whole garlic cloves into his ersatz salami sandwiches.

'Makes it taste like real,' he munched, 'instead of just bread on bread.' He waved his knife in the air, half smiling. 'Jules et Jim. In the film, they lost only two.' He swallowed. 'We lost seven.' He took another bite and munched for a few seconds. 'Like I said, life is always larger than fiction.'

'So. A Pyrrhic victory?' I muttered. Eliezar swallowed another mouthful.

'Oh no. Probably had to be. And anyway,' he smiled, 'Carthage has long gone. We are still here.' But there was no sparkle in his eyes as he said it. For the vatikim, his group from Romania, it was a body blow from which they never fully recovered.

The village pump

A wooden shower-sandal crashed against the corrugated iron partition that separated the men's and women's showers. 'Down with bourgeois inhibitions,' shouted Gidon. 'Away with all artificial barriers!' After the sudden silence that followed, came a responding thump from the far side.

'Get knotted, hooligan!' was followed by shrill cries. Laughter rippled through the hot water that splashed over our naked bodies and onto the concrete floor. It was a good-natured hour, washing away the weariness of the day's work, a time to be refreshed and prepare for the evening ahead — a moment in the day when one felt a true feeling of togetherness, of community.

The showers were our village pump. After having each spent the day in widely separated places of work, they were a meeting place where the steam, the sweat and the nakedness created a special atmosphere in which to exchange news and views. On the men's side, someone would tell of Yoske skidding the John Deere into a ditch, another of Itzik not sleeping in his own bed last night. Others dissected the latest decision of this committee or that, or commented on the latest political or economic crisis and, being Israel, there was invariably something on which to comment. Occasionally, heated political arguments would break out under the cascading water, continuing through the towelling and right up to going out into the evening sunlight, inevitably to be renewed the next day.

Across the partition on the women's side, there was equally agitated discussion about committees or fruit-picking. But usually less vociferous and more about people, than things or actions: who had become pregnant — or hadn't — the new kindergarten teacher, or Rivka's row with Miriam. Kibbutz sex equality hadn't changed traditional spheres of interest overnight. Above all, the communal showers provided a forum where matters could be mooted informally, before they came to committee or general meeting — a sounding board on some new proposal or a tentative approach to help organise a festival or nominations for a committee. All relaxed and non-committal.

The thin corrugated sheet between the men's and women's showers was no sound barrier and through it, someone might be arranging a coffee evening, a husband telling his wife that he would collect the kids, someone requesting a neighbour to collect the laundry when they went up to the clothes store. Unusual happenings like accidents, leavings or cock-ups, were immediately picked up through the partition.

'Who did you say?' would come through the corrugated iron. And ears would prick up, to be broadcasted rapidly around the other side: 'hey, did you hear that?'.

It was the same in every kibbutz. Right from its very beginnings the showers were a hallowed institution, an essential part of the egalitarian, communal life. And a complete folklore of "shower gossip" had developed, with its own language and innuendoes and humour. In the revolutionary twenties and thirties, some kibbutzim went even further and established mixed showers, to do away with the very barriers against which Gidon had humorously heaved his wooden shower-sandal. But they were short lived — an egalitarian step too far.

Hot off the press!

Together with the dining hall, the showers were one of the first communal buildings erected. Washing away the sweat and grime of a hot day was the essential prerequisite for relaxation after work. A shower, a cup of coffee and a change of clothes, and everyone felt renewed. Then it was time for socialising, for the kids and for the evening activities. And hot water was the essential ingredient. Even more so in the winter months, when the cold wind from the sea blew through the joints and nail holes in the tin sheets of our simple corrugated iron structure.

Our hot water system was Aharonchik's, the plumber's, baby. A water tank made from an old oil drum on the roof provided pressure; the boiler was a large steel cylinder with a central chimney running through it and heating was by a diesel-oil jet burner, bought from a disused factory in Tel Aviv. The tangle of iron pipework to the showers bore more resemblance to avant-garde sculpture than plumbing, but it worked — usually. And when it didn't, there was trouble.

Avri, the farm manager, knew that it had packed up again as

soon as he saw the small group standing outside the showers one
afternoon. They saw him too, before he could slink away.
   'What's up?' he asked. As if he couldn't guess.
   'No hot water again!' snapped Yoske, adding with a suitable
curse, 'no fuel oil.'
   'So why hasn't someone brought up a drum from below?'
   'We would,' muttered Joe, glaring at him, 'if it hadn't been
allowed to run out. No *Hanukah* miracles here, mate,' he grunted,
alluding to the miracle of the tiny cruse of oil that had burned in
the temple for eight days. Ordering fuel from town, was the job of
Zeev, the storeman. But Avri had moved him to the *falkha* for a
week to help with sowing the winter wheat before the rains came.
And the grey skies over the last few days threatened just that at
any minute. Avri glanced around the accusing faces. It was
November and a bitter wind blew from the sea, penetrating right
through our work clothes. Facing a cold shower was no joke. Nor
would it get rid of grease and grime and chaff. And for those with
kids, greeting them in dirty working clothes couldn't be considered. It was a crisis.
   Joe was furious. This time it was no fuel oil. The week before,
the jet air burner had broken down. Last month, a pipe had burst.
And to cap it all, the old corrugated iron hut, erected six years
before as a "temporary" measure, was being held together by wire
and willpower, whilst the promised permanent building was postponed year after year by more urgent items in the investment
plan. Rightly or wrongly, being the farm manager, Avri knew he
would be blamed.
   Bringing up the regular drum of diesel oil was entrusted to
Abba, a huge, red-faced, white-moustached parent of one of the
Romanian members, a character straight out of Tolstoy. With a
bony horse and small cart, Abba ran essential deliveries around
the kibbutz.
   '*Davai. Davai, Neveileh!*' he would shout at the poor creature in
a mixture of Russian and Yiddish, as it lugged a load of boxes and
barrels up the steep track, '*Davai!*' But he was absolutely reliable
and never failed to replenish the heating oil. But now, the main

storage tank was empty. To make matters worse, just a month previously, when the old burner had packed in, Abba said it needed a new one. Aharonchik, stung by the interference, insisted that he could repair it in the workshop. It only needed a small spare part, he said. The treasurer maintained that he couldn't find it in Tel Aviv and meanwhile days dragged by without hot water and revolt threatened.

Abba hadn't waited. Pulling the useless mechanism from under the boiler, he trotted his horse and cart down to the wadi, collected driftwood from the winter floods and made a huge pile of kindling by the showers. For the next two weeks, as each person came up to shower, he took a branch or two, broke it into small pieces and added to the fire under the barrel. All evening, flames and sparks shot up from the chimney and from the fields below, it seemed that at any minute our showers would up anchor and sail away into the Mediterranean.

Like some Jaques Tati film, the farce continued. Aharonchik continued to insist that it only needed one small spare part. Reubek moaned that he couldn't spend all day swanning around the junk yards of Tel Aviv — he had enough to do, running between the banks to avoid his cheques bouncing. Meanwhile, Abba continued to bring up loads of wood from the wadi and the chimney belched flames and smoke into the sky, well into the night. But at least we had hot water.

Avri looked into the boiler shed and cursed. He'd managed to cut the Gordian knot of Reubek and Aharonchik and to purchase the new burner, and after a thorough overhaul everything had been working perfectly. Now, it had run out of oil. In retaliation at being taken away from his stores job, Zeev had neglected to order the tanker. It wasn't really Avri's fault, but he knew he would be blamed at Saturday's general meeting if nothing was done.

'Can't light a fire underneath this time mate,' muttered Joe.

'Okay,' he said. 'I'll get the jeep and drive over with an empty drum to our neighbours.'

'Wait,' said Yoske and Joe. 'We'll come and give you a hand.' To ensure hot water, there was never a lack of volunteers.

The showers stayed that way for many years. As long as there was hot water and plenty of it — for occasionally someone forgot to check that the water tower hadn't emptied completely, or the oil hadn't run out again — we suffered the old tin hut. But as our numbers grew, it became more and more crowded. Everyone finished work around the same time and with each additional person entering, the concrete floor grew dirtier and muddier. Pulling on clean trousers became a juggling act as you carefully rolled up the free trouser leg to avoid dangling it in the dirt, then unfolded it in stages as you wriggled the leg inside it.

But apart from the hot water, the most difficult problem to solve was that of obtaining a pair of *kaf-kafim*, sandal-shaped pieces of wood, held on with rubber straps cut from old tractor inner-tubes. With constant use, the rubber often exceeded its module of elasticity and, without warning, would snap just as you let someone else in under the shower head, leaving you to hop back to your clothes like a lame frog.

Survival gymnastics in the showers . . .

'We're running a million pound enterprise but can't bloody well spare the carpenter to make a few more sets of kaf-kafim,' was the constant cry. Soon, obtaining even one kaf-kaf became a luxury and across the dim interior, you could hear the shouts. 'After you with the kaf-kafim, Gidon,' or 'Hey, I bagged those from Itzik,' whilst those without them had to wait under the showers until a pair, or even one, came free. In the meantime, the prized kaf-kaf had somehow taken on another meaning: a nickname for someone as thick as two short planks!

Eventually, the day came when the new showers actually made it into the annual investment budget. Six months later, a gleaming white concrete building with its ceramic wall tiles and newly painted benches and doors, stood in the middle of the courtyard in all its glory. No longer did Abba have to hump drums of diesel oil up the hill; a tanker replenished the large storage tank at regular intervals. And with a gleaming terrazzo-tiled floor and sufficient space, even the once sought after kaf-kaf lost its pride of place. But no longer could the two sexes enjoy common scandals and banter across the tin sheeting.

In time, more and more people moved into new houses which had their own small showers. The communal showers were used less and less and eventually only by the volunteers, who now enjoyed the same conviviality and esprit that we had known. It was progress and it was bound to happen. But something had gone. We had lost that informal space where everyone met, laughed and argued together after work: our village pump. And it symbolised our changing society — from a commune, to a collective of individual families.

Shula and the baby

Shula hadn't got up for work again. When Hannah went to knock at her door, she said she couldn't care less, wasn't getting up and anyway, she was leaving. It wasn't the first time she had threatened either or all.

Shula had tried working in the orchards, then the poultry, then assisting in the kindergarten. She didn't know what she wanted really, except to have her own home and to be with her new baby, Hanan, now six months old. Dissatisfied at work and unhappy with the baby being in the children's house, there seemed nothing to hold her in the kibbutz. Except Daniel. And Daniel wasn't leaving.

Daniel just accepted the situation as it was.

'Look mate,' he would laugh in his Yorkshire flavoured Hebrew, 'I work enough for the both of us.' And to be fair, Daniel, with his mop of curly black hair, tanned face and prominent teeth worked like a Trojan. Single-handed, he'd built up the piggery, from almost nothing into a money spinning concern: 'Just me and Abu Yusuf,' he'd grin, alluding to the huge white boar.

Daniel and Shula had been married for about five years. They were still a very affectionate pair, coming up to the dining room in the evening arms tight around each other and often, off to bed early. Like perpetual honeymooners, we joked, sometimes wondering how Daniel found the energy to work through the whole day. 'Make 'em tough up North,' he'd say, with his raucous laugh.

Daniel learned of the latest crisis when he came in for lunch. 'It can wait,' he muttered, stuffing his hat into his pocket. He finished eating before going down to their room where Shula was sitting on the bed in a cotton dressing gown, sewing a blue ribbon onto the baby's hat.

'What's up love?' he smiled, planting a kiss on her neck as he ran his fingers through her long brown hair. Shula put down the sewing.

'I'm tired Daniel. Dog tired,' she said, clutching her hands in her lap, her eyes red and puffy. 'And fed up being put in the clothes store.'

'But you're only there for four hours.' Daniel sat down beside her. 'You'd have finished by now.' She looked at him, her face pained.

'Oh, Daniel. Do you know what it's like working up there? The idle chatter. Sorting out laundry. Sewing on other people's buttons.' She hammered her fists on her knees, 'I hate it. Hate it. Hate it.' And she meant it.

We always joked that a man left the kibbutz for two reasons: one, he didn't have a wife; or two, he did. For Daniel wasn't alone in his predicament. Shula was symptomatic of a deep-seated problem which was occupying the greatest minds of the kibbutz movement and on which reams and reams had been written: 'The Problem of the Woman in the Kibbutz.'

Despite the kibbutz's proclaimed ideals of liberating women from their traditional domestic roles, whilst the men worked mainly in the fields and orchards and workshops, the women were sucked into caring for the increasing number of children and the growing services sector. Some women did want to work in childcare and in education and saw it as their vocation, but most hadn't given up studies or town life in order to look after children. Nor had they any wish to exchange domestic chores for the communal ones, even if they did have formal equal status with the cowsheds. And with the baby still young, Shula worked only four hours, making her choice of workplaces even more limited. Like most pioneering societies, the kibbutz had less women than men. And as the kibbutz grew older and people paired off, it became more a commune of families and the single men became a community of ageing bachelors. They often felt on the fringe, as festivals and timetables became moulded around the needs of parents and children. Some left. Some didn't — perhaps preferring bachelorhood in any society. Others may have been gay, though it was unheard of, or rather, unrecognised at the time. A few took "bachelors' leave" to go to town or another kibbutz, in the hope that they would meet a partner. The few women who did not find a partner, generally left too. So marriage was always seen as an important stabilising factor for the kibbutz and weddings were celebrated with great gusto.

But marriage did not resolve the problem of the woman's place of work. And if a woman was already dissatisfied at work, the problem became even more acute when the children arrived.

Most kibbutzim then had a system of *Khinukh Meshutaf* — Collective Education. It had developed historically and not purely from ideology or child psychology. In the early kibbutzim, labour was always in short supply and economic necessity demanded that women be released to join the workforce. In addition, everyone lived in small rooms which had no space for cots, changing tables, fridges to keep milk fresh and so on. So whilst a few women cared for the children in the children's houses, all the other mothers were free to work anywhere. As time passed, it was felt that this method of bringing up the children in their own "children's society", was the system most suited to the kibbutz. From this, an overall psychological and pedagogical theory and practice of collective education was developed which, we felt, was superior.

It started as soon as mother and baby came home from

hospital. The baby went straight to the babies' house where a trained nurse looked after it. This part of the system received a 'bad press' from some of the older kibbutzim where there was a strict routine of access hours to the babies' house — more probably inherited from a central European rigidity about child rearing. With us, as with many of the newer kibbutzim, the mother was free to drop in any time she felt, to come to nurse and feed during the day and when it was awake, to take baby to the room to play. The intention was also to give the mother a chance to rest for the first few weeks after labour. When the infant woke between meals, the nurse would change it and the mother could be rested and fresh when mealtimes came.

New mothers had two months off work to nurse and feed the young babies and had all the assistance and advice they needed from an experienced babies' nurse. This was especially valuable after birth complications and for those with their first child. Afterwards, mothers worked only four hours a day and only after some months did they work a full day again. But despite all these physical advantages it was harder on the nursing mother than it seemed. And Shula just didn't want to accept it.

'You don't understand, Daniel,' she continued, leaning against him. 'Who do you think has to get up and dress at three in the morning, to traipse along to the babies' house and feed Hanan?'

'But if the baby was here, you'd be woken even if it only whinged.' He put his arm around her shoulder. 'Hanan being in the babies' house gives you a chance to rest,' adding with a short laugh, 'and me!'

'Yes. But you don't have to go out into the cold and damp. If Hanan was here, in the room, I could just get out of bed to feed him. And anyway,' she continued, 'I don't trust that night duty nurse, Shlomit. What does she know about babies?'

'But Elanah looks after him most of the time, love. And even you know she's brilliant. Look how she's helped you through the first two months.'

Shula grudgingly nodded. But it changed nothing. The baby had become her main, and perhaps her only, interest amidst the general dissatisfaction of her life on the kibbutz. Added to her frustration at work, it became a constant battering ram against Daniel's resolve.

'It's just unnatural,' she said. 'A baby should be with its mother all the time.' She clenched her hands, 'I want Hanan here. With me, Daniel. He's my baby!'

'Look, love. Mine too. And we've been over this all before. Do you think that in town he would be with you all the time?', his voice betraying the weariness of their repeated arguments. 'You'd have to work as well as me to make ends meet, and Hanan would be with a baby minder or in a crèche for much of the day anyway.' Shula just stared at the wall opposite. Although she accepted the logic, she couldn't help feeling what she felt.

We regarded children as the responsibility not only of their parents, but also the community as a whole. From the child outwards, the family, the school and the kibbutz were in concentric circles, avoiding the disharmony of separate and contradictory environments that were often created in town. The children were cared for by a trained child nurse, the *metapelet*, and remained in groups of five or six until they went to kindergarten where two or three groups were amalgamated and progressed together through to school. Their peer group became a parallel family in which they developed a deep comradeship and empathy for one another — budding kibbutzniks!

The kids loved it and thrived in the system. They came home at four in the afternoon, after the parents finished work and received all the love and attention for the few hours before they went to bed, whilst most of the time enjoying the security of their group and the care of their trained metapelet, whom they liked and trusted. They spent much of the Shabbat day off with the parents as well. The children's houses also had toys and equipment that no individual working family could have provided.

Our education system continued into primary school within the kibbutz and then on to a co-educational boarding high-school, shared between several kibbutzim. We had our own project-based curriculum, influenced by the ideas similar to those of A.S. Neil,

Finding a hand for everyone . . .

which promoted an all-round development of the child and not
just academic excellence. And there were no exams. In the high-
school years, the pupils also worked for a few hours each afternoon, which gave them a sense of contribution to, and identifica-
tion with, the kibbutz.

No system is perfect, and in later years some of the children
told of their fears at being left alone at night. But it was nothing
like Huxley's *Brave New World* as was sometimes depicted in
anti-kibbutz articles and polemic, and we felt that there were
many more advantages than failings. It had to be compared not
with some non-existent idealised childcare system, but with the
"normal" nuclear family, which has certainly created its own crop
of problems. Above all we saw no contradiction between loving
our kids and their sleeping in the children's houses, as well as
their being looked after whilst we were at work. We felt we were
educating a generation of sociable, non-violent, co-operative,
physically and mentally healthy human beings. And, all in all, the
fathers saw much more of their young children than they would
in town. In the evenings, we sometimes listened outside the
shutters as the children chattered sleepily to each other before

they fell asleep, content and secure in their room with their friends and Daniel, like many of the fathers, would give his baby its first bottle at dawn before going out to work. New fathers often had the tell-tale smell of sour milk on their working shirts all morning where the infants had burped up.

To Shula though, it was 'unnatural'. Whether she sincerely held these views or was using them to get her own way, we never knew. It didn't really matter. For when the mother was disgruntled at work and didn't want her child in the children's house, there was a void that nothing could fill.

She and Daniel talked for another few minutes until he stood up.

'Look. I've got to get back, love. Couple of volunteers are coming up to help muck out the pens.' That evening, he would see Barukh, the work organiser, and try to find a different place of work. Shula shrugged. And with a final kiss, he went out.

Everyone loved Daniel and enjoyed his infectious, ribald sense of humour. Once he deliberately let the boar into the farrowing sows' pens just when some prudish *sabra* mothers brought the children to see the animals on a Shabbat morning.

'Look, Mum. Abu Yusuf is doing it!' the kids would jump and point in their own natural way, compounding the embarrassment. Daniel loved it. Apart from being a great worker, he was a fine tenor in the choir as well as the life and soul of the cultural committee who, at that moment were in the thick of preparations for the *Hanukah* party. And despite the problems she created, everyone really liked Shula. We tolerated her failings in the hope that she would eventually find a satisfying place of work. In the meantime, we just had to hope that as Daniel was happiest in the kibbutz, she would accept the situation.

That evening, they came up for supper as though nothing had happened. The work organiser added four more hours to those Shula already owed to the work roster, but no one really believed they would ever be repaid, just keeping things on an even keel and hoping the storm would pass. Either Shula had to give in, or Daniel. We hoped that it wouldn't be him. We couldn't imagine him in town — he was such a kibbutznik. Unfortunately, many marriages were like that, one half, heart and soul in the kibbutz and the other half just waiting to leave.

'Bloody Plato and his searching halves,' Yehuda moaned. 'Why does it always have to be like that?'

The success of Daniel's piggeries were also due to the food situation in Israel in the fifties and early sixties. With a general shortage of meat, beef and lamb were highly-priced. Ham and bacon had therefore become popular amongst the majority, non-religious, Israelis. It also sold well in the Christian Arab sector. And Daniel loved working with the pigs.

'Look mate,' he would grin, 'they're a bloody sight more human than people.' And as each batch went to market, he would commiserate with a bottle of black beer. But soon, things were to change for the worse.

In the coalition government, the power of the ultra orthodox religious parties was growing as the ruling Labour party relied more and more on their support. Eventually, new laws were passed, forbidding pig-breeding in Jewish settlements. For a long time, the kibbutzim managed to resist the restrictions and Daniel continued his merry way, breeding and sending pigs to market. But it was a rearguard action. Judgement day eventually arrived when Reubek, the treasurer, came to the Farm Committee one evening, looking shattered.

'The government have just brought in a new regulation,' he said. His face was drawn and tight; the piggery brought in much-needed ready cash. 'Milk from farms which also keep pigs won't be allowed into *Tnuva*, the main dairies.'

'But they can't stop us,' said Avri, the farm manager, 'We're shareholders in Tnuva.'

'So are the religious kibbutzim and smallholders' villages, and the Rabbis say it will make all their milk "unkosher"!'

'Can we fight it?' asked Itzik.

'Not really.' Reubek threw a copy of the letter on the table. 'They'll refuse to collect our milk.'

Closing down the piggery would knock a hole in our budget.

But the cowshed was a much larger part of our economy, and growing. We called down fire and brimstone on the bearded, black-coated Mafia, but furious as we were, all the committee knew it was a fait accompli. Daniel was at the committee meeting too; he'd seen it on the agenda. For once, there were no jokes, no wide grin, no taking the mickey out of Reubek — and before the end, he slid out of the door without a word.

Over the next few weeks, we desperately sought an economic replacement for the pigs. Some suggested geese, or turkeys, others sheep, but we didn't have any pasture land. Slowly, it became apparent that there just wasn't any direct alternative. And with this, Daniel's world crumbled. True, he hadn't come to kibbutz just to raise pigs. There were all his other activities too. But he'd invested so much of himself in the piggery and had such an empathy with Abu Yusuf and the older sows: 'Part of the family,' he would laugh. Now, we had to sell the lot. Last to go was the old boar, snorting his way onto the back of a pick-up truck. He was bought by an Arab farmer in Galilee. Daniel watched, tears in his eyes. Then, blowing his nose into a huge grey handkerchief, he wound his way down to his room, without a word.

Daniel went to work with Issy and the boys in the cowshed and the old sense of humour seemed to return. The winter passed and he helped to organise the Passover celebrations in the barn, and kept coming to the choir. And the efforts continued to find Shula a place of work. But, like our fight with the rabbinate, Daniel's was a losing battle. Shula's days-off continued to multiply and her arguments with Hanan's metapelet grew more fraught.

'Can't see an end to it, mate,' he confided to Issy as they climbed the hill after morning milking. For once, Issy had no answer.

They left in May. It was a terribly hot day. Shula hugged Hanan in the cab, Daniel sat on the back of the truck with their clothing and furniture, trying to smile as he waved goodbye. This time the tears weren't in Shula's eyes, but ours.

They found a small flat near Petakh Tikva and Daniel,

resourceful as ever, got a manager's job in a small factory. But to make ends meet, Shula had to work in an office in Tel Aviv and Hanan went to a local nursery. She couldn't be with her child most of the day, but now there was no kibbutz to blame. Yet whenever one of us visited them, Shula seemed happy enough. But fate, or the gods wouldn't let it stay that way.

Like most of us in border kibbutzim, Daniel had been exempt from army reserve duties. The army regarded us as "on call" all the time. But now, like every man in town, he had to go on active service for a month every year.

It was about three years after they'd left, on a warm spring day in the Jordan valley. Daniel's ambulance unit was on border watch. He was already a paramedic from his conscript days. Across the river on the hills opposite, Jordanian Arab Legion troops were on manoeuvres.

'Keep an eye out,' his company commander called over the radio, 'they're unpredictable.' Daniel, lying on a stretcher in the sun, raised his head and laughed.

'No worry, mate. British officers trained the Arab Legion. They can't help but notice the large red Magen David on the ambulances.' He lay back and closed his eyes again. 'No problems. You'll see.'

The distant explosions seemed part of the manoeuvres. Daniel didn't move. Two salvos of six-inch mortar bombs straddled the unit. When the dust and smoke had gone, so had Daniel. Life is so unfair.

Whose hand on the plough?

The barley harvest came as usual in April, but that year, with it came the scorching *khamsin* winds that blew in straight from the eastern desert.

'The grain is spilling out of the ears,' Dudik snapped at the farm committee meeting. 'If we don't work round the clock, we shall lose half the yield!' Dudik was the head of the *falkha* — the cereal crops. The crisis was made worse by a plague of field mice which was already wreaking havoc, felling the corn stalks like tiny trees and nipping off the ears to drag them down their burrows. 'We haven't enough manpower ourselves, for both day and night shifts,' he continued. 'So we'll have to hire outside combine operators.'

Gerry sat up.

'Hang on. When was this agreed?'

'It's already been decided,' grunted Dudik.

'Not yet it hasn't,' snapped Gerry. 'I'm a full member of the committee and this is the first I've heard of it.'

The farm committee was one of several elected every year, to manage the affairs of the kibbutz. Apart from the treasurer and general secretary, there were three other members and it was chaired by the farm manager. '

'Anyway,' Gerry continued, 'hired labour has to be approved by the general meeting!'

Our objection to hired labour wasn't an abstract principle. Throughout history, whenever communal settlements had abandoned a planned, all-year-round economy based on their own labour and exploited cheap labour for seasonal cash crops instead, it had led to their demise. Hired labour and private property were the two principal destructive elements to communal living. And in these crisis years, the dangers were intensified by outside political pressure.

The fifties were times of mass immigration, causing severe unemployment. As a publicity move, the government of Ben Gurion was urging the kibbutzim to hire workers to alleviate the situation and some of the older kibbutzim up North affiliated to his party, had done just that. The kibbutz movement however, was less than four percent of the population. The numbers that we could all employ wouldn't even nibble at the unemployment problem, but it would be a Trojan horse that would eventually destroy the specific nature of the kibbutz. Dudik's proposal was the thin end of the wedge and we called for it to be put on the agenda for the next general meeting.

By chance, the day before that Saturday's meeting, Gerry and I had to go out with two others to load up sacks of barley from our fields in the Negev. After a two-hour drive, we turned off the Beer Sheva road and bumped along a rough track through the loëss-soil badlands, raising a cloud of fine white dust that hung in the air and settled over us and everything around. In the distance, the tiny red speck of our combine harvester was crawling along the contours of the yellow fields.

With grating gears, the lorry backed over the stubble and up to the first pile of sacks. They looked heavy even before Giora let the tailboard down with a loud clang. Gerry and I grabbed the first sack, swinging forward and back, then full power forward and up onto the deck. Then the next and the next, whilst Eli and Yoske piled them up in the front. Forward, back and up; one two three, again and again, arms aching, backs crying out, but there was no stopping. The only break was the truck's short reverse back to the next pile. Finally, with all the sacks loaded, exhausted, we rested and waited for the combine to pass.

The churning red monster crawled towards us making a scalpel cut in the standing barley and leaving neat contour lines of straw over the undulating ground. Behind it, dust and chaff blew away with the breeze.

'Come to see some real work for a change,' grinned Dudik, 'instead of lazing around in the orchards?' He moved the gears to neutral and removed his goggles, leaving white circles in his dust-blackened face. Arik was tying sacks on the platform behind him.

'Look, mate,' replied Gerry. 'If you weren't up on wheels, there wouldn't be a single ear of corn cut. Anyway,' he added, laughing, 'typical of you *Kulaks* to sit and drive, whilst we serfs load the grain for you!'

We handed up the food and a milk churn full of lemonade cooled in the cowshed's refrigeration tank. The two of them would easily finish it off by the end of the shift, to make up for the sweat they had lost. Dudik nodded to a clutch of straw lying on the grey soil.

'See what the little bastards are doing.' The ears had been nipped off and nearby, were two small mouseholes leading down to their burrows.

Despite our difference of opinions, the good-natured banter continued, the humour helping to cope with the hard physical labour. But it was difficult to maintain eye contact, each aware of the undercurrent of conflict which would be out in the open at the next day's meeting. In the meantime, attracted by the heat and sweat, clouds of *barkhash*, tiny black biting midges swarmed into our ears and eyes and through every opening of our clothing like a plague. We slapped our heads and flailed our arms like windmills but it was useless. Arik and Dudik were already swaddled up in thick shirts and scarves and hats to combat them, despite the heat.

Loading the last few sacks from the combine chute, we drove off, leaving the barkhash to find new victims. I looked over to the east. The fields stretched endlessly into the distance, to where the foothills of the Hebron mountains disappeared into a grey haze along the Jordanian border. Just a short while ago, all this had been wasteland where Bedouin grazed their black goats on thorns and sparse grass. It was still liable to drought every few years, but by good husbandry and hard work, thousands of tons of grain were being added to the country's larder at a time when it was sorely needed. And in the isolation and danger of this border area, it was the kibbutzim who had risen to the challenge, with *felakhim* like Dudik and Heskel. It gave us plenty to mull over as we drove back to the kibbutz. For without a solution to manning the three shifts, round the clock, ourselves, all our principles were useless.

Attendance at the general meetings varied according to the agenda. Not since the heated arguments in the wake of the Sinai War had there been such a full house. That night, the tables down each long side of the dining hall were soon filled up with the usual groupings: the Sabras taking up one whole side, the English at two corners, and the Romanians at the other two and down half of the other side. All the *felakhim*, together with their wives or girl-friends had come, sitting close together around two tables. Giora stood by the door: 'To carry out the casualties,' he grinned.

As usual, some people had brought the weekend edition of *Al Hamishmar* to the meeting, Eliezar doggedly trying to finish the crossword. Two or three others struggled with the chess problem while some of the English took the opportunity to polish off unde-manding air-letters to their families. And, *de rigeur*, there were the knitters.

At every activity, whether it was a lecture, a discussion, or even a concert, some of the women inevitably brought their knitting — almost always sweaters or pullovers for the children. The kibbutz supplied the wool and it saved on buying ready-made clothes. Equally inevitably, during a crucial moment in the discussion or at a soft chord in the music, a needle would clatter to the tiles, invok-ing silent outrage.

'At least we do something useful in all that hot air,' Aliza would retort as we spilled out afterwards.

The meeting opened with the usual announcements by Dani, the general secretary, followed by a request from the plumber to report dripping taps to save water. Yoske suddenly appeared from the kitchen with half a dozen tin jugs of water, which he distributed amongst the tables.

'Just to keep it all cool', he grinned whilst we all laughed, thankful of the light relief. But the atmosphere remained tense, everyone waiting for the main item on the agenda.

Joe was weighing up the odds. The Romanians, the old timers, were the most sanguine. Having fought all these battles before, they sat quietly, apprehensive that whoever won, the confrontation would do more damage to the kibbutz than good. A few, like like Shosh and Eliezar still held to their ideals and would support us. Amongst the Sabras, many would vote with the felakhim, either pragmatically agreeing with them, or out of group solidarity. But Gadi and Yeremi and a few more, would side with us to uphold the principle.

'Could go either way,' muttered Joe.

Dani introduced the item, putting the two sides of the argument as fairly as he could. After he finished and sat down, there was the usual silence. Through the open windows, warm air blew in from the khamsin winds, 'so thick you could have cut it with a knife,' Arik said afterwards. No one wanted to speak first.

'Right,' called Yoske, 'That's decided then. Let's move on to the next item.' One or two laughed.

'Shut up,' snapped Shlomit, Arik's wife. 'Try and be serious for a change.' She was furious at the way the other felakhim had almost ostracised Arik, because he too objected to hiring outside tractor drivers. Again there was silence.

'Right,' Dani stood up, 'we'll vote on the motion to allow two hired combine operators to work in the falkha for this harvest.' It was a ploy. Calling the vote always invoked a reaction. It did and all eyes turned to Joe as he stood up.

'Look. The falkha can manage by itself,' he said slowly, 'if Arik and I work the combine as well. But we'll need two more to stand guard on the night shift.' He glanced at Dudik. 'And that's my proposal.' He sat down and again there was silence. Suddenly Shmuelik spoke. He didn't bother to stand up.

'We haven't worked nights at Tel Melicha for the whole season because of the danger of infiltrators from Jordan,' he snapped. 'And Joe knows it.'

'But we can. With a guard. And . . ,' Joe retorted. But before he could finish the sentence, Heskel jumped up.

'Maybe. But with Bedouin drivers, we don't need guards.' He looked around the hall. 'It will be so much simpler. Like we've agreed.'

Eliezar put down his pencil, rested his hand on the newspaper and looked up.

'Like who agreed?' he said, slowly and deliberately. Crossword or no, Eliezar missed nothing. In the tense atmosphere, Heskel had prematurely let the cat out of the bag. Not only hired labour, but local Bedouin on top? The Bedouin semi-nomads who had once roamed the arid south of Palestine had been "settled" in barren areas without tenure to the land. Now many of their younger generation had learned to drive and operate farm machinery as a way of eking out their impoverished existence.

Zeev, the farm manager, and Boaz, looked away, but no one answered Eliezar's question. For a moment there was absolute silence. Dudik glared at Heskel then suddenly stood up, leaned forward and slapped his hand on the table.

'Look. I am the head of the falkha,' he snapped. 'If I can't manage it the way I think fit, the kibbutz can appoint someone else to do it.' It was his trump card. But he'd been forced to play it too early and it didn't work. Yehuda was already on his feet.

'It's not the point,' he called across the hall. 'You can't decide to hire labour on your own.'

'I didn't,' snapped Dudik, 'Zeev agreed all the time . .' The rest of his words were drowned in uproar.

Elected for a two year period, Zeev, one of the Romanians, was now in his second turn of office after a break of only three years. It had only served to increase his naturally autocratic tendencies. Despite gaining few privileges from positions of office and usually having the best of intentions, it was symptomatic of how a few "experts", even in a direct and open democracy like ours, could begin to gain control of vital functions. Now, Heskel's slip of the tongue had exposed a private arrangement, which had not even come to the farm committee.

Zeev sat quietly, his balding head shining in the fluorescent light and saying nothing. We knew what he was thinking; he'd said it more than once: 'Bunch of kids playing at being farmers; think they can live off principles.' From that point on, however, Dani didn't need to prompt. From all sides, for and against, the arguments echoed across the dining hall. Until it was almost midnight. Then there was silence again. And with everyone waiting, the farm manager knew he would have to speak.

Zeev spoke a perfect, grammatically correct Hebrew, which we envied; better even than most of the Sabras. He stood up and, speaking softly, tried to make light of the whole affair.

'Dudik came to me and we discussed the situation at Tel Melikha. He is the one who is responsible for getting the harvest in and the situation is drastic.' He paused and glanced casually at Joe and Gerry. 'We just haven't the manpower for Joe's suggestion and anyway, we are speaking here of a one-time, short, limited period. So there's no need to make a big issue out of nothing.' Gerry leaped to his feet.

'What do you mean, nothing? First we hear of hired combine drivers. Then it turns out to be Bedouin drivers, without guards even.' He pointed at Zeev, 'Are you saying we can't even defend ourselves?'

'Bedouin don't need guards,' replied Heskel. 'Arabs won't shoot at one of their own. If you knew more about the country,' he sneered, not missing an opportunity to remind us that we "foreigners" knew little of the Middle East mentality, 'you wouldn't ask damn fool questions.'

'Oh sure,' shouted Gerry. 'And I suppose you've made an agreement with the *fedayeen*: not to shoot without asking name and tribe first, eh?' He glanced around the hall. 'Look, I don't relish the night shift, nor being a sitting target. I'll admit it.' He pointed at Dudik. 'But you're just as scared. You, Boaz and the rest. That's why you suggest the Bedouin and you know it. But I can tell you; either we work nights and guard ourselves, as Joe suggests, or we don't work night shifts at all.'

'And half the harvest will go to waste!' jeered Heskel.

The discussion had now turned. It was no longer a question just of hired labour, but also of self defence. For over half a century, ever since Jewish pioneers had settled on the land, they had fought to defend it themselves and not rely on hired Arab guards, like the Jewish landowners of the previous century. Self defence had become a principle. Now it too was at stake and Gerry's last remarks provoked a new bout of vociferous argument.

As with most discussions on farm matters, despite our formal sex equality, the women took little part. Sylvie, Zeev's wife, sat tense and drawn. Arguments like this led to bitterness and people refusing to work with one another and to some leaving. It was not how she had envisaged kibbutz life: 'Living together, decently,' she would say again and again, 'that is surely the most important kibbutz principle.' She was also worried about Zeev. To be farm manager, you needed support and co-operation. There was no coercion in the kibbutz. If he alienated one section or another, his job would become impossible. And then there were his migraine attacks. Stubborn as he was, the strain was beginning to tell, and if they lost half the harvest, Dudik and Shmuelik would be the first to lay the blame at his feet.

Dudik had sat quietly, elbows on the table, whilst the tumult raged all around. He leaned his head on his hands, the scene at Tel Melikha running through his mind: the ears of barley drying out, grain spilling onto the ground and armies of mice nibbling away. All that year's hard work going to waste and all for some damn stupid principle. When he had taken over the falkha two years before, it was an ailing branch of the economy. Only by dint of their crazy working hours and hard graft, had they kept the Negev lands in production, driving thirty miles and back, to prod

the soil after every spell of rain. 'Go and pitch a tent out there like
the Bedouin,' chafed his wife, Bilha. 'Then you can count each
drop as it falls!' She had suffered his long absences, worried sick
each evening he returned late. Only three days ago, a neighbouring kibbutznik had gone up on a mine. Now, feeling the light
touch of her small hand on his back, Dudik wondered why he
bothered. He was tired of all the hot air, all the arguments. Tired of
these up-in-the-air idealists. And of Zeev backing him, then not
backing him. No. No one appreciated what they had done. Why
the hell should he bother?

His thoughts were cut short as Dani rapped on the table.

'Well, Dudik. Why not take up Joe's suggestion for a trial
period? We can always come back to other proposals.' Dudik
looked up, his curly, fair hair tousled, his face flushed. The rest of
the hall fell silent.

'I don't care a damn what you decide.' He flicked his wrist. 'If
Joe and Arik think they can handle things better than me, let them
take over. I've had enough.' And that was just how he felt. Heskel
and Shmuelik half smiled: let them all see how they would get out
of that one.

'Dudik,' said Dani gently, knowing Dudik's quick temper.
'That's not really an answer.' The night was already tomorrow
morning and nerves were becoming more frayed. At that moment,
Eliezar raised his hand again.

'Tell me, Zeev. After the orange picking business,' he said
slowly and deliberately, turning to the farm manager, 'didn't we
decide that all hired labour issues came to the Secretariat?' He
paused, then added, as if by-the-way, 'And what about pay-
ments?' Everyone looked at Reubek. The treasurer would have
had to make ready cash available for the Bedouin. He must have
known of the plan too. Again, there was silence. Yoske detached
himself from the door post.

'Right.' He clanged an empty jug on the table. 'That's it.
Dismiss all the Secretariat. New elections.' He turned to his wife,
Tzipora, 'Come on darling, there'll be no time left for bed.' A
ripple of laughter momentarily broke the tension. Tzipora glared

back daggers, but stayed where she was and Yoske sat down and everyone waited for the next move.

Dani meanwhile, was anxious to close the discussion and bring it to the vote. It was nearly one o'clock. 'Right,' he said, 'All those in favour of Joe's suggestion, for a trial period?'

'It won't work,' muttered Heskel. 'You'll see.'

'What about you, Dudik. Can we agree?' asked Dani, desperately trying to reach a consensus. 'At least to give it a trial?'

'Do what the hell you like,' snapped Dudik, 'all of you.' He got up and strode across to the door. 'I've had enough. Someone else can take over.' And he walked out. Zeev stood and looked around the hall.

'Great,' he said. 'Now everyone can be happy. As if branch organisers grow on trees.' He glared towards us. 'Like a bunch of kids playing farmers.'

'Don't try that one on us, mate,' yelled Gerry. 'We won't give in to blackmail. No one is indispensable.' He pointed at Zeev. 'You neither. No one!' Uproar followed and ended only when Eliezar folded his newspaper and raised his hand.

'Well,' he said. 'I move Joe's proposal. But with a proviso that the farm committee, together with the felakhim, work out the details.' It was a typically clever move. Neither Zeev nor Reubek could oppose it. And the most Dudik's friends could do, was to abstain. Then just before the actual vote, Heskel threw one last bombshell.

'It's pointless,' he snapped, 'No one will agree to do guard duty out there, anyway.' He nodded towards Gerry and Joe, 'Talking is easy. Let's see if you're prepared to do it?' For a moment, there was absolute silence. The practicalities of implementing the proposal threatened it, even before the vote. But the smile under Heskel's moustache faded as a soft voice chirped from the corner.

'Well I'm prepared to take my turn if needed.' Everyone turned to look. It was Len, the last person anyone would call a 'fighter'. A family man with a new baby less than three months old. 'I just felt

Bringing in the hay — most of it . . .

that everyone should be prepared to defend their work and their home,' he'd said later, in his no nonsense, Brummie way.

Many people abstained, including Zeev, but the vote was carried by fifty-three to twelve against. We jumped for joy and cheered as the figures were announced. Dani tried to calm things down and went out to the lobby where Dudik stood.

'Look. Give it a try, Dudik. Give it a try. After all, with Heskel and Shmuelik as your friends, who needs opponents.' As Bilha came to stand by him, Dudik shrugged, turned and walked away, saying nothing.

For us, the night was not yet over and as usual, after a hectic general meeting, we crowding into Gerry's room to boil up coffee, munch dry biscuits and analyse what had happened. We would have gone on until dawn, if Avri hadn't thumped on the wall from next door.

'Screw your principles,' he shouted. 'This man's principles are a good night's sleep!' We agreed that he had a valid point and dispersed, weary but contented. A battle over principles had been won. Yet no one had any illusions that the war was over. The proposal still had to be implemented and guard duty out there so near the Jordanian border would be no picnic. But one thing was without doubt. Those who had voted for the proposal would have to show a personal example.

A matter of trust

We had changed shifts in the evening, to allow the truck to get back onto the main road before dark, and were sitting on upturned orange boxes, drinking coffee and munching cheese sandwiches as the sun set.

'Don't get up to any mischief whilst we're gone,' called Avram from the driver's cab as he engaged gear.

'No chance,' grinned Joe, 'we're not members of the local night club.' The truck lumbered across the stubble, then away up the track, its red tail-light glowing like a firefly in the gathering dusk. Heskel and Boaz had gone back with the lorry; Joe and Gidi were taking over the combine. I was on guard and the three of us were now alone, still with the tensions and bitterness of the previous Saturday's acrimonious meeting, yet having to co-operate to get the night's work done.

The combine harvester, with Joe and Gidi aboard, moved off, chewing its way over the barley in a halo of dusty, yellow head-lights which grew fainter every second. Darkness came quickly and soon only a soft glow above the ridge betrayed the combine's presence. With the night and myself now left to each other, I sat again on the upturned box, rifle across my knees, staring into the darkness. It was a matter of trust, mutual respect, common aims and shared ideals. Wasn't that what the kibbutz was all about? Trust amongst ourselves. Without that, we would always have conflict. So how was it that we had come to this bitter impasse, a situation where relations had become so strained?

In novels or films, people of differing and conflicting views are often thrown together. But it is usually an enforced situation — the army, being marooned, or an air crash. Here, we were voluntarily living our normal, everyday lives and would continue to do so into the foreseeable future. Despite differences, we still had to get on with one another, trust and work with each other day after day, have our kids in the same children's house and our wives or husbands working together. We had no illusions that everyone could be bosom pals. But to live with sharply opposing views and constant conflict in our community of a hundred or so adults, was something none of us had ever contemplated.

The kibbutz had been settled immediately after the War of Independence, by a group from Romania. Idealistic and highly politicised, they'd lost half of their group through ideological splits, as well as to the tough conditions and the border tensions. And whilst they still subscribed to their original ideals, many had tired of the constant struggle to maintain them and preferred the quiet life. Our group, from England, was probably even more idealistic. Many had given up university places, often cutting themselves off from family and friends and had rejected the materialism of the affluent society. The kibbutz, for us, was the embodiment of all we believed in, politically, socially and nationally. And whilst we understood the mental and emotional fatigue of many of the original settlers, we were completely unprepared for the problems posed when the large Israeli born group, the Sabras, joined us in the mid-fifties.

The nucleus of the Sabras had, like us, come through the socialist-Zionist youth movement. On finishing their army service, they had been determined to establish their own independent kibbutz.

But very many of the young kibbutzim had been hastily positioned to secure the borders of the new state and were now severely undermanned. So most new groups were sent to reinforce existing settlements. This Sabra group however, continued to fight tooth and nail to be allowed to establish their own kibbutz. And to add weight to their campaign, they had appended many smaller groupings and individuals who had scant regard for the specific ideals and values of kibbutz and were merely passing the time until they moved on.

In addition, both the Romanians and our English group had gone through a severe selection process before coming to the kibbutz. The faint-hearted and the insincere had dropped off along the way. For the Sabra group however, this selection process only began when they had finished their army service and came to the kibbutz, so it still contained many who still believed in nothing except their own egoistic wants and careers and had no intention of staying. These, together with the "add-ons", formed a large periphery which outnumbered and often outmanoeuvred the idealistic nucleus of the group.

As if this wasn't enough, having failed to persuade the authorities to let them create a new kibbutz and been sent to reinforce our kibbutz, the Sabra group was now determined to mould it as though it was their own independent settlement. Needless to say, both for them and us, it wasn't a good start and it wasn't long before conflicts erupted which were to shape the whole future development of our kibbutz. And the previous weeks' boisterous general meeting was just one result.

I was thinking about this as it grew dark. It was a moonless night with brilliant stars above and not a breath of wind. Yes. We had won this particular battle, but the constant struggle to uphold our principles was wearing. And if it continued, would we too end up like many of the "old timers": our hearts willing, but body and spirit unable?

Eventually, with my mind exhausted, I sat peering into the darkness and as the noise of the combine faded, anxiously listening for the crunch of a footstep on the stubble, for a stone kicked in the gully — for anything which might betray unwelcome visitors. At night, the ears are more reliable than the eyes and at every rustle of a mouse or the whirr of a swooping owl, my heart missed a beat and my finger twitched on the safety catch. The rifle was already cocked, with a bullet in the breech and the safety catch on. To draw the bolt in this silence would have been heard half a mile away. But if a *Fedayeen* group decided to cut through the area, who would be the watcher, I wondered, and who the watched?

In the daylight and from a distance, our gently undulating fields merged into a flat plain — something like we imagined the prairies. But on a closer look, they were dissected into badlands by deep clefts and *wadis*, scoured out by centuries of sudden winter rains. Precipitous sides, often fifteen feet high, spelled serious injury or death to a careless tractor driver. But unlike the prairies, it wouldn't be the Comanches raiding across the nearby border, but desperate and highly-trained men clutching Carl Gustav automatics and like us, fighting for what they believed in.

Most of us had served in the army and had seen action. But it was one thing to summon up adrenaline to fight a battle. Quite another to have the nerve to sit on a tractor, night after night, in the knowledge that someone out there in the dark might be pulling a bead on you at that very moment. Or to stand guard, alone like this, miles from anywhere. Our hope was that 'it would be known', through the Bedouin, that the combine crew had an armed guard, though a .303 would not be much use against a bunch of determined men with automatic weapons.

In the silence of the night, without much effort, my mind wandered back to the heated discussion. Trust. Yes, trust. It had begun to break down long before this and, looking back, I realised that the rot had already started last year with Heskel and the deep ploughing.

The kibbutz had this gigantic plough — like some ancient Pharaoh's war chariot, rust and all. It had a chisel point as thick as a wrist, furrow wheel over a metre high and a huge wave of curved steel blade. It ploughed only a single furrow at a time, but could reach down over three feet, straining every one of the hundred odd horsepower of our huge D6 caterpillar tractor. Plunging deep into the rock hard earth, it broke up the hardpan which other ploughs couldn't reach, turning up sods that had never seen the light of day, soil rich in leached-out minerals. But it was very slow. And very costly.

We'd bought it to prepare the ground for our new orange groves and the alfalfa pastures. Since then, it had lain idle in the garage for over two years. Now we had won a contract to break up barren dry-lands further down in the Negev, land earmarked for smallholders' villages for new immigrants from Morocco, Yemen and Persia. It was paid piece work, per *dunam*. And we sorely needed the income.

For Dudik and Boaz and Heskel, as for many of the Sabras, kibbutz was about work. And work had to be with machines — the more powerful and the more modern, the better. With a flair for handling and repairing anything mechanical and a reputation of getting things done, they relished breaking any previous records at ploughing or harvesting. True, they also liked the camaraderie and the sense of pioneering, of creating something from nothing. But principles such as equality, sharing, self-labour, were by the by. Kibbutz for them, was first and foremost, a successful farm — the *meshek*, the economy.

With the previous year's harvest in, they'd begun to work a double shift on the deep ploughing contract — ten hours of dust and jolting, and the smell of hot oil, stopping only for food and fuel. They loved it. It was the real thing. Joe also took turns, but couldn't understand why he was ploughing less than the others during his shifts; he was the only non-Sabra *felakh* on the contract. What was even stranger, was that none of the others teased him over his apparent tardiness as they stood outside the dining hall each evening, discussing how many dunams had been ploughed up that day.

'Some of them must be raising the plough,' Joe said quietly one night at supper, 'must be.' He looked round then continued. 'Look. You put the tractor in gear, set the throttle and it pulls. At the same depth, it can only go at one speed, more or less.'

'You sure?' I asked, 'That's a pretty serious allegation. Doesn't anyone check?'

'Oh. Sure. The settlement manager did at first. But now they just let us carry on. Everyone trusts us. Trusts kibbutzniks!' Joe glanced at his watch said goodnight and went out. Yehuda and I watched him go then chatted about what we had just heard. 'Just what Joe needs right now, eh?' muttered Yehuda. I nodded. This crisis couldn't have come at a worse time for Joe. Relations between himself and the Sabras in the *falkha* were already at a low over his new girlfriend, Ruthie.

The Sabras had a somewhat puritan attitude to sex; a result of growing up in the new, tight-knit, pioneering society of colonial Palestine, Issy reckoned. Ruthie was a member of their group but was different and didn't regard virginity as sacred. Joe wasn't against sowing a few wild oats and, going home one night, he'd happened to overhear her room mates bitching to Dudik's wife about her "immodest" behaviour. He was furious and like Gerry, didn't keep his opinions to himself. Bursting into their room, he yelled: 'If you frustrated cows were lucky enough to find someone to lay you, you wouldn't need to gossip about someone else's love life!' And stormed out, slamming the door fit to bring it off its hinges. Half the kibbutz had heard and now, together with this deep ploughing business, life for him in the falkha would be even more tense. But Joe had no intention of letting it slide and would fight it to the end. He hadn't given up his studies in London to be just another gentleman farmer. Either we lived our lives according to principles, he said, or there was no point in struggling to create a new community and society out here in this heat and dust.

The work continued, but a week later, it blew up. Heskel, being one of the girls' boyfriends, couldn't resist the temptation to get back at Joe. As we came up for supper one evening, we heard him mocking Joe's productivity that day.

'Listen, mate,' Joe snapped, his short fuse already strained, 'I'm ploughing a full metre deep. Not just eighty bloody centimetres, like some!' Heskel turned a deep red.

'Watch what you're saying,' he yelled. 'Go out and measure, if you like. Plenty others have.'

'Sure,' said Joe. 'There's always enough time to lower the point if you see the area supervisor coming. But the new settlement manager doesn't bother; they trust us. Kibbutzniks have principles, they think.'

'Are you accusing me of raising the plough?' Heskel roared, shaking his fist. 'I'll knock your bloody teeth out if you say that again.' Suddenly, he turned and walked away. Personal violence was unheard of in the kibbutz and Heskel knew he had overstepped the mark. Boaz and Dudik glared at Joe, but said nothing.

'Just goes to prove it,' muttered Joe as we went in to eat.

Over the next few days, Heskel's dunams shrunk to around those of Joe's. He'd hit a hard patch, Boaz tried to excuse. But whether he had raised the plough point or not, was now irrelevant. The mutual trust within the falkha had gone and the seeds of resentment had been sown. Soon, it would spread to other areas and last Saturday's general meeting was just one example. Yet I still hoped that now, with the bitterness behind us, tempers would cool and somehow, more friendly relations could be re-established between the different groupings. Especially now, when we were practising what we had preached: putting our principles where our mouths were as Heskel had taunted. Which was how I found myself on guard out here, alternating nights with Gerry and Yoske.

The night drew on. My eyelids grew heavier and I pined for dawn to come. Suddenly, at about three in the morning, a rustling came from the gully below me, followed by a scraping sound. Something was climbing up into the uncut barley, which would give it good cover. I crouched low, my heart thumping madly as I tried to make some kind of horizon against which it would be outlined, even vaguely. Could it be a group of infiltrators on their way back past Tel Tziklag to the border, or were they deliberately trying to get the combine?

The noise grew louder, the scraping more frenzied. It could only be one or two individuals whatever it was, but that would be enough. Carefully, I released the safety catch and, just as the lights of the combine came over the nearby rise, I raised the rifle and aimed at the rim of the gully. Suddenly, a misshapen bundle bounded up and hurtled past me, snorting and grunting as it went, long, white-tipped back quills quivering in the faint light. A porcupine! Dangerous enough in its own right, but what a relief. So great in fact, that I had to relieve myself there and then.

At that moment, the combine picked me out in full glare of its headlights. Joe couldn't resist the opportunity, as the churning machine came alongside.

'You'll get it shot off if you're not careful,' he called.

'Bloody porcupine,' I puffed. 'Sounded like a whole damn platoon.' Gidi tied another sack and sent it down the chute, without a word. Just a smile and a nod.

'Anyway. Be light soon,' said Joe. He engaged gear and pulled away towards the east, where a faint glow had appeared over the Hebron mountains. I sat on a pile of sacks, waiting for the dawn. Following all the bitter arguments, Gidi's nod was the most I could expect. Perhaps he was trying to make contact. After all, neither Gerry, nor I, nor the others like us, needed to risk our lives out here. We could have let it all just slide. Perhaps, even grudgingly, he respected that we were indeed prepared to put our principles, and our lives, where our mouths were. For that was the difference. We could not be like the politicians or the ivory tower ideologues, or the abstract academics, pontificating what should be done yet never having to do it personally. In the kibbutz, either you practised what you preached, or lost any respect or influence.

At last, dawn broke. I opened the bolt and flicked out the six bullets: one from the breech, five from the magazine; six sleek, silver agents of death. I couldn't help contemplating the paradox. We were here to make the desert bloom, to bring life to this barren earth. We had to rely on weapons of death to do it. I glanced at the swastika on the breech: a Czech-made, ex-Wehrmacht rifle to boot. The sun rose and with it came a terrible weariness. Exhausted by the long, tense night, I slumped onto the swollen sacks of grain and fell fast asleep.

The truck was less than fifty yards away when I woke.

'Fine kind of guard you are,' shouted Avram, grinning. I sat up and rubbed my eyes.

'What kind of a night did you have,' asked Arik who had come to relieve Joe.

'Oh. Pretty uneventful,' I grinned. 'Nearly shot a porcupine. Not much else.' The combine crawled up and stopped. Joe and Gidi jumped down and took off their dust covered hats and goggles. Avram looked over the piles of sacks.

'Not a bad night's work.' He glanced from Gidi to Joe, then back again, adding mischievously, 'You two should work together more often'. We all laughed, even Gidi. Yes, it could be a great feeling to be all working together towards the same end. That morning, for a brief moment, it felt that things were improving. But, waiting in the wings, there was always a new crisis.

Dining out . . .

In ancient days, the Macabees celebrated the miracle of the cruse of holy oil that burned for eight days. In our dining hall, it was the miracle of the everlasting tin of jam that never gave out.

From the very beginning, the dining hall, however primitive or bare, was the focal point of our community. Eating communally was a defining aspect of kibbutz life, an expression of our "togetherness". Mealtimes also providing the opportunity for everyone to meet.

Before we had kids and had to be present and ready for when they came home from the children's house at 4 o'clock, the first place we made for, following the weary climb up the hill after work, was the dining hall. Sitting round the tables in our grubby working clothes at *arukhat arba*, tea time, we exchanged news and gossip and jokes over a cup of weak tea — no milk — before continuing on to the showers.

Tea consisted of a few slices of black bread and often of ersatz plum or cherry flavour jam from a large catering-size tin. We didn't bother with plates, just lay the slices on the tabletop and smeared them with jam, hands still muddy or greasy imparting that special taste.

We loved the jam. It had the viscosity of axle grease, probably contained more vegetable pulp than fruit and must have been full of all those artificial colourings and preservatives that would make a modern "foodie" cringe. But in a limited diet, the chance of something sweet was a luxury we didn't question. Jam, however, was a relatively expensive item and after a while, constrained by her tight budget control, the head cook took to diluting it to make it go further. At first, we didn't notice. But our suspicions were aroused when, as the weeks passed, despite our daily depredations, the same tin was forever half-full. We were celebrating a latter day miracle: the everlasting tin of jam — 'and without divine intervention,' said Geoff.

Gradually though, the preserve became so fluid, it wouldn't even stay on the knife and had to be spooned onto the bread. Eventually, after the specific gravity must have dropped below 1, even the cook decided that it had had its day. Alas. No more mira cles — until the budget could stretch to another tin.

Another feature of our tea, was a bargain buy of a nondescript spread, vegetable or part-animal, we never found out, named — would you believe it — 'Tea Time' in Hebrew transliteration! And with most young kibbutzim being in similar financial straits, 'Tea Time' became a nationwide kibbutz institution and the butt of innumerable feuilletons and cartoons in our magazines of those early days. 'Give us this day, our daily Tea-Time,' we joked. But whether it was watery jam or the strange spread, aside from the socialising, this crude snack played a vital part in filling a hungry stomach, between lunchtime and supper.

As in most young kibbutzim, our first dining hall was a large wooden hut with a corrugated tin roof. One luxury was a tiled floor, whereas most of our huts had timber ones. In order to cram everyone in at mealtimes, there were long tables with benches down each side, and squeezing in an out during busy mealtimes required skilled acrobatics. It was during this period that the kibbutz institution of the 'kol-bo', came about. This was a small aluminium bowl, set in the centre of the table for everyone to put in scraps from their plates, such as salad peelings, left-over crusts, egg shells etc. The idea was to leave your plate free for actual food and avoid littering the table top. It was ugly and unappetising, but it was functional and, failing to find a better solution, the kolbo remained with us and most kibbutzim for a long time.

After a few years, in a daring and expensive move to make things more homely, we changed the long tables to tables for six, but still with the benches. This was a great improvement, except that like most solutions, it created new problems: 'part of the dialectic process,' Joe muttered. If you sat at one end of the table, you had to constantly ask those in the middle to pass bowls of food or salt or whatever, from the other end. If you sat in the middle however, you barely had time to eat, having spent most of the mealtime passing dishes from one side to the other. Joe reckoned it was further proof of the law of relativity. Either way, it was an agonising decision which had to be made each mealtime. As was that of the soft-boiled egg.

Work started at six each morning and, aside from those working far away, we all came in for breakfast between eight and half past. Apart from bread, salad vegetables and white cheese, the mainstay of the meal was an egg — soft or hard-boiled. And for the cooks, about forty of each kind had to be ready for this mad rush at eight o'clock.

With the hard-boiled eggs there was no problem. Bringing the pot to the boil and keeping them in there, even for twenty minutes, didn't matter. With the soft-boiled ones though, once the water was brought to the boil and the eggs immersed within their wire basket, those at the bottom would get the full three-and-a-half minutes, but those at the top or in the centre of the basket got less. So a critical decision had to be made: whether to give the whole lot another minute for those in the centre to be fully soft-boiled — in which case those on the outside would be hard — or to give them all the correct time, whereupon some would be left runny.

That was the cook's dilemma. Ours, when we came up to eat,

was more vexing: whether to take the easy option and go for the hard-boiled egg; they were a cert. Or to opt for a soft-boiled one, which was a gamble that made picking a winner in the national lottery child's play. And being the staple of the meal, if the egg was runny, you would have to grin and eat it regardless. This agonising choice had to be faced every morning — a trauma from which some of us never completely recovered.

The first years of our kibbutz coincided with a period of austerity in the new state, called *tzenna* — similar to the food rationing regime of wartime Britain but without the ration books. The huge immigration and the Arab boycott had all compounded the shortages and many foods were scarce. We were not subsistence farmers and had to buy most of our food from the income of our large-scale modern farming enterprise. And when crops failed or disease struck the livestock, budgets were tight and items like meat almost non-existent. So was yellow cheese, until some Jewish organisation in America found out and diverted to Israel, at a low cost, huge amounts of yellow cheese. A consignment landed up in our dining hall, in large slabs, and for months we ate yellow cheese with our bread, in lieu of the 'Tea Time'.

Then there was the period when eggs were in short supply, so we were exhorted to eat olives. 'Six olives equal an egg', we were assured. We ate kilograms of them. And as for chicken, either you were sick — or the chicken had been. Vegetables were the one product which was plentiful, so in lieu of meat we were served fried aubergine slices, the cooks trying to convince us that it was just like fried liver. It coloured my attitude to the egg-plant ever since.

At times, though, it was no joking matter. Agricultural work creates a huge appetite and there was a period when, after returning from a lunch of vegetable soup, pasta and a thin sauce, our stomachs still felt half empty. Luck had it that on the sand dunes behind the banana groves were ancient vines which provided us with large bounties of tiny grapes throughout the autumn. Even more fortunate was that by the time winter came, our food budget had been increased, eggs were more plentiful and the new breed of white-feathered, double-breasted turkeys was being bred all over Israel. This too had its down side. You could have leg, breast, white meat, black meat, fried, roasted, sliced or Wiener-schnitzeled — as long as it was turkey. Still, it was a great improvement on the aubergine "liver".

The old dining-hall hut served us for many years, painted innumerable times to spruce it up. It was also used for celebrations, the weekly general meeting, the daily work roster, choir practice and more, its elastic sides accommodating whatever came. Each year, a new, permanent building was put into the investments plan — and taken out again, as more pressing economic needs took precedence. Eventually, as the kibbutz grew in numbers, we came in line to receive a loan for a new dining hall from the settlement authorities. There was a list of priorities in Jerusalem and if we didn't want to take an expensive bank loan, we had to wait our turn. Finally, when it came and we could build a bigger and permanent building, the authorities also decided that being a border kibbutz, ours had to have a reinforced concrete roof to provide protection in case of sudden bombardment. This meant more money, so we had to wait again.

Eventually, it took shape, together with a large, state of the art kitchen with steam cookers and all the latest equipment, which cost almost as much as the building itself. It cost even more, as the architect had forgotten about the gigantic new refrigerators when he designed the doorways; we had to knock a hole in one of the side walls to take them in. Luckily it was only of lightweight blockwork.

The modern kitchen was also a determined attempt to redress the balance of the perceived lowly status of the kitchens. Despite our principles of equal value of all work, old prejudices die hard and even with the new building, the old problems of staffing remained.

The head cook was called the *economit*. Symbolically, the word has a feminine ending and it was invariably a woman who was elected to the job, often very unwillingly. The *economit* was a specialised job which did merit esteem and those who took it on

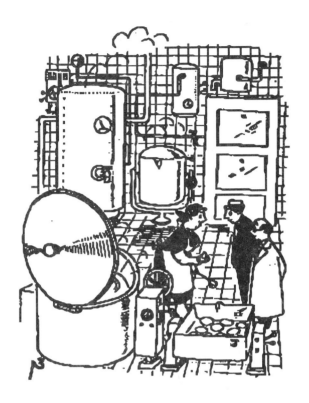

'Wonderful. But there's just the problem of the soft-boiled egg . . .'

went out to nutrition and budgeting courses. But it was still "the kitchens" and entailed a constant struggle with limited budgets. In our case, it also involved satisfying palates previously accustomed to Eastern European or English or Middle Eastern cooking. And despite the modern equipment and prestige, women who came to the kibbutz, hadn't done so to swap the domestic kitchen for the communal one.

Egalitarian principles or not, this was long before "new man" was envisaged. It was as true then as now, that most hotel head-chefs were men, but we didn't have anyone like that. Most of the

men could rustle up a decent camp-fire meal or manage the morning porridge, but when it came to real cooking — something with
flavour and imagination — none of us had that culinary wisdom
that girls imbibe from mothers, or were taught in school. And
when you are feeding a hundred people, if the meal is unpalat-
able, it's not an upset — it's a disaster.

Like many other principles, sharing all kinds of work was
easier in theory than in practice. In retrospect, despite the demand
for men in the heavy field-work, our kibbutz, like many others
who failed in this respect, should have made more effort to
destroy the image of the kitchen as women's work. We could have
elected and sent out men to study nutrition and cooking, to
become the *econom* — and relieve the *economit*. The fact that
women were persuaded at all to take on the task, was due to an
acceptance that it was for the good of the community. True, there
were disgruntled men who reluctantly agreed to work in the
orange groves instead of the garage or workshop where they
wanted to, but the kitchens were a particularly acute problem.
Later, as the ethos of 'finding oneself' began to replace this pre-
paredness to put the community first, it became more and more
difficult to persuade people to fill positions such as the cooks, and
outside chefs were employed. Strangely — or perhaps not so —
these were often men.

What we did do to try and redress the balance in the kitchens,
was to reserve the washing-up chores and serving in the dining
hall, for the men. And in the evenings, these were an additional
toranut rota on top of our day's work. There was the famous
cartoon of a government official asking to see the director of the
kibbutz factory, only to find him up to his elbows in soapy water
in the kitchens . . .

But however modern the new dining hall, there were problems
even it could not resolve. One was the serving the meals. Apart
from the person-in-charge, most of those doing the serving were
on a week or two's enforced stint from their regular jobs, or
between jobs or, in the evenings, on rota after a day's work. The
positive side to this, was the egalitarian "levelling out" principle.

Every man everywhere, from the garage or field crops or orchards, had do a spell in the dining hall in their slack seasons. Functionaries like the treasurer and farm manager did a longer spell when they finished their term of office, and volunteer workers always provided a proportion of the serving staff.

The work wasn't that easy, starting at half past five in the morning with washing the large, tiled floor of the dining hall. At first, all the chairs were placed on the tables which were then moved to one side to allow half the area to be cleaned. Then the whole lot was moved to the other side and the process repeated, before hurrying to set the tables and chairs in their final positions and to lay them out in time for the first breakfast. At the end of every late night general meeting or film show, you could hear next day's servers calling out: 'Put the chairs on the tables before you go, please!' in an effort to make the next morning's work less stressful. Later, in their usual innovative way, kibbutzim invented a kind of manual fork-lift trolley which raised each table with its four chairs "in situ" and wheeled them to the side and back again, as well as wheeled squeegees and polishers, etc.

Today, many kibbutzim have self-service in the dining hall, but in those days, it was *hagashah* — being served at the table. As soon as the dining hall began to fill up each mealtime, the servers came round with trolleys of food and drink for each table. Which was fine, until someone wanted more, or an item was found missing, or cold, whereupon the accepted practice was to raise the bowl or jug high, so the servers could see it. Often they did. But when things got hectic and the servers were pushed to keep up with the steady flow of newcomers, it was touch and go whether anyone would take notice.

After a while most servers became adept at the "server's glance." Head held high and facial expression as if looking around, their actual focus would be on a line about eight-foot high around the walls as they hurried about. Out of the corner of their eye, they might see the raised jug, but remained intent on doing something else. Today, when I see this phenomenon amongst temporary café and restuarant staff in London, Paris and elsewhere, I would lay odds that they had finely honed their talents whilst working as volunteers on a kibbutz.

Another problem was that of the *mishmerot* — "sittings". The dining hall was always too small to accommodate everyone at one sitting, so those who came up late had to wait until the dining hall emptied and had been prepared again for the second sitting. As an impatient crowd began to form in the entrance lobby, in an effort to speed things up, one of the servers would begin to clean off tables as soon as the diners rose and even before if, like Issy, they took their time whatever: 'It's my home, mate,' he would sigh, 'and I can eat as long as I like . . .' One of those serving would be a table cleaner who trundled around a small trolley with buckets of hot water and cloths. But any request to him for more coffee or soup was met with a raised hand: '*Ani smartoot!*' — I'm only the dishcloth!

With the larger dining hall eventually came tables for four, which did away with the agony of sitting in the centre. But the more intimate seating created its own problem. Most of us would eat the evening meal after taking the children back to the children's houses, usually partners together. This meant sharing a table with another two, often a couple. Now although we were all *khaverim* — comrades — we were not all bosom pals. And in times of fierce differences such as the debates over hired labour, or private property, sitting at the same table with someone with whom you had just had a slanging match the night before at the general meeting, or a recent argument at the work roster, was decidedly awkward. Then there was the odd *nudnik* — pain-in-the-neck characters — who could easily ruin a meal. And of course there were the surreptitious liaisons, where sitting with the other half's suspected could be dynamite. So you would occasionally see couples standing in the lobby, ostensibly looking at the work roster or some other notice, but really waiting for someone else to occupy the vacant places at a particular table. Communal living was never intended to overcome all normal human responses — or failings.

Yet, despite all, the system worked. And as the years — and the *tzenna* — passed, so we had a more varied diet, and meat and chicken often appeared on the menu. On Friday afternoons, the baker from Ashkelon brought lovely *challah* white bread, and we had tea and toast with the kids in our rooms or on the lawn outside. Soon, the tea time snack in the room with the children became the norm, often with the addition of home-made cakes, fruit from the orchards or melons from the fields.

With our rising living standards, more and more food could be taken to the rooms and if one partner finished work late in the evening, we made supper on the veranda instead of going up to the dining hall. Being a hot country, soon there was a demand for personal refrigerators so that we could keep more and more varied food at home. Their acquisition added a tidy sum to our investment budget but the fridges were popular, and "domestic" meals became more common.

It was some years yet, before, in many kibbutzim, 'eating out' became mainly confined to work times, the dining hall in the evening becoming the realm only of volunteers and new groups. But long before then, inevitably, along with the communal showers, the chit-chat tea time in the dining hall had disappeared for good, and the miracle of the everlasting tin of jam, had become just part of our folklore.

Come the revolution . . .

It was our first aniversary celebration. Up on the hill, long tables, covered with patched white bed sheets, were laid with biscuits and cakes on paper plates, fruit, jugs of orange juice and the odd bottle of wine. Guests and dignitaries had been invited from all over the country, and blue and white national colours fluttered everywhere with red flags flapping alongside them.

Above the tables, a huge white banner was stretched along the front of the stone blockhouse. On it, a bold slogan in scarlet Hebrew letters broadcast its message across the sand dunes:

'One more house for our people,
One more bastion for the working class,
One more Red Flag on the road - - - - !'

Painted out, by order of the Party head office in Tel Aviv, were the words: 'to Suez'.

Nakhum stared up in disbelief, clenching and unclenching his hands. He was nearly six feet tall and well-built, with a bristling mop of curly, fair hair. Swivelling round, eyes burning and face as red as the flags on either side, he stormed:

'The kibbutz is an integral part of the international class struggle. No one had the right to delete a single word. No one!' He walked across, stood under the slogan and raised his fist, 'We must encourage the workers of Egypt, of Jordan and of Syria, and all the other Arab countries to join the Israeli working class and fight for Socialism.' He pointed to the banner as though the Arab *felakhin* two miles away beyond the Gaza border could see it.

'And on this, our first anniversary,' he continued, as though in the throes of electioneering, 'despite the border, we shall send this message south, through Gaza and across Sinai, over the Suez Canal and to our Egyptian comrades along the Nile!'

The Party officials invited to the celebration didn't view it that way. They could see the headlines in the following morning's papers: 'Left wing kibbutz proclaims expansionist tendencies into Egypt!' happily bracketing us with Beigin's chauvinists on the right. Or paradoxically, at the same time sneering: 'Red kibbutz enlists Israel's enemies for their class war . .' And so on.

'To hell with the yellow press,' Nakhum snapped, 'and our own reformist backsliders. It's gross interference.'

Politics, for us, was a serious business. On the Left, it always is, each party or faction convinced that only they have the correct ideology, only they have the key to the revolution and to the millenium. All others have betrayed the working class, the revolution, the party, Marx, whatever. And no one took it more seriously than Nakhum. To avoid spoiling the celebrations, however, he agreed to let it rest for the moment. But as soon as everyone had departed, he demanded a special general meeting. And we knew there would be trouble.

The following Saturday evening, the dining hall was crowded and the atmosphere, hushed and tense. It was the early fifties, the Cold War had reached the Middle East with a vengeance and the spokesman from Tel Aviv was explaining, yet again, the Party line opposing the recent Soviet-Egyptian arms deal. In a corner by the kitchen door, hunched over a table sat Nakhum, his face growing more clouded by the second. Suddenly, he sat back and slapped his broad, mechanic's hand on the table. He couldn't listen to any more of this claptrap, he said, it hardly differed from the official government propaganda, adding that blanking out part of the anniversary slogan was just another sign.

'The Soviet Bloc is anti-Zionist, because the World Zionist Organisation is dominated by rich American Jews,' Nakhum continued, 'and it is against Israel because Ben Gurion is kow-towing to the USA. And,' he added, 'whatever its failings, the USSR is the bulwark against American and British imperialism.' The speaker, standing at the centre table, twitched his glasses and disagreed, gently, wanting to avoid a head-on confrontation.

'The Soviet weapons would be used primarily to attack Israel,' he said, 'and as socialists, we should oppose the deal because the weapons could just as easily be turned against Egyptian workers.' Nakhum sprang up. His face, already flushed, had turned a shade closer to crimson.

'Soviet arms supplies to Nasser are justified,' he said. 'They are to defend the Egyptian revolution against British and American imperialism. And tell me,' he shouted, pointing at the spokesman, 'what will you do if the Red Army brings the revolution through Turkey and Syria and stands ready to cross our northern border?'

For a few seconds there was absolute silence. The speaker coughed and cleared his throat, trying to formulate an unprovocative response. Suddenly, from the opposite corner by the entrance doors, Zeev stood up, hands gripping the table edge.

'I don't care whose bloody army it is,' he shouted back, 'I'll pick up my rifle and go and defend my homeland.' Nakhum span round to face him.

'The Red Army will never come as conquerors,' he retorted, 'only as liberators!'

'Balls!' shouted Zeev, 'Russia is playing power politics like everyone else!'

Uproar followed as voices joined in all around, some supporting one side, some the other. Desperately, Mikha, the secretary, thumped on his table, trying to restore order. The questions and discussion had been going on all evening, but entrenched attitudes had only hardened. It was nearly one o'clock and it was up again for work at six. But by now the hotheads of both sides were in full cry.

Mira looked up at her husband, her long, dark hair hanging over her smooth face. Slowly she shook her head and looked down again. Politics was Nakhum's life, his reason for being here. It was not a game like it was for some, but a deep and sincere personal conviction, which was why she loved and respected him, but also feared where the acrimonious debate would lead.

At that moment, in the midst of the slanging match, Nakhum's supporters on the tables around him stood up and started to sing "The Internationale":

'Kum hitna'era am khelecha . . ,' 'Arise ye starvelings from your slumbers. Arise ye criminals of want . . '.

From the far end, not to be outdone, Zeev's group stood and gave voice to "Hatikva", the Israeli national anthem:

'Kol od belevav, penima . . . ,' 'As long as our heart beats, a Jewish spirit will sing out . . . ' Soon the dining hall had divided into two unequal choirs, The Internationale being in the minority. Not that the others were less committed socialists, but the arguments, the frayed tempers and the late hour, had banished all rationality. Twenty minutes later, the special general meeting, called to resolve 'The Affair of the Banner', ended in complete chaos.

Castrating the slogan, for that was how he saw it, was, for Nakhum, symbolic of our Party leaders' abandonment of basic principles. And his protest marked the start of a series of ideological confrontations that bedevilled and rocked our kibbutz and many others throughout the fifties and into the sixties, leaving casualties strewn along the way.

With Nakhum, it began even before the kibbutz came to settle on the border and after the anniversary celebrations, as he had walked down from the hill with his arm around Mira, he recalled those days in the temporary camp in Rehovot, and the bitter arguments.

'For this we left Romania?' he said to her as they crossed the small green patch of lawn they'd planted the year before. 'For this

I argued with the Jewish communists of Anna Paulker, that a Jewish proletariat will only be created in its own land. That only then will we materially contribute to the revolutionary struggle.' Mira gripped his hand but said nothing. Liberation by the Red Army from Nazi occupation and almost certain extermination, had left many of them with an emotional, as well as an ideological affinity to the Soviet Union. 'So much for our revolutionary party,' Nakhum muttered. 'So much for all the arguments with Paulo and Itchou and the others, eh?' Mira tried to calm the waters. Ideologically, she was with Nakhum. But the Kibbutz was more than just politics.

'Look,' she said, 'if the Party appears too extreme, Nakhum, it could alienate people in town, especially the new immigrants. Give it time.'

'There is no time, Mira,' he said firmly, 'Either we are with the socialist camp, or we allow Ben Gurion's government to help America to take over the whole Middle East.'

Nakhum and Mira were amongst the founder members of the kibbutz and part of a highly-politicised group who left communist Romania in 1947. Seized as illegal immigrants by the British and imprisoned in Cyprus for a year, they arrived in 1948 and were soon organising local political meetings in Rechovot, where they were temporarily camped, canvassing the orange groves workers and local packing houses. In 1949, when the group was about to move to create a permanent settlement on the Gaza border, a small section broke away and decided to remain behind. There was no way of furthering the class struggle out in the desert, they maintained. Their real place was there, they said, amongst the workers in Rechovot. Despite all attempts at persuasion, when the trucks finally moved off, the splinter group remained behind. Within a few years, some had joined the Israeli Communist Party. Eventually, most became functionaries in government offices and generally did very well, conveniently and quite readily forgetting their revolutionary political ideas.

Between Nakhum's group and those who had remained, there was no more than a cigarette paper's thickness difference of ideology. But it was memories of that hard-fought battle that now made Nakhum, and those who thought like him, so vociferous and militant over the banner. And it stuck in his side like a thorn.

Our situation wasn't that simple. We were socialists — revolutionary socialists — believing that it was the only way to bring about a new society of justice and equality. We were, however, also Zionists, maintaining that Zionism was the national liberation movement of the Jewish people and that, like any other people, we had a right to self-determination in our own homeland. Unfortunately, all other revolutionary socialist parties throughout the world, headed by the Soviet Union, were anti-Zionist. So we had continually to prove ourselves 'holier than thou', to be accepted by them as socialists. It was of course an uphill and completely unrequited struggle, and despite strenuous efforts, we were always out on a limb.

Nearly half a century later, it is possibly difficult to grasp this undimmed belief in socialism and the Soviet Union. But during the slow return to normality after the trauma of the Second World War, we felt that without the Red Army and the heroic stands of Leningrad and Stalingrad, Hitler may never have been defeated. And surely a people that made such sacrifices for their country and regime must have believed in them. True, the Russian control of Eastern Europe was oppressive, but apart from Czechoslovakia, most of those countries had been quasi-fascist in the thirties and had sided with the Nazis during the war. In addition, Mao Tse Tung's communist victory in China, Castro's Cuba and the Asian national liberation movements had all added a completely new dimension: no longer was it an isolated Eastern Bloc, but a world movement. It seemed that world Socialism was on the march.

On the other side of the equation, America was in the grip of the McCarthyist witch-hunt, blacks were still being lynched in Mississippi, militant union leaders had been assassinated and the old western Imperial powers were desperately trying to hang on to their colonies in Asia and Africa. And for all its faults, the Soviet Union was seen to be the main ally of these new liberation movements and of progressive forces throughout the world. And we were by no means alone. Many eminent and respected intellectuals and groups throughout the western world thought likewise. This was also the time that the Big Powers began using the Middle East countries as pawns in the power game and Ben Gurion's government had sided with the United States as a bastion against Soviet influence. It isolated Israel from the Eastern Bloc, where there were still large Jewish communities and also from the Third World, whose friendship we needed to counter the influence of the Arab and Moslem states. Above all, it made Israel an active participant in the Cold War.

Within Israel, we were then the only Zionist party to regard the Palestinians as a people with equal right to independent self-determination in their own state, alongside the state of Israel. This prompted vicious "patriotic" attacks not only from the chauvinist Right, but also from the ruling Labour party. Disillusioned and isolated, the Israeli Left found itself on the defensive, creating fertile ground for divisions to appear and it was against this background, that Nakhum's traumatic general meeting took place that Saturday. And broke up in chaos.

During that week and the weeks following, the arguments raged in the cowsheds and the poultry houses, the workshops and the young orange groves. Were we an integral part of the revolutionary socialist world or weren't we? Were the Party leadership becoming social democratic pinkos? And, more relevant, was the kibbutz a vanguard of the Israeli working class, or an idealistic utopia in the desert and a political dead end? The extremists on both sides wouldn't give an inch, but gradually things simmered down into a *modus vivendi*. As Mira had said, the kibbutz was more than just politics.

For those like Nakhum, however, it was the prime ingredient, and from that day he stopped coming to the general meetings. In the garage workshop, he answered in monosyllables. We recognised his protest, but thought it would blow over, especially as Mira continued to head the education committee; she was our first trained teacher. But her usual enthusiasm was lacking too, her eyes dull and at times moist. In the dining hall, she and Nakhum would often sit through a meal hardly exchanging a word.

We feared what was coming and one month later, Nakhum stood up at the general meeting to make a personal statement.

'Israel,' he began, 'is fast becoming a tool of American imperialism in the Middle East.' He then continued that the Party wasn't fighting against this tide and the only way to do that was to mobilise the growing proletariat in the towns. The kibbutz was too isolated to play any significant part. 'Socialism,' he concluded, 'is now more important than Jewish nationalism and for that reason,' he paused and looked around the dining hall, 'I am leaving'.

We listened in absolute silence, shaken, even though it wasn't unexpected. When Eliezar had called round one evening, Mira had been in tears trying to make Nakhum see things in proportion. We knew that if it hadn't been for her, the crisis would have come sooner. Many had tried to dissuade him throughout the previous week, so there was nothing to add. Nakhum knew his own mind and the hall remained silent. Two weeks later, he, Mira and his two year old son left, with nothing apart from their bed and blankets and a few clothes. They put up in a dingy room on the outskirts of Tel Aviv and he took a low paid instructor's job at an agricultural school.

During the weeks following, about fifteen others declared themselves 'politically aware' and left too. It was a pattern that was to repeat itself at each crisis. A few did indeed share Nakhum's stubborn convictions, but more were merely jumping on the ideological bandwagon as an excuse to leave. It saved face, without needing to admit that they were just finding the going too tough. Nakhum's leaving was tragic and very, very sad. He was a kibbutznik, body and soul, as was Mira. It was a terrible blow, but his political leaving wasn't the last of its kind. Nor was the crisis.

The whole problem was exacerbated by our kibbutz belonging to the 'Artzi' federation of kibbutzim, in which there was an 'Ideological Collectivism'. Since our lives were collective in every way, it seemed quite natural to hold common ideological beliefs which strengthened our social, economic and cultural cohesion. In fact, all the more permanent communal settlements of previous eras were precisely those who had a common, usually religious, ideology. In our case, it was political. We chose it voluntarily and those who did not wish to follow it, left for other kibbutzim or to town. For practical political purposes, we were part of the United Workers Party, MAPAM. In town, however, when Party members disagreed, it rarely affected their home or family lives. But for us, every ideological split also provoked social and personal crises, resulting in bitterness and leavings, and in the mid-fifties it returned again.

Mordekhai Oren, a leading Party member, was arrested in Czechoslovakia on charges of spying for the United States. It was ludicrous, akin to accusing the Pope of adultery! Oren was not only a member of one of our kibbutzim, but also way out on the left wing of the party. This charge, coming in the wake of the Stalinist — and usually anti-semitic — trials in Poland, Hungary and Czechoslovakia, was rapidly destroying any remaining illusions we had about the Soviet Union. But the dilemma was agonising. Either we had to believe Prague, that Oren was guilty, or accept that the Czech regime was corrupt and certainly not socialist.

Into this stew stepped one Dr. Mosheh Sneh, a leading Party member from Tel Aviv. Either we were part of the revolutionary camp led by the Soviet Union, he said, or we were against it. Oren might be a tragic error, but in the present international struggle between East and West, he maintained, we had to support the Czech socialist regime, adding, for full measure, that Zionism was irrelevant, since the internal Israeli political struggle was now paramount. A small minority in the kibbutz came out in support of Dr. Sneh and once again, the arguments raged at work, in the showers and on the lawns after work, and also in the general meetings to which Party spokesmen were invited.

This time however, our own kibbutz federation intervened. The threat of dissociating ourselves from the World Zionist Movement was a matter of principle and undermined basic tenets of our ideological collectivism. In addition, Dr. Sneh, meanwhile, had split away to form his own party. So this time, said the party

spokesman, the kibbutz had to take a stand; either those supporting Dr. Sneh, the Snehists, disowned his views, or they had to get
out.

Many of us were unhappy with this outside intervention. But
our kibbutz movement and Party were already on a collision
course with the Israeli establishment and the government was
accusing the Left of alienating American Jewry and its vital financial backing, of being pro-Arab, of betraying Israel in the international scene, etc. etc. After the famous banner incident, for us to be
seen as anti-Zionist as well, would have been politically
disastrous.

That Saturday's general meeting had all the same features of
the one a few years before with Nakhum and the Communists.
Each side proclaimed its adherence to socialism and argued over
minutae such as whether we were Marxist and Leninists, or
Marxist-Leninists (the hyphen, or not, being of paramount ideological significance). Like I said, on the Left, politics is always a
serious business.

Perhaps it might have all blown over. But in the existing
environment, the 'Snehists', headed by Rakhel, were pushed into a
corner by the kibbutz federation representatives. The result was
the leaving of another ten people. Less than half were actual
Snehists. The others, as before, waverers and the fainthearted,
seized the opportunity and slunk out. There was no singing of the
'Internationale'. No 'Hatikva'. It was all sad and subdued and, as
before, three of the dissenters were leading kibbutzniks. Four
were also members of the choir and two were nursery nurses. And
with them went six children, depleting our school still further.
Once again, we strove to pick up the pieces and continue.

By now, towards the end of the fifties, Khruschev's and others'
revelations about Stalin had destroyed any of our residual faith in
Moscow. Many even threw out the socialist baby with the Stalinist
bathwater. No longer did the walls of the dining hall resound to
political arguments, or the beams of the cowshed roofs quiver
from ideological hair splitting. Apart from a few stalwarts, apathy
became the order of the day and when the next ideological test

came, it was from the Right, as anti-Arab sentiments and militaristic chauvinism began to surface within the kibbutz. And it wasn't a pretty sight. It too was a minority. But by then, the majority had become too fed up with politics to care. A plague on all their houses!

Nakhum would have seen the irony. His road to Suez was now firmly blocked by fanatical, right-wing Jewish settlers and by the Intafada in Gaza. And those of us in the kibbutz who retained some real socialist ideals and still adhered to a collective ideology, had now become the minority.

In the late sixties, just before the Six Day War, I bumped into Nakhum at the bus station in Tel Aviv. He was working for the ministry of agriculture; Mira was a head teacher in Rishon. Both doing quite well and they now had three kids.

'Politics?' I asked him. Nakhum brushed back his thinning hair and smiled. We shook hands, I sent regards and he went on his way. Never did make the revolution.

'. . . and keep the Red Flag flying.'

Visitors and volunteers

As he ate lunch in our dining hall one Shabbat, Anthony Nutting showed us his gold watch, a present from King Saud of Arabia. The king's portrait was on the dial. It was noon and we were all amused as the hands covered the bearded face. Nutting had resigned as Foreign Secretary in protest over the Anglo-French invasion of the Suez Canal. He was now on a tour of Middle Eastern countries and a first secretary at the British embassy in Tel Aviv had brought him down to our kibbutz. He was surprised to hear that we were opposed to Israel's collusion with the Anglo-French invasion of Egypt, and more surprised that a sizeable Israeli minority thought likewise. The strangeness lay in the fact that left-wing Socialist Zionists and a Conservative arabophile were of the same mind over the Suez Crisis.

Nutting was just one of a constant stream of visitors to Israel who wanted to see kibbutzim for themselves and we were one of the kibbutzim to which English-speaking visitors were recommended. Most visitors were sympathetic but not all. Like the apocryphal tale of a delegation of American Women Zionist's during the McCarthy era. Despite their distaste for what they regarded as our 'communist' ideology, they appreciated the modern cowshed, the murals in the dining hall, the immaculate children's houses as very impressive and so normal. But as they were about to depart, one matriarch turned to their kibbutz guide.

'Of course,' she smirked, 'you people believe in free love, don't you?' The kibbutznik paused, then sighed.

'Perhaps. But I'm afraid you are a little too old.'

Since its very beginnings in the 1920's, the kibbutz has held a fascination for people of all shades of opinion, but misconceptions are still rife. Books like Koestler's 'Thieves in the Night' in the thirties, promoted the free-for-all ideas that caught the American lady's attention and all visitors inevitably brought with them a baggage of preconceived ideas and notions. At times, we felt that there were as many ideas and prejudices regarding us, as there were visitors.

One of our first such experiences, was with the journalist Paul Johnson, in the days when he was still way out on the Left. Climbing the hill, he looked out to the sand dunes, then down to our farm buildings and the red roofed huts.

'Impressive,' he pronounced. 'But after all, you really can't call yourselves socialists.' We soon became aware that like him, many on the far left to whom we looked as natural allies, dismissed the kibbutz as utopian and escapist. We were not a little peeved, but he was our guest so we humoured him. Still, despite all its ideological failings, the kibbutz has yet to emulate his political somersaults over to the Right.

Over the years, we discussed, argued and joked with a steady stream of English-speaking visitors of every shape, size, colour and ideological leaning. There was the late, Labour MP, John Mendelson.

'We have nationalised all heavy industry and transport,' he said, 'and when we nationalise land, we shall have achieved socialism in Britain.' We questioned him about worker participation, about education, the House of Lords and housing, but his replies were vague. Having remembered the great promises after the '45 high, we felt that the Labour Party had already lost direction. He thought us rather too idealistic. More encouraging were the many progressives and free-thinking socialists, like Tony Benn.

The first secretary from the embassy who had brought Nutting, came several times, often bringing others with him. He showed genuine interest in the workings of the kibbutz and we became quite friendly. However we kept him away from our mortar pits and trenches up on the hill, told him that the armoury was the emergency food store and steered him round to the farm and out to the new orange and banana groves.

'Tank tracks,' he observed on one visit, looking at the dirt road down to the sea.

'Must be our Caterpillar D6 tractor,' I replied, not even convincing myself. He winked then looked again and murmured ever so politely.

'I was once in the armoured corps.'

It was rumoured that Britain had a plan involving Israel giving up non-essential border areas in exchange for a Arab recognition. He may have been sussing out just how viable our particular area was. So it was, *khabdehu ve'khashdehu*, as we say in Hebrew: 'respect and suspect.' And with pro-Arab sentiments at the Foreign Office and British officers still in command of the Jordanian Arab Legion, the 'suspect', was high on the list, albeit with typical English politeness.

He also brought the new British ambassador who came heavily escorted by the Israeli military. They were not taking any chances of sparking off an international incident in our wild border area. An Israeli major sat in on the welcome, perhaps to check that we would not reveal any military secrets. As it was, we had more serious logistical problems. Mikhal insisted that we could not serve the ambassador tea in our scratched plastic cups. Elizabeth, the daughter of the Mayor of Sheffield and originally a volunteer who had married in, saved the day by unpacking her delicate bone china tea set, a wedding present. We looked on with horror as the ambassador, stressing some point or other, waved his cup and saucer in the air fit for it to drop at any moment. Later, we wondered what the Israeli major made of it all.

The embassy secretary brought me a blue glass vase from Hebron. In those days, with monthly skirmishes between Israeli and Jordanian units, it was as if it had come from another planet and I still have it. We also accepted the invitation to the annual Queen's birthday party at the embassy. After the Suez Crisis, Israel needed all the international friends she could muster and we felt this was our own small contribution . . .

Then there were the writers. Maeve Binchy returned several times; so did Lynn Reid Banks who wrote about us in *The Observer*. She set part of one of her novels on our hilltop settlement, before marrying a member of another kibbutz up north. Bob Hoskins spent some time with us before he became famous, and returned to visit even when he was. And then there was the international press.

The first aerial jet dogfight between Israel and Egypt took place right above our heads over the *wadi*, resulting in the downing of three Egyptian Vampires. Two weeks later, a convoy of cars descended on the kibbutz; reporters from the then popular weekly magazine *Illustrated* arrived with the intention of running a feature: 'British settlers on the border'. For two days, they hustled and bundled groups of us into the trenches and up to the watchtower, photographing us from every conceivable angle: Mikhal and Peretz pointing rifles through the roses over sandbags; Yehuda herding the cows with Sten gun over his shoulder; Issy up by the watchtower at night with searchlight beaming above his head. It was all great stuff for the folks back home and our families bought dozens of copies to show to their friends. It completely disrupted any normal routine for the few days the camera crews were there. But again, Israel needed friends and if it helped, why not? And it brought yet further waves of reporters for months after.

Following the Suez campaign, in an effort to break the diplomatic isolation sponsored by the Arab states in Africa and Asia, Israel provided a large number of agricultural advisers overseas

And over there. A typical kibbutz!

through the United Nations. It also welcomed Third World graduates, especially in the field of agriculture, and what better place to show them than the kibbutz. We spent hours of our precious free time, showing them around; having them to tea at the same time as trying to be with the kids and so on. But it was a soulless task. These students of agriculture and economics had no intention of returning to their villages and raising standards. In vain we explained that the success of Israeli agriculture and development didn't lie with the ministries in Jerusalem and Tel Aviv, but in having those with vision and expertise at the sharp end and that their talents would have most effect by personal example out in the villages. But despite their good knowledge of English, we seemed to be speaking different languages. Their priority was to get a career job in a black suit in the ministries in Lagos, Nairobi or Colombo. They probably thought us crazy.

Our system of collective education brought psychologists and sociologists aplenty who, without knowing the language and on the basis of unrelated work experience, didn't hesitate to write learned articles and books about us, often wide of the mark. Bruno Bettelheim wrote his famous 'Children of the Dream', comparing our system to his home for very disturbed children, after spending only three weeks in a kibbutz. On what other society would anyone have the *chutzpah* to do that? Thirty years after Koestler's book, people were still spreading misconceptions.

Perhaps the most difficult were the Japanese. In Japan, a similar movement to that of the kibbutzim was started by a Tokyo professor. There were already tens of settlements and thousands of adherents and, although it had a strong religious flavour, firm ties were established between them and the kibbutzim in the '60's. And as the only foreign language with which they were vaguely acquainted was English, we were targeted to welcome them as well. So two or three young Japanese would suddenly arrive with a letter of introduction and we would spend an awkward evening trying to explain things, to which they would smile and answer 'Yes,' each time. It took two or three of these visits for us to realise that when they said 'Yes', it did not mean agreement, nor understanding, just that they had heard.

More welcome, and of greater significance, were the Volunteers, people who came and stayed a while to give a hand. There must now be tens of thousands, throughout the world, who have spent a few months or more on one of the kibbutzim. The volunteer movement actually started from within Israel itself, but it became international as a result of the Six Day War.

In April 1967, Nasser blocked the straits of Tiran. Throughout May, war threatened and young people from all over the world, identifying with Israel's David against the Arab states' Goliath as it seemed at the time, began to arrive by plane and boat. However, just as this trickle began to turn into a huge flood, the Six Day War broke out in June, closing the airport and ports. When the war ended, thousands were still waiting and once flights were resumed, they came all the same. Most ended up on kibbutzim that were desperate for labour, with many of the men still in the army and huge backlogs of farmwork to make up from the priorities given to defence. From then on, word got around all over the world: there were these great places to tune in and drop out for a few months. True you had to work, but there was sunshine and all was found. There were good-looking men and suntanned girls. So, along with the trail to Katmandu and back, the kibbutzim were the 'in' place. We didn't mind. Most of the volunteers fitted in well. Some made strong personal relationships. One or two married and tried to stay. But somehow, lacking the ideological commitment, most went back to their original lands, sometimes keeping contact in small local volunteer associations and networks.

We couldn't fathom out why some came, or stayed. But all were welcome. Judith was an aluminium magnate's daughter and quite stunning, with brown wavy hair; she could have been a model. She worked wonderfully in the orchards and even marched with us on May Day in Tel Aviv, yet always kept much to herself. Then, after six months, she was gone and never heard of again. Renso, an electrician, came from Milan. He was always joking and helped out in the carpenter's shop. He fell in love with Tzipi, a vivacious, strong-minded girl originally from Morocco. He went back with her to Italy and returned again, travelling back and forth several times. Then it broke up. Or did it? We never were quite sure. Alma came from Boston, after quitting the first troupe that danced *West Side Story*. She was a wonderful worker with tremendous repartee — giving more than she took as the boys tried to flirt. But hers was a story in itself .

Roger became a stalwart of the dairy herd, but eventually the call of the Outback down under, proved too strong even for him. From Paris came Chantal, long blond hair and wide eyes. She fell in love with one of the boys who'd been badly wounded in Sinai and wanted to stay and marry him. He felt he would be a burden and wanted to be independent. After a year and a half she left, heartbroken. Maurice from Marseilles came three or four times and was infatuated with Miriam. But she was married, happily.

Marion from Scotland had come at the instigation of her parents, who wanted to stop a nice Jewish girl from marrying a Catholic. She had nymphomaniac tendencies and some of the bachelors were quite sad when she went home. Ed came from Philadelphia. He stayed for nearly a year then came back several times to try and stay. Something didn't click, difficult to know what. Many of the young Jews who came from America however, felt that they were God's gift to Israel and the kibbutz. They were full of complaints and suggestions, couldn't work and generally were a serious pain in the neck. The best workers were the Aussies, Kiwis, Dutch and Scandinavians. The English tended to get drunk too often.

The origins of the volunteer movement were in the weeks leading up to the Sinai War, or the Suez Crisis, as it was known outside. Quite suddenly, in the autumn of 1955, the Egyptian army moved in force into the Gaza Strip and it was realised just how woefully inadequate our defences were. So people in town were given time off from work, to come and help out in kibbutzim along the borders, digging shelters and trenches and stretching new barbed wire fences. There was a group from the Inland Revenue, who had to put up with our jokes about tax inspectors as the blisters swelled on their hands; followed by a dozen geology students from Jerusalem, just before their exams. Despite a gruelling day's work, they stayed up late, quizzing each other about tertiary rocks and strange-sounding fossils. But our favourites were a group of dockers from the port of Tel Aviv.

Huge tourist hotels and a broad esplanade now cover the old docks area, but at the time it was still unloading cargos and exporting Jaffa oranges. And they were still the original dockers from the thirties, Jews brought over from Salonika with leather brown faces and arms like oak boughs, wearing dark blue peaked caps and speaking a heavily accented Hebrew. They had been the lucky ones. Ten years after they came, Hitler wiped out their entire, ancient community. They helped dig trenches, made up manpower in the fields, anything. And we, who had come to conquer physical work and ended up aching from it every evening, admired the effortless way they shouldered hundredweight sacks of grain or picked up loaded boxes of fruit as though they were light suitcases. Most had never even visited a kibbutz, certainly never lived on one, and during the fortnight they stayed with us, were curiously amused at our communal way of life and lack of money.

Both sides were genuinely sad at their going back to the port which, a few years later, would be closed down for good. They were a dying breed from a lost community. We promised to keep contact 'after the crisis was over' and invite them down with their families. Then other groups came, the Sinai War started, and we never did.

During the tense weeks leading up to the Six Day War, a group of 'old timers' from kibbutz Hazorea up north came to help us deepen the trenches and dugouts. Many stayed for six months or more, roughing it out with us despite being of pensioner age, and further groups came throughout the following years to help out generally and give us the benefit of their experience.

The volunteers who came in the sixties brought with them a fresh breeze of new ideas from the storm that was sweeping the West during that decade. Many became close friends, feeling free to come to our rooms, providing intellectual stimulation and new slants on our way of life. We dearly hoped that some would stay and join us, add to our social composition and bring new talents and additional vitality as well as augmenting our permanently undermanned workforce. Hardly any did. By the seventies, we could no longer make the effort to repeatedly respond to new faces and relationships, knowing by now that they would inevitably be transient. So the volunteers became just another part of the workforce, living in huts on the far side of the kibbutz, lounging by the swimming pool after work and spending their evenings together. Eating as a group in the dining hall, they rarely connected with the kibbutzniks in any deeper way, then left after a few months to go on their way.

After the Lebanon War and with the changing image of Israel in the world media, volunteer numbers dropped but a steady stream continued to arrive. Some even married in, but few couples stayed on the kibbutz. Finally, more and more, we felt that young people from the West were just using the volunteer movement to get away from unemployment or a cold climate. Or both.

No doubt the curious will still come to visit and volunteers will stay for a short while or longer. Their welcome will vary from kibbutz to kibbutz. Some may decide to remain. But would they be the drop-outs and misfits? Or will the kibbutz still have a sufficient residue of ideals to attract those seeking a positive, alternative purpose to their lives?

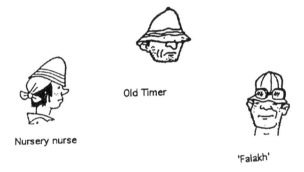

Old Timer

Nursery nurse

'Falakh'

Metamorphosis of the kibbutz work-hat
- the *kova tembel*.

Culture
vulture

youngster

Tough nut

Organiser

To Mount Sinai . . .

The dining hall was packed tight, everyone was laughing and singing with the accordion twirling away and sweets and biscuits and orange juice all round. It was the end of November 1956. The Sinai War was over and the boys had returned from the fighting.

With British and French troops holding the Suez Canal, Israeli army and air power had destroyed Colonel Nasser's new army and conquered Gaza and most of Sinai. Biblical allusions to the ancient Hebrews overcoming Pharaoh were coming through thick and fast in the media, and especially in popular song. 'To Mount Sinai' was just one of the ditties spawned by the brief war. It had become a battle hymn and now rang around the dining hall again and again:

'. . Look now, how the bush burns before Mount Sinai
Ho, Flame of God, Here are your Youth
Ho Flame of God, Here are your chosen ones . .'

But despite the relief and rejoicing, many of us had misgivings about the justification for the war. Eliezar in particular was having trouble celebrating, and winced every time the refrain crashed out.

'Just listen,' he muttered, crunching a biscuit, 'if the patriotic jingoism wasn't enough, now we have to listen to this quasireligious twaddle.' He slapped his hand on the table. 'Suez was an imperialist war by Britain and France to regain possession of the Canal. We, Israel, did their dirty work for them. And now we, kibbutzniks, socialists and internationalists are celebrating. I ask you . . ' But it was not so simple. Many felt that Israel had been justified to take advantage of the Anglo-French assault on the Canal Zone, to settle scores in Gaza.

With the rise of Colonel Nasser in the early fifties, Soviet arms had begun pouring into the new union of Egypt and Syria. Throughout the summer of 1956, infiltration by Palestinian *Fedayeen* from over the border intensified. Tractors went up on mines and even villages further inland, were attacked at night. Week after week, we put out ambushes down in the *wadi* and increased night guard strengths. It affected our daily work, frayed the nerves of mothers with young children and certainly nibbled away at our internationalist ideals creating a general hardening of attitudes.

Israeli reprisal raids on fortified police stations at Gaza and Khan Yunis were followed by the Egyptian army shelling kibbutzim along the border, causing several casualties and much damage. Israel had replied by bombarding Gaza town causing even more casualties. But when an Israeli 'red berets' attack on the Jordanian village of Qibya left many Arab civilians dead and wounded, the arguments between doves and hawks about the reprisal strategy in general, became even fiercer.

Within the kibbutz, this was not merely ideological hair-splitting. With Egyptian artillery only a few miles away and many of the boys called up in the parachutists and similar elite units, it was a matter of life and death. Opinions became more and more polarised, some supporting the government's 'bloody nose' tactics whilst others, like Eliezer, continued to maintain that the only solution was a political one; to negotiate a peace and a settlement with the Palestinian refugees, from whom the Fedayeen drew their strength.

The watershed came with the Suez. At first, reserves were called up, then released, then called up again. Israel is a small country. Everyone knows someone "in the know" and rumours began to circulate of an even more massive reprisal action; of seizing the Gaza Strip; of bombing Cairo and parts of Jordan. Finally, our political party newspaper, *Al Hamishmar*, began to hint of, and caution against, 'joining international intrigues'. It was obvious that something on a quite different scale was being planned. What no one knew, was that Ben Gurion had already gone to a secret conference in France and agreed to collaborate with the British and French plan to seize back the recently nationalised Suez Canal. At the same time, they hoped to topple Nasser and his pro-Soviet regime.

November began beautifully sunny, the autumn lingering on with hot days and cool, clear nights. We began the winter ploughing and prepared for the grapefruit picking. But life couldn't continue as normal. Newspapers and the radio reported increased shipments of Soviet weapons to Nasser and large concentrations of Egyptian army units in Sinai and Gaza. We were ordered to prepare for . . we didn't know what, but something big.

Normal working continued only with the livestock and some essential crop irrigation. Lawns turned yellow and flower beds wilted. All other labour was diverted to frantically digging new trenches to the children's shelters and clearing the perimeter machine-gun emplacements of thorn bushes and rubbish. With the help of volunteer groups of workers from town, heaps of sand rose everywhere and the chances of falling into a trench in the dark increased daily by geometrical progression.

Somehow, Shoshannah and the cultural committee managed to continue organising the Friday night cultural evening which, by chance, was for November 7th, celebrating 'October 1917' and commemorating what we then still considered the first socialist revolution. Despite everything, we still felt a resonance of the liberation of the Russian workers and peasants to our own liberation and our socialist ideals. Every year, we played records of Prokofiev and Shostakovich, and sang *Kalinka* and *The Birch Tree*.

We read from Mayakovsky and Sholokhov, and from the famous war novel, *Men of Panfilov*, those famous lines, when the commander asks his men what they are fighting for. And when they reply in the abstract: 'The Homeland', he makes them spell it out: their village, their home, their wives, their children, their achievements. All of which we felt and identified with; defending our own homes and our homeland.

But every year it was becoming more problematic. First, the revelations about Stalin, then the mock trials in Prague and now the military pacts between Moscow and our Arab neighbours. Here we were, preparing to celebrate the Bolshevik revolution, but if war came, we would be facing Soviet weapons and planes. How could we celebrate October? Yet to cancel it, we felt then, would be to deny our socialist ideals; agree to Israel becoming allied with the USA in the Cold War. But events overtook the arguments. On the evening of 6th November, a security alert was announced. By

Wars come and go — a tree is forever.

the next morning, the children were down in the shelters and we were all manning the trenches.

The first sign of anything unusual was a small convoy of merchant ships steaming down the coast towards Gaza. Previous to this, we had never seen anything larger than a fishing boat so close inshore. Subsequently, we heard rumours that they were American boats evacuating foreign personnel from Gaza. But to this day, that convoy remains a mystery. That afternoon, the 7th, we took up action stations and the same night, the radio announced that Israeli forces had crossed into Sinai: 'in pursuit of infiltrators'. All work, apart from that with livestock, the children and kitchen was cancelled. We left our rooms and assembled in our fighting units, taking turns to sleep in nearby huts. The Sinai War, known elsewhere as the Suez Crisis, had begun.

For two days and nights we took turns in the trenches, staring across the dunes and peering into the darkness, fearing an Egyptian army night attack. Anxiously, we listened to news broadcasts of our forces in Sinai, heading for the Canal. Then on the third evening, Dudik, our platoon commander stumbled into the hut, hot and flustered.

'We have to get up on the hill and stay there,' he gasped breathless. 'Headquarters says that refugees from Gaza are being organised to march north. And we have to stop them!'

For a few seconds, we just sat and looked at his face which was working like mad.

'Stop them? How? Shooting? At unarmed men and women? And children?' He just nodded, as though unable to believe it himself. Yet we couldn't let them just walk past and into Ashkelon and on to Tel Aviv. There would be chaos. Confrontations. Israelis settling their own accounts. And behind that human shield, would come the Egyptian army. It didn't bear thinking about.

That night and all the next day, we lay in the trenches up on the hill, scanning the dunes to the south. Each movement of a goat or a bird, each wisp of smoke or dust cloud made everyone jump and point their guns. And again and again, the murmured arguments: if they really came, could we bring ourselves to shoot? I noticed that even Dudik, despite his militaristic views, was also shocked at the possibility. That, at least, was encouraging. For myself, I had decided to fire in the air, or at the sand in front. I hadn't come out here to kill innocent civilians. Those people had a cause, they had to be resettled and compensated, with perhaps a proportion allowed back into Israel, when peace came.

In the end, mercifully, the alarm proved to be false. The following morning, the Egyptian General in Gaza submitted his surrender almost without having fired a shot. But then, that afternoon, out of the blue, came the news of the combined British and French invasion of Suez and their ultimatum to the Israeli army to stop short of the Canal. Immediately, the political arguments started again.

'Just like I said,' thundered Eliezar, 'it was all planned in advance. And we have been tools of British-French imperialism to retake the Canal and bring back that corrupt playboy, King Farouk.'

'Couldn't care less,' said Dudik. 'If it helps to kick Nasser in the balls and destroy his army, so be it. And if it gets us into Gaza to sort out the Fedayeen bases, even better!'

'Rubbish. In the long run,' snapped Eliezar, 'we shall pay for it. We'll lose support of the unaligned countries, alienate even the progressive Arab forces and push peace back even further.'

'No point,' snapped Dudik. 'They're all a lost cause.' He leaned forward, his face hard. 'Look, Eliezar. Just find me one Arab leader, just one, who is prepared to talk to us. Then we'll see.' And to that, we had no answer. The fiercest debates were yet to come but the war was not yet over. The arguments had to wait.

That night we still kept guard, but everyone was more relaxed. Then early next morning, just as we thought it was all over and were dismantling our positions up on the hill, a puzzling message came through from area headquarters. The kibbutz was to organise a platoon to be ready for active service by ten o'clock that morning. At first we took it as a wind-up. Gaza had surrendered, the army was in control of most of Sinai and our part in holding the northern border of the Gaza strip was over. But sure enough, at around ten thirty, about twenty-five of us were mustered to climb onto our truck, loaded with weapons and ammunition. We knew that this must be for real; Gabi, the elected kibbutz commander, had donned his yellow boots. We always joked that when Gabi wore his yellow boots, the security situation was getting tense. . .

We drove to the border near the Erez check point, where we met other platoons from neighbouring kibbutzim, equally baffled, until the area commander drove up in a jeep. It appeared that the military government convoy sent to take over the administration of the Gaza Strip, had come under fire at Beit Hanun, a village a few miles north of Gaza town. With every active army unit down south or on the Jordanian border, we were the only fighting force left in the whole area!

It was a hot day and the sun beat down as we spread out then charged up a steep hill and into a gully. I was carrying two heavy packs of two-inch mortar bombs as well as a rifle over my shoulder and a full ammunition belt around my waist. Alongside me, Joe carried another pack as well as the mortar.

'Forgot my passport,' he puffed as we crossed the unmarked border into the Gaza Strip. Then the joking was over. Bullets ricocheted and whined as they struck the purlins of a steel-framed barn at the top of the next rise — someone knew we were coming. Crouching and shuffling forward, we sheltered behind bales of straw and then edged towards a ditch. Across the main road to Gaza, about a hundred yards away, a machine gun was firing at us from a dugout. We opened up with all our weapons and the firing stopped. But as soon as we tried to move forward, they fired again. We could be here all day. Someone lobbed two grenades. They fell short. Then Geoff, our prize cricketer, tried a gigantic throw from the boundary. It almost succeeded, but the firing continued and we waited for the next move. Finally, under covering fire, Yoske played the hero. Crawling along a shallow ditch, he managed to lob a grenade right into the dugout. There was a brilliant yellow flash, an explosion, then silence. We charged forward, yelling and firing. In the dugout, a Bren gun pointed into the air and three khaki clad figures lay in the blood and dust.

'Was this all that had held up the huge convoy?' complained Itzik as we ran past. Suddenly he stopped. 'Just look at those smashing boots. I'm coming back for them later.' They were hard nuts, some of the sabras.

Fearing that there were more Fedayeen in the village in front of us, everyone fired at the mud walls and bushes, whilst Joe and I took the opportunity to shoot off a few of some of the mortar bombs. The range was too far but those damn containers were heavy.

'Cease firing!' shouted Gabi, as we let off two more rounds. But at least that left only one container to carry between us. Gingerly, we began to comb through the village, creeping along mud brick walls, kicking open gates and peering into huts. It was completely deserted and I had an eerie sensation of deja-vu, recalling the scene from Kurosawa's *Seven Samurai*, where the village is frozen and silent, though only a short while before it must have been busy and humming with normal activity.

We continued to search, but the hearths were cold and everything useful had been carried away. The villagers had probably fled early that morning. And just as rapidly as it had risen, the adrenaline subsided and I felt uneasy. This was an ordinary and quite poor village with mud huts, small rooms and rickety beds. There was the odd cupboard and oil lamps were tucked into niches in the mud brick walls. These were simple villagers, farming their land, like ourselves, but unlucky enough to live too close to the border to be left in peace.

In the last hut — just one room — three exercise books lay on the earthen floor. The evening before, by oil lamp, a schoolkid had been doing their English homework. I leafed through the pages. He, or she, could already read and translate. I wanted to find their name, to write to them through an intermediary in England after this was all over. Tell them that I hadn't wanted to come — that we hadn't started the war. That only five miles separated us and some day we would meet as neighbours. That we wished only to live in peace and that I bore them no ill. I never did. The road to hell is strewn with good intentions . . . Outside, in the gathering dusk, I found a blackened, battered *finjan* coffee-pot in the mud-dirt road. I hesitated, then stuffed it into my pack.

Darkness fell rapidly and we spread out around the perimeter of the village to keep watch. It was November and although it had been a scorching day, with the desert close by, temperatures soon dropped. In our thin, sweat-soaked shirts, we began to shiver as though it was midwinter. We organised a frantic search of the village for clothes or blankets. But everything had been taken. Eventually we found half a dozen Egyptian army jackets, small size — probably jettisoned by soldiers wanting to hide the fact if they were caught. The uniforms fitted like straitjackets but at least they were some kind of protection. However, within half an hour, we were all scratching like mad — fleas! So each one chose between keeping them on, or freezing. Either way, it was the worst night's sleep — or rather, no sleep — that I've ever had. The next morning's sunrise couldn't come soon enough.

For breakfast, all we had was some cold tea and dry biscuits. No one had anticipated being away for so long. Meanwhile, along the nearby main road, the long army convoy was finally rumbling its way towards Gaza. Mission accomplished.

We gathered in the courtyard of the UNWRRA vocational school opposite the village, to await transport home and glad of the warming sun again. Someone found a basket with pitta bread and olives — the gatekeeper's breakfast that he'd left behind. Starving, we grabbed a handful each and in two seconds it was gone. Suddenly, a grey Fergusson tractor roared out towards the front gate. Someone from neighbouring border kibbutz was driving it away. We stood in the roadway and protested. He waved us aside.

'To hell with it,' he yelled. 'This will replace the tractor those bastards blew up two months ago.'

'But this is a training school for refugee kids,' I shouted. 'They didn't do it!' to no avail and he drove off. But worse was to come. Throughout the classrooms of the low, concrete building were typewriters, tools, laboratory equipment, books and agricultural implements. Within a short while, some of the sabras began to look around.

'*Shallal!*' Booty, they grinned. Again we protested.

'Don't be stupid,' Uzi laughed. 'If we don't take them, the soldiers coming after us will!' That wasn't the point, we said. We had principles. They dismissed us as naive. This was war and anyway, the military government officers would take the lot if we didn't.

So once again, the two sides argued: Pragmatism versus principles, Left versus Right, ideals against a kind of nihilism that had sprouted from the general opportunism of the new state and disillusionment with the Soviet Bloc and Socialism. I felt sick and went to sit on the sand outside. Suddenly, there was a movement in the dark green orange groves, about two hundred yards away. Instinctively, I cocked my rifle and took aim, only to see a tall figure in a white cloak cross a path through the trees; it was just a *felakh*, a local peasant. What the hell was I aiming at? A second later and I could have shot him. I lowered the gun and eased out the bullet from the breech, feeling sick again at how war so easily corrupts.

We arrived home late that afternoon to cheers and laughter of relieved wives and friends, only to be treated like pariahs until we had thrown all our clothing into a huge tub by the laundry and showered away the flea bites. And that night we celebrated what became teasingly known as: 'The heroic assault on Beit Hanun'! Three weeks later came the much greater celebrations when the parachutists came back from Sinai. All but one. But despite the relief at the quick victory, controversies soon surfaced again. And not only about the political events.

Gadi, one of the sabras who had fought in Sinai, was sickened by the way some of the soldiers in his unit from town, had looted Egyptian military stores, despite strict orders not to touch anything. Others had seen Egyptian prisoners beaten, and in one incident, even shot. They were isolated occurrences, but he and others felt these to be a terrible betrayal of the high moral standards of *Tzahal*, the Israeli army; a betrayal of principles as deep as that which Eliezar felt on the political front.

Now however, with the war over and no need to close ranks, the arguments about the war and the role Israel had played, grew more acrimonious. Kibbutz federation and Party spokesmen went out to all the kibbutzim to lead discussions. Predictably, our general meeting soon broke into a slanging match along usual lines. The majority condemned Israeli participation in the Anglo-French plan, but some, especially many of those who had just returned from the fighting, justified it.

'I don't care who we allied ourselves to,' Dudik repeated. 'As long as it helped us crush the Fedayeen in Gaza.'

'We could have dealt with those without occupying Sinai,' we argued, 'or joining British and French imperialist plots.'

'It would have cost many more lives to go it alone,' came the riposte and the ill-tempered arguments continued until well after midnight. As tempers grew frayed there was almost a fist-fight with one of the boys back from the parachutists, something completely unknown before this. In the end, we didn't even vote; it was all too fraught.

In retrospect, we should have waited a month or two until emotions had calmed; it was too soon after the war. How could we expect the men who had just survived a baptism of fire, seen comrades killed and wounded alongside them, condemn as unjust the very war they had just been fighting? But we were young and impassioned.

So 'October' had been postponed indefinitely and we were holding this party instead. After all, the boys were home and back in the kibbutz, the Fedayeen were no longer in Gaza, and the nights were silent once more. And maybe the Egyptians would make peace?

'No way,' said Eliezar, as the singing continued. 'From war, you only make more war. And as for that damn holy burning bush . . .' The rest of his words were drowned as Avraham took up the accordion and started to play; circles were forming for the *horra*. We all rose, Eliezar included, and joined in. Tomorrow the arguments and soul-searchings would continue. But for now there was a celebration, and the dancing would go on well into the night.

Work — and more work

It was like any other day after work: five o'clock, showered and changed, and enjoying a quiet cup of coffee. The children were playing in the room and soft, late afternoon sun streamed through the fly mesh at the open window. Suddenly, Gidon poked his head around the door.

'Truck's arrived,' he grinned, 'and you're on *toranut preekah!*'

Toranut, was our term for the overtime rota, derived from the word *Tor,* (taking turns). This one was the 'unloading' rota.

Our truck would leave the kibbutz at dawn every morning, usually taking produce to market. It then spent the rest of the day picking up a list of items ordered by the purchasing controller and inevitably arrived back after work, and often after dark. But it had to be unloaded and left ready for the following morning.

'What's it brought,' I spluttered through a mouthful of bread and marmalade.

'Chemical fertilizer,' Gidon grunted. 'See you down by the ramp!' He hurried away to round up the other two on the list and I gulped down my coffee.

The toranut system resulted from our aim to be a self-sufficient labour force. It meant that every odd job, even the ones outside working hours, had to be covered by ourselves. So on top of a full day's work, we had the washing-up rota after supper, helping with the livestock or in the kitchen on Shabbat, extra guard duties in tense security period, loading-up the lorry so that it was ready to take off early next morning or, like this day, unloading it when it arrived late from town. And all these rotas stuck into our leisure time like a thorn in the proverbial . . .

The cowmen, who regularly worked night shifts, and those on seasonal long days sowing or harvesting, were excused. This left just a few dozen able bodies and, taking up four men at a time, this particular rota seemed to come round with unnerving frequency.

Changing back into my sweaty working clothes, I got ready to go down. The alternative would have been to stay grubby all evening until the truck had arrived, much to the disgust of our children who expected us to be showered, changed and ready just for them at four o'clock.

'Ah Dani. Glad I found you. You're on early shift tomorrow!'

Yoske joined me along the path and we hurried down to the fodder store where we found a four-ton truck-load of potash, brought straight from the docks at Haifa. The huge sacks, originally from Turkey, weighed at least seventy kilograms each and must have lain higgledy-piggledy in some silo for months. The potash had settled and, being hygroscopic, had solidified into grotesque shapes.

'Henry Moore couldn't have done better,' muttered Mosheh, staring at the misshapen hulks with open disgust, 'I bet Reubek bought this cheap as a damn job-lot.'

'Yeah,' said Yoske, 'perhaps we'll send them to the sculpture park in Jerusalem.'

'No chance,' said Gidon. 'Come on. Let's get the damn things off.'

In the early days, every sack of seeds, bran or fertilizer had to be manhandled one by one and stacked in the store. When the elevator came, it was like a gift from heaven, though the sacks still had to be taken off the truck and stacked up at the other end. It wouldn't help this time though. These sacks had to be stored in the fertilizer shed down by the banana grove.

Gidon moved the truck, switched off the engine and jumped onto the back whilst we dropped the tailboard.

'Just lower that sack gently onto my shoulder,' hissed Yoske. 'And gently, I said!' He arched his back and leaned against the side of the truck. Mosheh and Gidon dragged the sack towards the edge. As they slowly eased it onto his shoulder, Yoske's knees flexed, he trembled, then with a fierce curse, he slid aside and staggered away, and the sack fell with a dull thud onto the dirt roadway. It sat there, looking as permanent and solid as though it had sprouted from the earth beneath.

'Bloody hell,' he gasped. 'Those Turks must be supermen. I've never felt a sack like it!' We stood in a circle and stared, and then looked up at the fifty odd sacks still sitting on the truck like a miniature Himalayas. Gidon shrugged.

'It's got to be unloaded. Khaya is sending broiler chickens to market tonight.' Yoske and I rolled and dragged the sack into the shed and over to the far corner. And the next half dozen were given the same treatment. Except that the force of their fall broke the fertilizer into several smaller lumps, which made them even harder to handle.

We sat down for a moment to draw breath.

'It's simple,' puffed Mosheh. 'Next time we make sure that they import a few Turkish stevedores, together with the potash.' But we weren't in a laughing mood.

'Need a bloody mule to carry those things,' I said. Yoske's eyes suddenly lit up.

'Hey. What about Yankeleh's donkey?'

'Great idea,' agreed Mosheh.

'Don't be daft,' said Gidon, 'it can hardly drag the two-wheeled cart.'

'Balls,' scowled Yoske. 'You seen those huge, fat effendis they carry in Nazareth. Hundred kilos at least.' Eventually we convinced Gidon that it was worth a try and Yoske ran to bring it from the stable.

The animal, sensing that no good was afoot, refused to back up against the tailboard. Again and again, Yoske led it in a wide circle, until finally he succeeded in bringing it alongside.

'Now,' he snapped, 'use that pole and lever the sack onto its back. Gently mind you.'

'Okay, Archimedes,' smiled Mosheh. 'Give me a fulcrum and I'll lift the world.'

'Never mind the world. Just ease on the sack meanwhile,' muttered Yoske. 'The beast won't stand here much longer.' But as soon as the sack touched the donkey's back, it bolted, dragging Yoske about fifty yards up the road. Mosheh collapsed in a heap, laughing.

'Hey. That donkey ain't never heard of Archimedes.'

'No. Only Yankeleh,' said Gidon. 'Any more great ideas, Yoske?' he shouted, looking up the road. He hadn't. Neither had any of us.

'Bloody principles,' Yoske muttered. 'Reubek should have hired four blokes from Ashkelon to unload this lot.' And as we stood there, catching our breath and thinking of what to do next, I wondered yet again how long we could maintain this struggle not to hire labour. Would we have the will as well as the physical strength to keep this up — together with all the other rotas?

The toranut rota system was a necessary evil. With limited labour resources and not wanting to hire outside workers, day after day the elected work organiser tried to reconcile conflicting demands and couldn't. 'Like pulling a single sheet over a double bed,' Issy would say. 'Someone's always going to be left uncovered.' And so we had to rely on the rota system so that every job was covered.

As if this wasn't enough, every season brought its mobilisations, called *giyusim*: Most branches were run by a small group of regular workers who could never have coped with the large scale seasonal works. Private farms hired temporary workers, usually on piece work and poorly paid. We could not do this, hence the system of giyusim. For example, our cereal crops branch, the *falkha*, was completely mechanised. Ploughing, sowing, fertilizer-spreading, and harvesting, cutting and baling the straw and hay were all done by machines. But during the harvest season, the four or five people working there permanently could never bring home the hundreds of straw and hay bales, so essential for our dairy. Nor could the other overstretched branches release regular staff for days at a time to do this. On top of which, neither the truck, nor the tractors and trailers could be spared from their normal work during the day. So it was back to giyusim, which required two groups of four men every evening for three weeks, each of us having to take three or four turns. We usually finished after dark, barely having time to see the kids, before they went back to the children's houses.

Although bringing in the hay was amongst the hardest work, it was also the most pleasant and I wrote this at the time:

The afternoon sun is halfway down to the sand dunes but the day is still as hot as if it were noon. To our weary bodies it seems even hotter as the first bales are thrown up and we set them on the floor of the truck; two on the right side, two on the left, leaving space for only one-and-a-half bales in the middle. From then on, it is non stop.

Another heave, and up from the stubble come the next two. We balance them on their corners, one on each side of the empty space, then it's push and push and stand and thump and thump to squash them in level and tight — a *mishgal*, we call it, the biblical term for copulating, all to make the first layer tight and firm enough to build up the rest of the load. The truck moves forward and up come the next bales; then the second layer, binder twine cutting and chafing, and as before, two right side, two on the left, then . . .

'Ready for the *mishgal*?' shouts Geoff. And again the humping and thumping to squeeze them down, sweat streaming off the forehead and into our eyes, salt smarting and blinding, then dripping off to be soaked up in the straw.

'God,' snorts Yossi. 'Another *mishgal*. If only it was!'

The boys below continue to throw up bales; forward, back and up. Again and again in regular rhythm. Now the third layer, then the next, higher and higher, dust and sweat filling our nostrils, flecks of straw sticking between sodden vest and sweat-soaked skin, salt stinging the deep scratches from the sharp, cut ends and the thought of ice-cold water at the end keeping us going, until the final layer is up and the ropes are tied round.

At last comes the blessed journey home, lying on the top bales as the truck speeds down the narrow road, cooling off in the breeze rippling over our sodden backs. A few minutes of sheer relief before unloading it all into the dutch barn, which is as hot as an oven from the the sun beating on the corrugated tin roof. Until the last bale.

Exhausted, we clamber down, sweep off the truck floor and raise the sides. Then the mad rush to the milk-cooler room. Ice-cold water and freezing melons from the refrigerated tank whilst the sweat soaks the waistbands of our grimy trousers and streams down into already sodden socks. Finally, the weary slog up the hill to the long-awaited shower and, in the early days, often to find that all the hot water had been used up . . .

For regular, large scale jobs like picking fruit or weeding large areas, we had mobilisations of as many people as possible after work or on Shabbat, often involving the whole family. These were usually a drag, but the occasional *giyus* could be enjoyable, like when treading down the silage in the tall round silo tower. Again, this is from that time:

Everyone comes, with wives and kids, up the long steel ladder into the semi-darkness. Backs against the circular wall and holding hands, we trudge round and round, everyone singing in time and the kids hurtling into the centre where they can jump and roll and wrestle in the soft greenery, without fear of hurting themselves. On and on, treading and singing and laughing, round and round, packing down the blown, chopped maize stalks to squeeze out the air and make sure it ferments into sweet smelling silage for the cows in the winter. Round and round. Round and round, stamping and pressing until Gadi could see the programmed chalk line he'd marked on the wall before the last loads were blown in that day. At the end, laughing and joking, we sit on the fresh cuttings and tuck into biscuits and cool lemonade brought up from the kitchen. Finally, exhausted but exhilarated we climb back down the ladder and out into the cool evening to make our way in small groups up the hill to the children's houses. Then, as darkness falls, we head for supper in the dining hall, everyone flushed with a sense of achievement.

I was thinking about those moments, all our own labour, and all for our community — when a sack of potash rolled off the lorry and the ground shook by my feet, bringing me sharply back to the present.

'Hey dreamy,' Gidon called down, 'have a go at that one.' Mosheh and I bent to and began to roll and heave it into the store.

Every busy season had its crisis which we strove to overcome: a fruit crop to get to market on time, as with the the grape harvest, or potato picking, weeding the onions or sugar beet, and many more. But over the years, all this extra work in our spare time, created a weariness and reduced willingness. Eventually we met a crisis that we couldn't resolve, and it came with our first bumper orange crop, as the groves we'd planted began to bear fruit.

The Israel tourist board used to have a poster of a smiling girl

Yet another load for market . . .

reaching out to pick a juicy orange. Jaffa oranges were an icon of the new state. But we who actually had to do the job, hated orange-picking; day after day, the repetitive snipping-off of the fruit, dragging the loaded haversack from tree to tree and threading the ladders through the branches to reach those at the top. The picking started in December with the Clementines and Navels, then continued with the *shamouti* Jaffas for the Christmas export rush and dragged on and on until the Valencias in March.

As it was a profitable export branch, like many other kibbutzim, we had planted acres and acres in the expectation that by the time they bore fruit, the kibbutz would have grown in size and population to pick it all. We did grow, but not by that much. So despite schools' harvest camps and groups from the youth movement, who all enjoyed the week of orange-picking — and eating their fill, that particular year, with a large area still unpicked, the fruit began to fall. It continued to fall until in one section, the earth was almost red with fallen fruit.

So we began daily giyusim after work, again taking us out

during the children's time. On Shabbat too we went out; whole families with the older kids and even mothers holding young babies, pulling off fruit with their free hands, again and again. Until we had driven ourselves to a standstill. And still the fruit was dropping off.

For two weeks, arguments raged in the farm committee and at stormy general meetings and as always the kibbutz was divided. Some preferred to leave it rot, rather than start hiring labour; we would lose money, but there were greater things at stake. Others insisted on bringing in hired pickers from Ashkelon.

'It's the thin end of the wedge,' we said. 'Once hired labour comes in, every time there is a crisis, it will always be the easy option.'

'There's a bigger crime than hired labour,' thundered Yosef, adding that many unemployed people in Ashkelon who would be glad of the money.

'Since when is the farm manager so charitable,' quipped Joe. But in the end, this time we were outvoted and every day for the next fortnight, a van brought workers from town who were paid by the box, until the picking was over. We continued to argue about who was right. Perhaps it was as the famous Rabbi once said: 'You are both right.'

The custom of toranut and giyusim continued for many years but it became more and more difficult to maintain. Eventually, bringing in the hay was contracted out, as was the orange-picking. Other crops were sold 'off the field' to market traders who brought their own labour. We had built up an economy and a standard of living that could not be sustained by our labour alone and more than just the thin end of the wedge had penetrated the fabric of the kibbutz. It left us open to heading the way that other communal settlements had gone — gradually reverting to being ordinary villages and farm-owners employing seasonal labour.

All that though, was still some years away from those sacks of potash which somehow, by dragging and rolling and heaving, we managed to unload onto the storeroom floor.

'No way I'm going to heap them up,' muttered Mosheh.

'Blowed if I'm going to lose anything for this lot.'

'Me neither,' grinned Yoske. 'And you've got two kids already.'

It was nearly dark when we finished. As we shut the heavy wooden door, I glanced at the layer of grotesque shapes that covered the floor and couldn't help smiling. Henry Moore would have been proud.

We learned afterwards that our treasurer, Reubek, had indeed bought them cheap as a job-lot because of the condition they were in: 'Saved fifteen percent,' he crowed at the farm committee. But he never dared do it again. And Yankeleh's donkey? Well, after that, whenever he saw a sack of fertilizer, he bolted.

'Proof of Pavlov,' said Gidon.

'Sure,' agreed Yoske, 'but I bet he didn't have to unload his own chemicals!'

'Maybe not,' muttered Mosheh, 'but we have to.'

Too bright a flame

Aharon looked so ordinary. Nothing heroic about him at all. Pale, round face, receding fair hair and eyes blinking from behind steel-rimmed spectacles — sunken, grey eyes that for so long had stared through iron bars. The ruddy, full cheeks were deceptive, the results of three weeks of intensive nourishment after fifteen years in a Bucharest gaol, much of it spent in solitary confinement.

Hella sat beside him, anxious, glancing sideways from time to time with the dark, sad, yet beautiful eyes of an Eastern icon as he spoke. Her soft cheeks were furrowed with lines of worry, lines that mirrored the bars of his cell. Lines from waiting and from the despair and the misery of the many cancelled visits. But lines also, of determination, of faith in a loved one so callously ensnared in a web of Byzantine intrigue. We waited. Humbled. How do you survive all that and still come out sane? How does love bridge so many years of separation and cruelty?

Aharon sipped from a glass of water as he spoke, smiling across the dining hall to those he remembered. Fifteen years before, he'd been the leader of their circle. A fervent Marxist but also a committed Zionist. Suddenly picked up by the Securitate, to become involved in the Stalinist purges of the early Fifties. Accused of being a C.I.A. agent and diverting Jewish refugee relief funds to finance acts of sabotage.

He couldn't take them seriously. Felt it was some Kafkaesque situation which would soon resolve itself. Still incredulous even at his trial and defiant; pointing out that his judge had served the fascist Antonescu regime. He scoffed at the public prosecutor that he had more Marxism in his little finger than the other would ever have in his whole body. The public gallery cheered. They cleared the court and hustled him down again to the cells.

Weeks passed. Months. Not a word from Aharon. Nor from the authorities. Suddenly, the court was reconvened and again he stood in the dock, but now a shadow of his former self. Thin and pale, staring listlessly at the far wall as the public prosecutor read out a long and detailed confession: espionage, corruption of youth, defamation of the great leader Stalin, on and on. A tissue of lies, ludicrous and degrading. But then shock and disbelief as Aharon nodded agreement — to all the charges. Yes, it was his statement, his signature and freely given. In the stunned silence that followed, Hella collapsed and had to be helped from the courtroom. The others looked on, numbed, as he was led down to the cells, a hunched figure, eyes half closed.

Aharon looked up from the table and blinked through his glasses, half smiling. Yes, that had been his own signature. Yes, freely with his own hand. If you could call no sleep for days on end, voluntary; revolting food that you retched up as soon as it was down, of his own free will; screeching earphones and flashing lights, freely given. Yes, he had signed. Because he knew they would never stop. Either until they had what they wanted. Or until he was dead.

He paused abruptly and we sat in a stunned, horror-gripped silence. For a split second, his eyes glared. Yes. He signed, because otherwise they would have killed him, and he hadn't wanted to die on a lie. He was determined that one day, somehow, he would get out. And that thought was to sustain him. Make him fight to survive and let everyone know the truth.

We waited for him to continue. Hella waited too, slowly clasping and unclasping her hands. Waiting as she had always waited. Never doubting. Looking at him with her soft, dark eyes, as he finished speaking. Then gently shaking her head. No, she didn't want to add anything.

The evening was getting late. The frailty and weariness now showed clearly on his face. One last question. His future plans? We'd invited him to join the kibbutz and his friends. To come home. Aharon blinked again. Managed another thin smile. He'd been free just three weeks. In Israel for less than a few days. No, he'd never lost faith in his ideals. Still believed in Socialism. In Zionism. In the kibbutz. And the regime back there? He couldn't even begin to describe. All he wanted to do was to survive and tell the truth and, he glanced sideways — and to be with Hella.

She looked up and touched his arm, as though to reassure herself that he really was there. And, for the very first time that whole evening, she smiled.

As they walked to the waiting car, Aharon looked up. Turning his head slowly, he stared at the myriad stars in the black, soft Mediterranean sky and drew deep breaths of the cool night air. I had the image of a flickering candle that had spluttered to stay alight in the foul confines of a dungeon, suddenly bursting into brilliant, white flame as it reached the fresh air and burning brighter than ever before.

But Bucharest had bestowed no favours upon him. Aharon had been released because he had cancer. And the flame that had begun to burn so brightly in the free air of his homeland, now consumed the last vestiges of his wasted body. Six weeks later, he died.

Festivals and holidays

Christmas was cancelled for the foreseeable future, apart from for Gerry and Helen and a few others, who out of nostalgia tuned into radio Amman to hear carols. New Year's Eve and Easter and Whitsun were out too. Our holidays and festivals were Israeli and secular, but based on Jewish tradition and timed by the ancient Biblical lunar calendar. And we celebrated every one of them in a distinctive kibbutz manner, stressing their agricultural origin and relating them to the rebirth of our people and the return to the soil.

The first festival in our calendar was *Rosh Hashannah*, the Jewish New Year, which fell some time in September depending on the new moon. For the religious, it was a time to commence anew, reading the Holy Book from Genesis, and a time of introspection and individual soul-searching leading up to the Day of Atonement. For us, it was a time of collective reckoning, the opportunity to sum up our kibbutz agricultural year and to look forward to the next, and with the New Year, began the yearly cycle of festivals.

After a festive *Rosh Hashannah* meal in the dining hall, each branch of the economy reported on its achievements and problems, as well as profits and losses — and there were always some of the latter. Either way, it was a time to celebrate the old year's achievements and look forward to the next year.

The New Year festivities were also a time of 'changing the guard', for our internal elections and the kibbutz, being a self-contained community, required a range of committees and functionaries to organise and run everything from work and education, through to street lighting. Most of these tasks were in addition to the daily workload, necessitating devoting some of our spare time to carrying them out and no one received any more for doing this. As the years passed however, with more time in the evenings and on Shabbat taken up with the children, spare time grew more precious and people became less enthusiatic about taking on added responsibilities. So leading up to the New Year, elections to new committees and functions took several general meetings, many people being voted kicking and screaming into the various positions.

Three weeks after the New Year came *Succot*, the eight days of

Nominations committee at work.

Tabernacles which traditionally commemorated the temporary shelters of the Israelites during their wandering in the desert. Like most of our festivals, it was centred around the children, part of a conscious effort to ensure that our kids grew up with a strong and vibrant Isreali identity.

In the days leading up to the festival, outside each kindergarten or school, parents, teachers and children built a *succah*, a lean-to open-sided hut. Fruit and paper decorations were hung from a roof of eucalyptus branches and elephant grass from the banana plantation windbreaks. Much to their delight, the children ate their meals *al fresco* for a week — providing the first rains didn't come as a torrential downpour. Getting the succah dismantled and cleared away by the dads was less spontaneous, often demanding persistent nagging by the children's nurse.

In December, as in nearly every culture and religion approaching the winter solstice, came the feast of light. In our case, it was *Hannukah*, traditionally the time when the ancient Maccabees liberated the temple of Jerusalem and a small cruse of holy oil miraculously burned for eight days. Throughout the centuries in Europe, candles and fires with warm food and presents cheered the cold and the long nights. With us it was fried goodies all round; latkes and doughnuts, symbolic of that cruse of oil. Then, together with the parents, candles were lit on the eight branched *Hannukiah* candelabra in each children's house. We sang Hannukah songs about the Maccabees, the ancient Jewish freedom-fighters, paralleled with our own modern fight for survival, every boy felt himself a Yehudah Maccabee, fighting the Syrian Ptolomys, and every girl — Hannah, the brave mother, refusing to bow down to Greek idols.

On the first night of Hannukah, wrapped up in woollen hats and warm coats, we filed in torchlight procession down to the basketball pitch. Parents desperately shielded flaming paraffin-soaked torches against the strong winter wind, each torch casting eerie shapes on whitewashed walls and sending shadows flitting from tree to bush. Up on the water tower, a large hannukiah of electric lamps signalled across the sand dunes to similar lights on neighbouring kibbutz towers — part of a chain of light and hope shining out along the dark, silent border.

Tu B'Shvat, the new year of the trees, came each January. All over Israel, schoolchildren went into the mountains and deserts to plant new groves and forests. Each year our kibbutz gardener ploughed up a new patch of waste ground and after songs and a few readings, everyone dug a small hole and planted a sapling of pine or eucalyptus or casuarina, leaving the tiny tree, tossing and whipping in the wind and rain to put down roots before the summer heat. Year by year, we greened more of the kibbutz until it became one huge park.

Purim, early in March, was traditionally a joyful carnival time. Way back in ancient Persia, the king chose the beautiful Jewess, Esther, to be his queen and she in turn saved the Jews from being slaughtered by the king's vizier, Haman. For weeks beforehand, parents spent anxious hours helping the children to become animals, or dragons, or spacemen, or sleeping beauties as well as the more traditional villain, Haman or the heroine, Queen Esther. At the same time we were preparing our own costumes for the huge fancy dress party. Either it was warmer in Persia in the first century B.C. — or our forefathers had misjudged the season, because we froze in the chill winds that whipped across the courtyard, spending anxious moments on the way up to the dining hall trying to keep the costumes in one piece.

For the party, the dining hall was festooned with streamers, posters and coloured lanterns and a stage set up at one end.

'And by the clothes shall ye know them,' quipped Issy, as all manner of alter egos were exposed: Caesars and Cleopatras, my fair ladies, wizards and witches, chorus girls, batmen, etc. with prizes for the most original ones. On the stage were skits and satirical pieces on aspects of kibbutz life, often lampooning this or that kibbutz functionary, no holds barred. After that we would scoff the traditional 'Haman's ears', tiny poppy-seed cakes, and other goodies prepared by the kitchen. Finally, pulling the tables aside, we launched into hectic dancing, continuing to the small hours, costumes unravelling and being cast aside, heralding the

The Purim party poopers.

return to normality on the morrow.

On May Day, we celebrated our socialist beliefs. Red flags flanked the entrance gates and flew from the water tower. In the evening in the dining hall, we sang stirring Hebrew renditions of the *Varshvyanka* and the *Internationale*, with readings from Brecht, Mayakovsky, Howard Fast and others, wishing to express our solidarity with workers throughout the world.

Israel, at that time, was still a social democratic country — something like Sweden perhaps, and May Day was a public holiday. The ruling Labour party and the trades unions held huge demonstrations and processions through the towns. Floats were draped with hundreds of red, and blue-and-white, flags and tens of thousands of participants strolled in the bright spring sunshine. A contingent from the kibbutz always took part, sometimes travelling to Tel Aviv but often into our local town, Migdal-Ashkelon. It was populated by new immigrants, some plucked from almost medieval existence in North Africa and we felt it a duty to join the local emerging trades unions and bring them into the spirit of the festival. Our children came too in neat white shirts, waving red and Israeli flags whilst the bemused local townspeople stood and smiled and clapped as we marched and sang our way through the streets. But others were watching too and scowling: groups of heavily-built men, new recruits to Menakhem Beigin's *Kherut* party, our 'homegrown' fascists and an ominous sign for the future.

By the sixties however, the rapid embourgeoisement of the towns and the ever 'pinker' Labour party, drove May Day into a back seat. We continued to put out the red flags but only a few committed individuals bothered to join minority demonstrations still held in the main towns. In connection with the spirit of May Day, until the late fifties, we also devoted a special evening to the October Revolution. But as the years passed, especially after Khruschev's revelations and continued Soviet military support for Syria and Egypt, disillusionment with the Soviet Union did away with celebrating 'October'.

In May, the exact day depending on the Hebrew date, we held an open air assembly to celebrate Israel's Independence Day, observing also a minute's silence while remembering those who had made the supreme sacrifice.

Israel didn't have a Guy Fawkes but at Lag Be'Omer, in late May, we still had a bonfire night. Traditionally, it commemorated a victory over the Romans by the legendary hero, Bar Kochba. The kids ran around with bows and arrows and in the evening we had fireworks and a huge bonfire. On one occasion, immediately prior to the Six Day War, the older children had their own 'guy', when an effigy of Nasser, who had just blockaded the straits of Tiran, was ceremoniously burned. Ephraim, the head teacher, had some 'pedagogical' misgivings about that, but accepted that it was an opportunity for the children to release some of the tension and anxiety that had been building up inside them over the months — and in us too.

People have always grafted their own religious symbolism onto earlier pagan festivals and the Jews were no exception. The summer solstice festival *Shavuoth*, became traditionally associated with the time when the Ten Commandments were handed down

on Mount Sinai. But underlying Shavuoth was an agricultural festival, and in biblical times it was one of the three festivals when
pilgrims brought offerings of first fruits to the temple of
Jerusalem. For us, it was a time to celebrate the fruits of our own
harvest, symbols of our return to the homeland and to the soil.

We usually chose the clearing amongst the trees down by the
wadi, erecting a stage of straw bales between an old mud-brick
wall draped with flowering jasmine and tall palms on one side,
and a clump of feathery tamarisks on the other. Rows of straw
bales served as seating and between the front row and the stage,
an open space was reserved for presentation of the 'first fruits'.

First came the kindergarten children, in white headscarves and
garlands and white shirts, each bringing tiny baskets of corn ears
and vine leaves, followed by the schoolchildren who brought produce from their children's farm and decorated cages of doves and
rabbits. Then each branch brought its own offerings. With
Avram's fingers rippling on the accordion, playing 'Oh Mr.
Talleyman . .', Menakhem and Yehuda, in broad-rimmed straw
hats, brought in a thirty kilo bunch of green bananas slung on a
pole, imitating the biblical spies of Eshkol with their huge bunch
of grapes. Following them came Elisha and Issy with churns of
milk and a young calf, straining at the halter, its eyes bulging,
alarmed at so many people. Then came Khaya and the poultry
with baskets of gleaming eggs and cages of white feathered chickens. The orchards and vineyards brought choice produce in decorated boxes and baskets, all laid in front of the stage to form a
colourful mosaic as the celebration continued. And between each
offering, appropriate excerpts were read out from the Bible, with
poems and songs from the choir and presentations from the dance
group on the stage.

From the irrigated crops came Uzi, bringing huge cobs of
maize, gleaming potatoes and gigantic orange cattle-beet. Finally
with a loud roar, our red combine harvester rolled into the clearing, pausing in front of the stage to spill out a heap of golden
grain, whilst Gerry joked that Boaz and the boys from the falkha
couldn't do anything without being on wheels. Once, when we

thought everyone had finished, Ruth, the babies' nurse, came forward spontaneously with all the new mums carrying their babies. Everyone cheered and clapped this most significant of all the fruits of our community.

Of all our festivals, that of Passover, *Pesakh*, was the most unique and symbolic. Traditionally it celebrated the Exodus of Israel from Pharaoh's Egypt: our forefathers' journey from slavery to freedom — the Jews being probably the only people to equate the rebirth of nature at springtime, with the rebirth of their nation. This too had been transposed onto the ancient spring festival of the wheat and barley harvest which, in the Mediterranean, comes in April. And in the Jewish tradition of a family get-together, we celebrated both aspects at the first night Seder as a communal family: parents, children and grandparents all together.

Preparations for the Seder began as soon as we had recovered from Purim. The festival committee prodded the choir and drama groups into action, organised the readings and readers and sorted out contributions from the kindergarten and school as well as chivvying the artists into preparing decorations for the hall. In the early days, we all managed somehow to crowd into our dining-hall hut, but this soon became too small. The only other large covered space was our grain and fodder-meal store, so the first task of the festival committee was to convince Zvi to run down his stocks. Then, during the week before the Seder, groups of us would go down after work to pile the remaining sacks up against the walls, leaving a few as a base for a stage. Beni and Lilli decorated the walls with colourful scenes from the Exodus, shields of the ten tribes and harvest motifs, covering so much of the bare concrete blocks, so that long after the Seder had moved to the new dining hall, parts of pyramids, or the Red Sea, or huge wheatsheaves still peeped between the stacks of barley and bran and fertilizer sacks.

On the day of the Seder, all work in the fields stopped early and everyone lent a hand erecting tables and forms and taking utensils and food down from the kitchen. The procedings opened with the choir, followed by readings from our kibbutz *Hagaddah*. Unlike the traditional book which dealt only with the ten plagues and the Exodus, ours also told of the coming of Spring, of the first harvest, of our own and others' freedom struggles — reserving a special place for the revolt of the Warsaw ghetto, which took place at Pesakh 1943.

The readings, interspersed with dances on the stage and dramatic presentations, always concluded with a reading of the vision of Isaiah, of beating swords to ploughshears and spears to pruning hooks — a cry for peace and freedom, for that was the essence of our Pesakh. After all that, came the meal, always sumptuous however hard the times. And of course, perhaps the only occasion when the odd person drunk themselves a little too merry on the traditional wine. Becoming legless was usually a rare occurrence. Relatives and friends from town often joined us for the Seder but over the years, the unique kibbutz Seder nights became so popular that we and other kibbutzim eventually had to limit the number of visitors.

Finally, with the food gone and the readings over the children went back to their houses, many of the younger ones already fast asleep on their dad's shoulders. Everyone else charged up the hill and into the empty dining hall where we formed large, concentric circles, flinging ourselves into a wild *horra*, to begin the dancing that would last well into the night. Every year the same, yet each time anew; a celebration of rebirth and renewal, and of creativity. And of our own special kind of community.

High finance

Reubek sat down at the scratched formica table and dumped his briefcase on the chair beside him. Reubek was *Gizbar*, the kibbutz treasurer. He'd left the kibbutz at six and now it was eight in the morning. He glanced around the small café by the Tel Aviv bus station with its faded cream paint and metal framed windows, that probably hadn't changed since the owner and his wife had arrived from Poland in the forties.

'The usual,' Reubek called over to the counter.

'Two fried eggs and salted rolls and *kaffeh hafukh*: milk coffee,' muttered Khayim through the small hatch to his wife.

It was Reubek's early morning ritual, snatching a light breakfast whilst meeting treasurers from other kibbutzim and swapping news. After that it would be the daily trek round the offices and institutions: the Settlement Agency to see about a new loan for the cowshed, a bank or two to sort out accounts or pay in cheques, then the ministry of agriculture in the Kirya to chase up the next instalment of drought compensation. After that, it was off to the various suppliers and merchants to settle bills or, more usually, to extend credit and then on then to *Tnuva*, which marketed most of our produce. His final call would be at the *Mishkei Hadarom* co-operative, through which the kibbutz bought its supplies. Each day the same plod from office to warehouse to bank and the same arguments to try to balance the precarious finances of the kibbutz.

For the two-and-a-half years he'd been kibbutz treasurer, Reubek had followed the same routine. But today he was feeling unsettled. On the drive into town he'd begun to think much more seriously about his future. It wasn't a sudden urge. Over the last few months, he'd found himself becoming more and more frustrated by arguments with inexperienced youngsters in the farm committee and renewed confrontations over principles in general meetings. He'd been through all that before, more than once. Now, after fifteen years in the kibbutz, he just didn't need it.

Khayim slapped his rolls and coffee on the table and as Reubek sipped the drink and waited for the eggs, he ran his hand through his curly black hair, now slightly greying. His mind drifted back to the morning Nakhman had told him about Avrumkeh.

It was about two months ago. He'd sat down as usual to wait for his breakfast and, opening his briefcase, took out a brown plastic cheque-book wallet. Inside were not one, but three cheque books and he was wondering whether to use all three that day and if so, with which one to start.

'Playing the merry-go-round again?' Instinctively, Reubek slapped the wallet closed and looked up. Nakhman, the treasurer from a kibbutz near Gedera pulled back the chair opposite and sat down, 'It will catch up with you one day.' Reubek shrugged.

'*Ein breira!* No choice. Have to settle the last instalment on the furniture for the new classroom today.' Nakhman's glass of lemon tea had arrived at the same time as Reubek's eggs and rolls.

'Heard about Avrumkeh?' said Nakhman softly, glancing around to see who else was nearby. Reubek was dipping the end of a roll into the egg yolk. He stopped and looked up.

'Heard what?'

'Leaving kibbutz Goranim!'

Reubek took a bite then stared across the table.

'You must be joking. After twenty years? Why now?'

'Got a job in the Settlement Agency,' said Nakhman, munching a piece of toast. 'Came with a flat in Beer Sheva. Said he was fed up having petty arguments — no one understanding the problems, no one listening, no one respecting him.' He grinned. 'Said he's going where his talents were appreciated.'

Reubek half smiled.

'So what's new. Always been the same. Everyone makes fine decisions but in the end, the treasurer has to sort it out.' He took a gulp of coffee. 'And you?' Nakhman flicked his wrist.

'Me? No. I've got used to it. Anyway. I'm the kibbutz and the kibbutz is me.' He paused for a second. 'Still. Makes you think, eh?' Finishing his toast, Nakhman drained the last drops of tea and stood up, '*Lehitra'ot*.' See you. Reubek watched the short, balding figure bustle out to the street. Avrumkeh leaving? And getting a good position just like that? That was the third treasurer in the last year he'd heard about. Yes. It did make him think . . .

Now, finishing off his breakfast, Reubek took out the cheque-books as usual. According to the yearly farm plan, there should have been sufficient surplus in the bank by this month to settle quite a few of the outstanding bills. But that was before the drought last winter. And now there was the '*brokh*' with the guavas which, being a late season fruit, had always filled an awkward gap in the kibbutz cashflow. Apart from grapes, they were once the only fruit on the market at the end of the year. But now apples and pears from the new orchards up north were taking their place and that last consignment had gone for only half the usual price. He opened one of the cheque-books: the merry-go-round. There was nothing else for it until an advance payment on the sugar beet next month. Picking up the glass of coffee by its metal holder, he took a large gulp then began writing the first cheque.

'It works like this,' he'd explained to Yoskeh one evening by the work roster board. 'Suppose I need to gain a week's respite, say, for a large payment. So I write a cheque to be presented at the

Bank Leumi branch in Safed. Well, it takes three days to clear and meanwhile I write a cheque for two days time from Bank Hapoalim in Hedera to the one in Safed. That will also take three days to clear. Then,' he continued, though Yoskeh had looked as though he was lost already, 'then I write a cheque from where we will have a bit of credit, say Bank Leumi in Tel Aviv, for six days time to the one in Hedera.' He smiled. 'Then it's Shabbat — so no money goes out until the following week!'

It had sounded all so simple to himself too. The problem was that the juggling act had to be done several times each week and with so many balls in the air, sooner or later the whole thing could come tumbling down. Like it did to the neighbouring kibbutz last month and the Settlement Agency had to step in to cut all their budgets and prop them up. But it wouldn't happen to him.

Sorry. Not till the next budget.

Reubek thought again of what Nakhman had told him and half closed his eyes. Most of the kibbutz shied away from the job of treasurer, it reminded them too much of the traditional Jewish trades they'd left behind. Not up to the ideals of manual labour and the return to the soil. He himself had managed the cereal crops for many years and still respected those ideals. Yet someone had to do these administrative jobs. The kibbutz couldn't function without them.

As a boy, he would sometimes accompany his father through Transylvania to buy wheat and vegetables from the peasants. He remembered the hard wooden seats on the slow train and his father, red-faced with a huge paunch, tearing off hunks of black bread to eat with a leg of chicken. Before the Germans came. At times he wondered whether he had inherited this financial acumen from his father, a trait he too had once despised and rejected on leaving to come to Israel and to the kibbutz. Yes. he'd been through all that. Now he was prepared to acknowledge that he enjoyed the challenge of managing the finances.

Reubek had been kibbutz treasurer once before, six years ago. Then it had been much tougher. Their collective learning curve as farmers had just begun, times were very hard and the turnover much smaller, leaving no room for manoeuvre. And for good measure, there were those two consecutive years of drought. It had been in the early fifties when, with many other kibbutzim, they had answered the government's call to cultivate the new lands of the arid Negev south for desperately needed grain for the waves of new immigrants — Zionism, the pioneering spirit and all that. But it left them deep in debt for many years and the experience had left its mark.

The treasurer was elected for a three year term and like that of the work organiser, it was a thankless job. But unlike the work organiser, who only lasted six months or a year, not everyone had the head for figures or the ability to be treasurer. And as the kibbutz economy grew and diversified, a 'Buggin's turn' situation had evolved: four or five people who could and were prepared to do the job. 'We're creating a financial hierarchy,' Gavriel had com-

plained in the general meeting when Reubek was elected this
time, '— a threat to our kibbutz democracy!' And only last week
at the farm committee, he and Yehuda had accused Reubek of
manipulating figures to prove that without hiring outside labour
from Ashkelon to weed the sugar beet, the kibbutz would lose a
third of the yield. Yet they wouldn't take the job of Gizbar themselves, would they?

Reubek was a founder member of the kibbutz. He'd been
through the camps in Cyprus and worked on the roads in Rehovot
before settling in this desolate border area. He too had enjoyed the
early enthusiasm, the earnest discussions on principles. He didn't
like hired labour either. But sometimes you had to be flexible. He
took another sip of coffee. Yes. Gavriel and his rigid principles —
just like Nakhum and his politics. And where had that got them?
Half the kibbutz had left after all those arguments. Sure, it was
great in '49 when they started out, young and idealistic. But you
couldn't live on principles and international Socialism. Now after
more than a dozen years, the main thing was for the kibbutz to be
economically viable, otherwise they wouldn't survive, principles
and all.

Reubek stared at the table top, thinking that if half the sugar
beet yield was lost through not completing the weeding, they
wouldn't get through December without taking a short term,
higher interest bank loan. Why could no one understand that? He
played with the metal glass-holder and was still thinking about
Avrumkeh when Yitzkhak, a treasurer from another kibbutz came
to join him. It was Yitzkhak's fourth term as treasurer in twenty-
five years; not many tricks that vatik old timer didn't know.
Reubek ordered another two coffees.

'*Nu*. How goes it?' asked Yitzkhak. Reubek sipped his coffee.

'So. So.' He sighed. 'Another damn stupid argument about
hired labour last night. Think they can live on air, our idealists.'
Yitzkhak nodded, then called over his breakfast order to the
counter and as they began to swap news of this and that, Gershon
from another young kibbutz joined them. Again there was surprise and comment about Avrumkeh's leaving. And the thought-

ful silences between as Reubek mulled over the recent arguments in the farm committee and at the general meeting. Was he the only realist?

From the outset, the kibbutz had naïvely over-estimated the ability of agriculture to support our ever-expanding housing, social, educational, health and cultural needs, the costs of which were rising at a faster rate than that of our net income. We were ignorant of the hard reality that, throughout the world, agriculture provides most people with a low net income and that the majority are peasants or day labourers barely eking out a living. Even the well-managed farms in developed countries could hardly succeed without government aid in one form or another. And the verbal battles with Reubek — and with almost every elected treasurer, were all part of a continual struggle to retain our principles and to live only from the fruits of our own two hands. Unfortunately, many of the most profitable crops required short bursts of large amounts of labour, which we struggled to meet with our own resources. And we were convinced that with initiative, modern methods and our collective spirit, we could be self-sufficient and still attain a reasonable standard of living.

But we were not only building a farm; we were creating a new village from nothing: roads, paths, landscaping, main services, drainage — the lot. We also underestimated our need to budget for a continually rising standard of living. When we lived in huts, ate a simple monotonous diet that allowed chicken only when one of us was sick — or the chicken was — there was so much else going on that we just didn't consider our standard of living. We were creating something from nothing, making the desert bloom, conquering physical labour and pioneering a new form of society. Over the years however, as the first flush of enthusiasm paled and many of the stalwarts left, raising the standard of living became the principal aim of a growing and eventually dominant section of the community.

Apart from all that, we hadn't taken account of the natural hazards in agriculture: frost in the orchards, drought in the cereals, mastitis in the dairy herd, pests in the cotton, and the rest, which often drastically reduced our anticipated income Then there were the hidden costs of living on the border: four able-bodied people on guard every night, one person half time engaged with security matters and liaison with the army, ambushes in the wadi and extra guards during tense situations and so on. In the late sixties, when the government costed all these items for the border kibbutzim, it came to many millions of pounds. Grudgingly the finance ministry paid up, but too little and too late. And from all the above, we had a severe cashflow problem.

By its very nature, agriculture takes months or even a year to pay back on any crop, and years to repay the planting of orchards and orange groves. In addition, modern farm machinery is ever more complex and expensive, requiring high initial financing. As a result, nearly all farmers everywhere, are in permanent debt to the banks. We used to joke that from six to eight each morning, we worked for the banks. Only after breakfast did we work for ourselves. We were lucky. Kibbutzim less organised than us ended up working till lunch for the banks! And later, with loans pegged to the dollar in an inflationary climate, this burden of interest was eventually to submerge the whole kibbutz movement.

At the outset, we kept our borrowing to long term loans on low rates of interest from the Settlement Agency. But as the kibbutz grew, the number of children increased, new houses became larger, the dining hall and kitchen more modern, etc., and we were forced to take short term, higher interest loans. With them came an ever-increasing burden of debt to the banks and now, no longer were bank loans required purely to tide over until the harvest, but more and more the loans were financing this higher standard of living. We didn't want luxuries and we tried to keep a rein on budgets, but essentially we had middle class expectations and desires, but a 'working class' income. And it took all the juggling acts of the treasurer to keep us sufficiently in credit everywhere. But we felt that in their efforts to keep the whole enterprise running, functionaries like Reubek often began to lose sight of the whole picture — of why we were here at all.

Now, as he sat in the café nearing the end of his three-year term

Sure. 30,000 for that — but 120 for my new mixer? No!

of office, amongst the same old formica tables, eating the same salted rolls and fried eggs, Reubek was thinking about all this too. In a private family, you live off what you can earn. In the kibbutz, he had to do battle with each branch manager or each children's nurse, all convinced that their needs were paramount. But only he, and a few others like the farm manager, seemed able to see the whole picture. And despite all his efforts, their financial situation was still as precarious as when he started. It only added to his unsettled mood as he contemplated what next.

In two month's time, when his term of office was over, the kibbutz wanted him to take charge of the orchards. But he knew he'd never get on there with Barukh and Elanah. And the cereal crops which he'd once managed had been taken over by younger members. So he'd probably have a spell in the dining hall whilst deciding where to work. 'Essential proletarianisation', Gavriel had joked, but Reubek had felt he meant it. And then there would still be all those arguments about hired labour, democracy, equality and collective decisions. He dreaded having to go through all that again with the English and the Sabras.

There was something else bugging him, something that hadn't mattered as long as he had been busy in Tel Aviv or Beer Sheva nearly every day. He was becoming aware of how many of his original Romanian group had left and just how few of his old friends were still around. In fact, he'd be working mostly with people with whom he had no special friendship. As he finished up his breakfast, Reubek continued to reflect on his winding up as treasurer.

Over the years, he'd given a lot of himself to the community and had no regrets about that. But times were changing. Perhaps now he would give something to himself. Yes, for himself. By chance, the previous week, he'd happened to run into Avrumkeh in Bank Leumi. Avrumkeh was now an area finance controller for the ministry of housing. Came with a new *Swallow* car, a large flat in Beer Sheva, and working just eight to five and a half day on Friday.

With the large immigration and new settlement projects over the recent years, government offices had expanded and were desperate for people who had financial management experience and who knew the language and the institutions. They were given neat offices, secretaries to type letters, accountancy asistance and above all, they were given respect for the job they were doing. Like Nakhman had said: somewhere where their talents were appreciated. No, he didn't need the constant confrontation with the kibbutz when he was only trying to do his job. Nor the insinuations about living it up in town and of trying to be an autocrat, and the feeling that everyone was waiting for him to finish his stint so that he could be 'down in the ranks' again, feeding the cows or picking oranges. He was past that. He'd done his bit for the pioneering life. Yes, perhaps it was time to let someone else have a go. Why not?

But there was Hannah. She'd trained to work with children with special needs, and although she couldn't be released from managing the kindergarten, she was happy in the kibbutz. And their children were doing well. Still, kids were resilient. But if he was serious, he had to discuss it with Hannah, very soon. Meanwhile, he would have a chat with Elkhanan in the Settlement Agency later that day to see what was around first. Finishing his coffee, he said 'Shalom' to the others, picked up his briefcase and went out.

Three months later, Reubek handed over to Offrah and went to work in the dining hall, polite and efficient, even managing a smile now and then. The worry lines dropped from his forehead and we teased him that he was losing weight after the good life in town. But just two months after that, he and Hannah announced that they were leaving. No one was that surprised. Barukh said he couldn't get used to being just an ordinary member of the kibbutz and doing manual labour again. Maybe. We'd all been relying on Hannah to weather the crisis until he found a satisfying place of work. Perhaps if she'd been allowed to work where she wanted, it would have helped; now we would have to find someone else to manage the kindergarten anyway . . .

At the time, we were probably too inexperienced in financial management to appreciate the problems and give Reubek his full due. He didn't help, often inclined to be officious and off-hand as gizbar. But still, he was a kibbutznik and had a lot to contribute. And there was Hannah, and the kids. So in the end, it was another sad loss.

Frost on the borderline

Israel has a Mediterranean climate. Mostly. I wrote this one winter.

I am fast asleep and imagine a knocking on the door to be a dream. But when the night guard taps on the door again and I recognise Shimon's voice, I turn onto my back and groan.

'Yes?'

'The thermometer's only two above zero,' he mutters. His boots scrape on the veranda tiles as he turns. Then his footsteps die away.

Still half asleep and trying not to wake my wife, I creak out of the warm bed into the darkness and pad over the ice-cold tiles out to the veranda. Groping for the light switch, I curse in the usual mixture of Russian and Arabic whilst pulling stiff working clothes over my pyjamas. There is no way I can get myself to take them off. Back in the room, I reach under the bed and grab the Sten gun. Pocketing two magazines, I creep out again to put on my boots, cursing the clear skies and still air.

Out on the path, the cold draws my skin taut as I shine the torch onto the max-min thermometer, hoping that Shimon has made a mistake. No chance. Through the beads of dew on the glass, the mercury is just above freezing point. No time to lose.

Running to the house behind, I catch Menakhem who is already lacing up his boots, and a few minutes later we are both haring down to the garage, calling out to the guard to unlock the rear gate.

'If we are not back in two hours, do something about it,' I yell, 'Okay?'

With an asthmatic cough and splutter, the old horizontal-two-cylinder John Deere chugs into life and with its pop-pop-popping waking half the kibbutz, we drive through the gate and out into the dark, freezing night, my warm bed becoming a distant dream. The frost claws through our clothes and penetrates right to my bones. At times like these, I see in a less favourable light the early pioneers who brought over Canary Island bananas for a trial. Now we are so successful that we even export them to Eastern Europe! Except that this is not the Canaries with their warming ocean currents. This is a Mediterranean country, bordering on central Asia. Every few winters, a freezing air-flow straight from Siberia reminds us of that, bringing with it nights of devastating sub-zero temperatures. And this was one of those nights.

We had tried everything in the books to protect the banana groves: burning old tyres, using smoke machines, giant fans, anything. Eventually, by chance, we discovered that the most effective means was to open the sprinklers which are mounted on twelve-foot-high standpipes and which irrigate the plantations. Ground water is at about eighteen degrees centigrade and the latent heat released when it starts to freeze on the leaves keeps them just above freezing point. In this way, the growing heart and developing flower inside the palms remain undamaged, and can sprout again in the spring. Now in this, our third cold winter, we think we have it all worked out and the night guard checks the thermometer outside my room every hour. If it drops to two degrees above zero, he wakes me. Then all we have to do is start up the electric pump at the well to send the water spraying out from the sprinklers.

Leaving the fence lights behind us, we drive along the dirt track to the well house, the John Deere exhaust popping and our headlights casting ghostly shadows on the roadside casuarina trees and prickly pear hedges. Menakhem is driving and looking out for pot-holes, whilst I balance on the drawbar, holding tight to the seat back with one hand. With the other, I clutch the Sten gun and peer into the darkness for infiltrators who might be desperate enough to have left their warm beds in Gaza to see what we had left out in the fields overnight. If the rabid jackals miss you, we say, there is always the chance of a stray bullet from the darkness.

Menakhem is whistling. It can hardly be heard above the racket from the John Deere, but he is whistling all the same, from Bach to Schoenberg and back again without a single misplaced note. He's usually whistling, that is when he isn't playing the flute. Menakhem is a virtuoso. He can play the flute as though it is a part of him; beautiful sweet notes, soft and clear. He is also our budding composer; studying one afternoon a week at the

Conservatoire in Tel Aviv, after a hard day's work in the groves. Not that we go a ball for all that atonal stuff he composes. But the cognescenti in Tel Aviv think he has a great future. So, as we do for Beni, our artist, we stump up the not inconsiderable tuition fees, proud that our small community has such promising talents.

Leaving the tractor chugging outside the well house, we run in and press the starter switch. A snap and a snarl, and the huge vertical-pump motor springs into life. With a whine that swiftly rises in pitch to a high scream, the full power comes through, corkscrewing the water up from fifty feet below and sending it away through the main pipeline. Menakhem is leaving the well house and is halfway through the 'Trout' quintet, when I glance at the pressure gauges.

'Hell,' I shout. 'The needle's not rising. The pressure's too low.' Menakhem takes an abrupt bar rest and comes back. We both look at the dials, tapping the glass with our knuckles, but the needle is stuck at one and a half atmospheres and refuses to budge.

'Some stupid bastard has left their own stopcocks open in the fields,' he says. We both think for a few seconds.

'The sugar beet!' we shout together. 'Bet it's in the damn sugar beet.' They had been sowing the day before.

'I reminded Yoske yesterday,' snarls Menakhem. 'I'll wake him up when we get back. I'll murder him,' he snarls, continuing with a string of unmentionable tortures he will inflict on the unfortunate Yoske. Extreme cold brutalises the most delicate of natures.

Back on the tractor again, we open full throttle to hurtle up the road to the sugar beet fields, keeping our eyes peeled as we pass through the orange groves. A month previously, our lorry was shot up just at this point as it came home late from town. The driver escaped without a scratch, though he needed a change of trousers when he reached the kibbutz. Ever since then we all treat that place with the greatest of respect after dark.

At the edge of the fields, we slow down; even in anger, there's no point in ironing flat our precious aluminium irrigation pipes. Walking away from the noise of the tractor, torch in hand, we try to listen for a rush of water, realising at the same time that we are perfect targets for an ambush. But we have to find those open taps. Sure enough, three are gushing full bore. I don't fancy being in Yoske's shoes tomorrow lunchtime, whether he's personally responsible or not. Menakhem has the proverbial artistic temperament. Again, we seriously consider waking him up when we get back, freezing wet hands and all. But that wouldn't be fair on Offrah. With a hiss and a gurgle, the stopcocks are closed and we rush back to the well. Sure enough, the pressure has risen; we are now the only ones taking water. Then it's out to the banana grove, to make sure that all the sprinklers are turning. If one remains blocked, the drifting spray from the others in this sub-zero temperature will cause more damage than if we had done nothing at all.

Leaving the tractor running, we scamper up and down every row of sprinklers, the wet banana leaves brushing and slapping against us. Sure enough some are not working. We unscrew the standpipe, blow out the nozzle of the sprinkler and screw it back on again, getting soaked in the process. The tractor, muffled by the palms, throbs in the distance, headlights casting faint beams over the tops of the huge green leaves. The sprinklers tck-tck-tck away as they turn, the water drumming on the leaves every time they spin round, soaking us again. Our bodies are growing colder and colder, but at least there's no fear of infiltrators in here — they wouldn't be so damn crazy.

The drive back seems to take ages. The adrenalin is spent and tiredness is taking over. With our blood thinned by years of working in the heat, the freezing night quickly penetrates the sodden clothes into our bodies. I feel as though I shall never again be a warm-blooded animal, ever. And slipping back into bed like this, will be inviting instant divorce.

Menakhem has finished 'Trout' and is into a snatch of 'Tanhauser'. We both go a ball on Wagner, despite the genius's anti-semitism and the fact that public performances in Israel are still *verboten*. Then, as we pass the mango groves, a group of shadowy figures runs towards us. Menakhem, halfway through Siegfried idyll, stops on a crotchet and pulls out full throttle, sending the tractor roller-coasting over potholes. Perched on the mud-guard, I grip the Sten gun and push the safety catch to automatic, whilst locking my legs around the steering column for support. All this cannot have taken more than two or three seconds, when suddenly one of the group runs into the headlights and waves. We recognise the uniform: it's one of our patrols and we breathe again.

'Stupid idiots,' yells Menakhem, amongst other curses as the engine drops to idling speed. 'Thought you were infiltrators. I was going to run you down.'

'Sorry friends,' the corporal spreads his hands. 'Our radio's packed in. Can I hitch a lift to your telephone? Truck's coming to pick us up'. As he climbs on the other mudguard, he rubs his arms.

'Heck. What a night. Bloody freezing.' Suddenly, he looks at Menakhem, then at me, then back to Menakhem. 'Funny,' he says, 'Didn't rain where we were!' Menakhem pulls out the throttle.

'It didn't where we were either. And as for freezing, mate,' he sniffles. 'You don't know what cold is!'

During the following years the cold Siberian winds seemed to come more often; then after the Six Day War, the Soviet Union and Eastern Europe imposed a diplomatic freeze and banned imports of our bananas. So we gradually phased them out and planted avocadoes instead. It wasn't the last time we had to battle with the frost, but Menakhem never whistled as well after that particular night. His lips seemed to have frozen into a different shape. And as for me, when I feel the cold each winter, I wonder whether I have ever completely thawed out.

One man's war

Kalman hadn't shown up for work. And suddenly we realised that we hadn't seen him since the start of the war. He was our building foreman, from Tel Aviv, and reliable as clockwork.

The Six Day War had been sudden and swift, victory complete. The newspapers came every day with more commentaries and predictions, but all the news had already been made. And whilst the world outside marvelled, analysed and quarrelled, we were counting the casualties. Day after day, new names appeared in the large, black-bordered boxes that covered the pages. None of this English stiff upper-lip of just a few lines of faint print on an inside page obituaries' column. Here, the names were in heavy block type with thick black borders. Bold and screaming. For two thousand years, Jews had been given much practice in mourning the dead.

There were still accounts of recent battles in the papers and impressions from the newly-occupied Arab areas, but mostly we scanned the pages for names of friends and others we knew, and for the fallen of neighbouring kibbutzim. A high number of kibbutzniks were in the crack units or were officers, and the kibbutzim had provided so much more than their fair share of casualties. Each fresh day brought the renewed sick feeling, as we recognised a name, or spotted another person from a kibbutz which had already suffered enough. God, or whoever might be up there, was never very even-handed.

In this highly politicised country, each party had its own newspaper and we mainly read *Al Hamishmar*, which represented our party. In town, however, most people also read one of the two evening papers, *Yediot* or *Ma'ariv*. These now had special editions several times a day devoted largely to obituaries. The inside pages were just chequer boards of large black boxes: four across, twelve down, each box a son, a brother, a husband, a lover. And each black border left a family shattered, sending shock waves through relatives and friends. In this small country, where everyone knows someone, hardly a family was untouched in some way by the grim reaper. Some names appeared three or four times as acquaintances and workmates clubbed together to express their condolences and family friends showed their grief. Other boxes, from more affluent families or from offices and institutions, were double or treble in size, while still others contained just three or four words, leaving an empty space, an emptiness that would be there forever.

We scanned the pages, so engrossed in those we knew well, that we couldn't take in others, slightly removed; nor did we receive the evening papers from town. So when Kalman didn't show up for work, although we were surprised, we didn't make any connection; the war had disrupted so many routines. And he was too old to have been called up.

Building and construction was the one area in which we allowed outside, hired, labour since they were investments and not a part of our basic economic activity. Foremen and tradesmen from town were employed by our Federation's building company, travelling from kibbutz to kibbutz as demand arose. And Kalman had been supervising our building works for nearly a year now.

Kalman came from Gallitzia, the old Austrian part of southern

Poland. Life there had always been an endless struggle for existence and the 'Gallitzianers' were noted for their endless energy,
for their infighting and for always being on the make. Kalman
was no exception. Having survived the Poles, the Nazis and a concentration camp, no one was going to get the better of him. Tall
and spindly, he had a habit of walking with his head set forward
like a battering ram, his body held at forty-five degrees, making
him appear shorter. His mouth was always half open, ready to
comment or command. 'I said put four nails in every cross piece,'
he'd say, when the the carpenter was doing just that anyway; or,
'Remember. Two-and-a-half buckets of cement to each mixer.
Don't skimp,' he'd snap at the labourers, having said it a dozen
times before. In return, the men would tease him horribly. And
with an apparent complete lack of sense of humour, he seemed
impervious to their chivvying. But Kalman knew his job and the
workers knew that too, and as well as being proficient, he was
extremely conscientious. So after that first week, when he didn't
show up for work the following Sunday, it seemed very odd.

On Monday, we phoned the Federation building office in Tel
Aviv. There followed a moment's awkward silence. Hadn't we
heard? Didn't we know? Know what? Kalman's son had been
killed; up on the Golan on the last day of the war. We were
stunned. His son! Kalman's only son. He was forever talking
about his son, telling us how he and his wife had worked their fingers to the bone to send him through technical high school; how
he was one of the top students in his year at the prestigious Haifa
Technical Institute and how he, Kalman, had made sure that the
boy wouldn't have to traipse around the kibbutzim or down to
Beer Sheva and Dimona, to make a living on building sites. He
would be an engineer, with his own practice. He, Kalman, would
make sure his son didn't turn out the second rate drawings that he
often had to work to. And he would put him up to all the old
tricks contractors like to play. We often joked that it was like the
old Bulldog in *Tom and Jerry* cartoons, patting his pup's head
'That's my boy, that's my boy . .' as he would rattle on about 'My
son Yoram . . My son this . . my son that. .' And now, the son was

no more.

It was mid-morning when we'd telephoned. I didn't wait. After hurrying across to the office to take some petty cash from Offra, I got changed.

'Pick me up at the Migdal turn-off at eight tonight,' I called out to Motele, as I ran past the garage and out to the main road to hitch a lift to Ashkelon.

At the central bus station in Tel Aviv, newsboys scurried along the platforms shouting: 'Ma'ariv. .Yediot. . Ma'ariv!' I bought a copy and scrutinised the inside pages on the local bus to Givatayim. How many more days? How many more litle boxes? How many more names? I recognised some names of boys we knew from neighbouring kibbutzim. Relatives had placed them in the evening papers so that their friends would see. Who the hell read our left-wing newspaper in the fleshpots of Tel Aviv? And then, there, on the centre page, staring out at me, I saw it: 'To Kalman and Hedva . . for Yoram . . from the Sokolov family.' Folding the newspaper, I gripped it in my hand. And was still holding it tight as I walked along the tree-lined roads of the work-ers' suburb.

Kalman held one too, as he answered my knock. The door was ajar, but I still knocked. One look told me that he would never be the same Kalman again. A grey pallor had replaced the ruddy complexion; the bright, ever moving eyes were dull and half closed; his shoulders were more hunched than ever.

'Sorry, Kalman,' I reached out my hand. 'We only heard this morning. From the office.' He shook it and turned to look behind him.

'Come. Come in. Hedva will be pleased. Hedva,' he called out, 'Someone from the kibbutz.' He glanced back at me. 'Come. Come in!' The same old repetitive manner. But the fire had completely gone.

The room was furnished simply, a dark mahogany formica sideboard and a glass cabinet, a highly polished, dark table with matching chairs and a large rug on the cream terrazzo-tiled floor. Over the sideboard, the mirror was turned to face the wall.

Beneath it were placed photographs: Yoram as a baby, schoolboy Yoram and the parents and, pride of place, in a large black frame, Yoram in uniform, with wide eyes and Kalman's nose, thin lips and pointed chin. The mother rose as I came in, short with greying dark hair, her eyes red behind thick-lensed glasses. Kalman introduced her. Hedva. We shook hands. She sighed and nodded towards the photograph then closed her eyes for a moment. No sight could have expressed her grief more. Then she looked up.

'A cup of coffee?' she said softly in a strong Polish accent, 'You've come a long way.'

'Please. Don't bother. I don't want to trouble you,' I said, in spite of the fact that I had missed breakfast and was starving.

'No trouble,' she said, turning towards the kitchen. 'No trouble at all.' She shuffled through to the kitchen in her carpet slippers. 'What else have I left to do?' she murmured. 'What else is there?' And in the silence that followed, came the clink of the kettle and a rattle of cups.

Kalman motioned me to sit down and waved towards the table. It was covered with all of that day's newspapers as well as those of several previous days. Layer upon layer, each folded to the page bearing the name of their son. As the mother came in with coffee and some biscuits, the door opened and a young woman came in: their daughter. She held out a copy of the latest edition.

'Look,' she said. 'The Rabinovitz's have put one in too.' Kalman snatched it from her hand.

'Here. Let me see. Let me see it.' He put on his glasses and brought the page close to his face, peering at the black bordered box. For one tiny moment, his eyes flickered with the old fire.

'Nice of them to remember,' he muttered. 'Yoram used to play with their boy.' He turned to me and held out the paper. 'They loved him.' Tears came into his eyes. 'Everyone loved Yoram.'

Hedva and her daughter sat in adjacent chairs and watched as Kalman grew more animated.

'Look,' he said, pulling a copy of *Al Hamishmar* from between the layers, 'your Federation, and the Building Department; they put one in too. Double space.' The kibbutz would have one in tomorrow, I said, apologising once more for not knowing. I couldn't help feeling that it would have been better in the evening papers, so their friends could see it and, more importantly, Kalman would know that they had seen it. But it was many times more expensive. Kalman picked up the latest edition again and perused it as though something new would emerge, as if through mentioning his name again and again, he would be conjured back to life. The mother reached out a shaking hand.

'Nu. Let me see already.' She adjusted her glasses. 'Hmm. The Rabinovitz's. Very nice. Very nice. They didn't put one in for Benzion's boy.'

'You see. You see.' Kalman nudged my arm, 'Everyone loved Yoram.' He waved his arm again over the pile of newspapers, as though they expressed a league table of whose son had the most black boxes; living from one edition of the evening papers to the next, from day to day, as if the more black borders there were, the less painful would be their loss. Perhaps it would be — and anyhow, who was I to judge?

As I sipped my coffee, Kalman asked about the kibbutz. Whether we had . . ?

'No,' I answered, somehow feeling guilty, 'Just two wounded . . and two tractors blown up in the fields.' I could have told him that we lost one in the Sinai War and that three had been killed in reprisal raids before that. But it would be meaningless. Only one thing mattered to Kalman at that moment and probably forever; Yoram had gone, and with it, the whole future for which he had planned and worked. What more could a person lose?

A slow, disjointed conversation drifted around the table, mostly about who had lost who and where and how. Neighbours came in, mumbled consoling sentences and were shown the latest black box. They told of the Cohens in the next street, this one's brother, that one's nephew and their neighbour's cousin in the tank corps. Everyone nodded and sighed: 'May you live to a hundred and twenty,' and went out, leaving Kalman to rearrange the newspapers. Eventually the daughter kissed them both, shook my hand

and went out. I could find nothing meaningful more to say and, after long spells of dull silence, I explained that I had to catch the last bus to Ashkelon. Kalman nodded and stood up and we shook hands warmly. I shook the mother's hand and wished her well.

In the doorway, Kalman thanked me again and again for coming. What a pity I had never met Yoram. What a brilliant engineer he would have been. Not like that idiot in the design office who couldn't tell a high-tensile bar from a number ten nail. We didn't mention his returning to work. It seemed the least relevant thing at that moment. On the bus home, in the gathering darkness I imagined I saw a reflection in the side window; Kalman shuffling the papers on the polished table, counting the black boxes and noting from whom, and his wife sitting silently on the edge of her chair, rocking gently back and forth to the ticking of the clock on the sideboard.

The kibbutz truck was late picking me up at the crossroads — as usual. This time I didn't care. The later back the better. I couldn't face everyone asking me: 'How's Kalman?', perhaps still with a faint smile as they recalled the hurried, slightly ridiculous gait, his bleached hat askew on his bald head and the way the workers teased him. The path down to my room ran past the half-finished shells of five new houses. His voice seemed to echo from the blackness within: 'Put four nails in, I told you . . . Where's Shlomo gone this time . . .' And I saw his shadow hurrying along the path towards me, eager to relate the latest progress of his son.

For a brief moment, I thought of whether he would return to finish the houses, but it seemed so irrelevant. I looked over the unfinished roofs and into the night sky, thinking about how he'd survived all those terrible war years, sustained, he once told me, by hoping for the future. And I wondered: how do you survive, when the future has gone?

The one who knew

Abu Salaam came to us as a building labourer along with half a dozen others from Gaza, after the Six Day War. At first, we almost sent him away. Short and bow-legged, in his tattered, baggy trousers and an off-white skullcap, he looked so old and frail — more like a doting grandfather than someone who would dig trenches in the blazing sun. But he worked well and picked up Hebrew much more quickly than many of the younger ones.

The months after the Six Day War were heady days. At last we could meet 'the other side'. Talk with them and show them we were not monsters. Try to explain. Hope that the politicians and the world statesmen would seize the golden opportunity to make peace and settle the refugee problem. And meanwhile, in our own small way, despite our past enmity, we wanted to help, to befriend and treat them as fellow human beings. But it took a little while before we managed to know each as individuals, rather than 'them'. And for me, it started with Abu Salaam, which apart from meaning 'the father of Salaam', by chance also means 'father of peace'.

Mahmud said that Abu Salaam had once been a *mukhtar*: a village headman. But then each one from Gaza had a story of what he had been and how much land he'd owned, and we often wondered where reality ended and the fantasies began. But with Abu Salaam, as I gradually found out, it was no fantasy and it started the day our regular bricklayers didn't turn up.

It was the second time that week and I guessed that the builders were running another job as well; probably cash in hand. The new calf shed was only half finished and the cowmen were going frantic setting up temporary pens in the corners of the Dutch barn. As I cursed and moaned, Mahmud nudged me.

'Why don't you ask Abu Salaam?' he murmured.

'Who?' I smiled. 'Old grandad?' He nodded.

'Abu Salaam can do anything. You try him and see.' I couldn't take him seriously, but he persisted. 'You ask him. See.' Desperate times breed desperate measures. I had to pacify the cowmen. We crossed the yard to call him and the old man climbed out of the trench.

'Blocks,' I said, going through the motions of bricklaying, 'can you build blocks? Walls?' Abu Salaam touched the side of his nose with his forefinger.

'*Ana aaraf.*' I know. And with an almost toothless grin, swept his arm in a semicircle, adding, '*Al kull.*' Everything. '*Ana aaraf!*'

Still sceptical, I borrowed Hanokh's building lines and trowel and set him on a simple, straight wall by the silo. Two hours later, when I came back, the wall was waist high with every block set true and joints filled.

'*Quais,*' Great, I said, not a little embarrassed. He touched the side of his nose again and smiled.

'*Ana aaraf.*'

From that day on, as well as bricklaying, whenever there was an awkward job — a metal frame to be set in concrete, drain to repair, tiles to lay or any number of odd jobs — Abu Salaam would take a look, rub his chin and then without a word, stride off to organise tools and materials to get it done. Everything was worked out and thought through to the last detail. And although the others often joked and teased him, when he spoke, they fell deferentially quiet and paid attention. And one day, he proved that in his story at least, there was indeed substance.

He was repairing a gulley in the milking parlour and as I came in to see how it was going, he pulled me outside and pointed to the brown dust and ends of straw that covered the cowshed compounds outside.

'What do you do with that?' he asked. It was the dry, powdered cow dung which turned to a quagmire in the winter rains. Every year we spent valuable labour scraping it up and dumping it on the fields and orchards. We also sold some of it to a merchant from Rishon for next to nothing.

'Why?' I asked

'I can take it away, if you want,' he said, winking. 'For cash.'

'Okay by me,' I replied, imagining him humping half a sack home each day after work for some small vegetable plot near Gaza, 'But see Gadi first, okay?'

That evening Gadi caught me in the dining hall.

'Wants the lot,' he said, eyes wide, 'Two-and-a-half lira a sack, we agreed!'

'Take a few donkey loads to get rid of that lot,' I smiled. There were at least two hundred sacks in each of the four courtyards. Gadi had already made the calculation. His forehead creased.

'We're talking big money,' he said. 'And from that old grandad?' I thought for a moment then shrugged.

'Well, let him take fifty sacks for a start. And we'll see.'

The following day after work, my son and I went down to water the new concrete silo floor to stop it drying out too quickly. He loved squirting the hose back and forth. At about seven o'clock, just as we were setting off back to the children's house, a battered green truck with a Gaza number plate chugged in from the front gate in a cloud of dust and on down to the cowsheds. As soon as it braked, four men threw out piles of old sacks and without waiting, jumped down and started to fill the sacks with the dry dung, using shovel heads and offcuts of plywood. A few moments later, a short man in a gleaming white *keffiyeh* headscarf and wearing a smart brown jacket and clean, beige *abaya* smock climbed down from the cab.

'Looks important, doesn't he?' said my son. The man had his back to me, but as I walked across, he suddenly turned and raised his hand, his yellow toothed smile beaming.

'*Ahalan we sahalan.*' Greetings, he said. I stood and blinked: Abu Salaam! It couldn't be. Recovering, I tapped the side of my nose with one finger.

'*Ana aaraf,*' I grinned. He smiled back, his eyes twinkling.

'*Aiwa,*' he said. '*Ana aaraf.*' And I saw that this was the real Abu-Salaam, every inch a *mukhtar* — a real 'chief'.

As we continued to work together, I came to know more and more of each refugee's past. And every one had his own, often very sad story.

One day, whilst loading sacks of cement onto a trailer, Yusuf and I were joking about Subkhi and his Israeli National Insurance stamps, (more of that later). Yusuf was tall and thin, with a ragged black moustache. Suddenly he stopped laughing and his face darkened. Lifting his left trouser leg, he pointed to a nasty scar on his shin.

'Subkhi is lucky. Not like me,' he grunted. Then he straightened up and pointed across the dunes. '"Ruh el beit!" Go home, the Effendi said to me.' He heaved another bag of cement onto the trailer and repeated, '"Ruh el beit." That was all he said!'

I waited for him to continue, wondering what the connection was with Subkhi. But in that Eastern way of tortuously winding up to a conclusion, I knew it might be some time in coming and carried on loading the trailer. Then, as we rested for a moment to draw breath, he began again, speaking in short phrases as he struggled with the Hebrew.

'We were working for that Effendi, digging a ditch for a new pipe. And just before makleh: lunch, it caved in. Buried three of us up to our waists.' He clutched at his stomach. 'Up to here. Two they pulled out straight away. It took three hours to get me free and my leg was bent double.' He crouched low to illustrate, 'The pain nearly killed me.'

I pictured the scene: heaps of yellow sand, a large white house set amongst the green orange groves, the day labourers in tattered white cloaks and baggy trousers. And Yusuf, groaning on the ground with the others clustered around him.

'When the Effendi came out,' he continued, 'he just looked around and shouted to them all, "Get back to work." Then he pointed at me, "Inta. Ruh el beit! You. Go home! How?" I asked. Perhaps he could bring a cart. A doctor. I thought my leg was broken. He didn't even look at me again. Just said, "Ruh el beit" and went indoors again.'

Sensing that I might have difficulty following his rudimentary Hebrew, mixed as it was with colloquial Arabic and Egyptian idioms, Yusuf slowed down as he continued.

'So I shouted after him: "What about my money? At least till the end of the week. My wife. Three children. Money for the doctor." But all he ever said, was,"Ruh el beit!" '

We loaded another sack, then he continued.

'The men carried me home after work, but I had no doctor's money and the hospital was on the other side of Gaza. So I went to the Bedouin on the sand dunes. Their medicine man wrapped the leg up in hasheesh. Then I had to lay down for a month whilst my wife begged and scraped. Ya'Allah, it was a hard time.' I bent down to pick up another sack, but Yusuf stood back and tapped me on the shoulder.

'That would never happen in Israel!' he said. 'Here, I get my wages every week. And if I fall ill, there's still some money from National Insurance'. He paused for a few seconds. 'And that's why Subkhi wants it to be correct.'

We finished loading and as he climbed on the trailer, I started the tractor and pulled away up the hill, thinking. Yusuf wasn't one to ingratiate himself for the sake of it. He knew us well enough not to have to put up a front. No, what he'd said was what he felt. Those few short statements had expressed his dilemma, the dilemma of all the refugees from Gaza.

When the kibbutz settled in 1949, the whole area was a deserted no-mans-land; all around were the remains of one of the last battles of the War of Independence. Assured that Israel would soon be defeated, the Arab villagers had fled towards Gaza with the retreating Egyptian army, expecting to return when the Egyptians regrouped and advanced again. They never did. Ever since, they had been treated as second class citizens by the Egyptian military regime and used as cheap labour by the landowners in Gaza. Having been dispossessed of their homes and their lands in that war of '48, now, after the Six Day War, they were working in Israel. But here even though they were not citizens, they received the going rate, paid their National Insurance and received the benefits when needs be. And it had opened their eyes as to the way they had been treated by their own people.

Yusuf's story and its dilemma must have been repeated a thousand times. But there were other stories. Like that of Ibrahim. When we went to pick up some shuttering planks from a neighbouring kibbutz, we drove the back way up a dusty track. Suddenly the carpenter pointed to a row of prickly pear bushes near the ruins of Beit Jirja.

'That was where my fields were,' he said matter-of-factly and softly, as though not wishing to offend. I looked at the cotton and maize crops of a Tunisian immigrant village that had settled there in '52, themselves refugees from the anti-Jewish riots in Djerba. I nodded but said nothing, again wondering: fantasy or not? Each worker from Gaza had mentioned at some time or other his fields, his house or his orchard. Added all together, they would have covered twice the area between Gaza and Migdal. The acres had multiplied themselves during their twenty year exile in Gaza. Yet for them, they were undoubtedly the reality.

Our fields and all those of all the nearby settlements had once belonged to those villagers. And it was graphically brought home to us in '67 when for months after the Six Day War, every Friday, their sabbath, cars and pick-ups would drive along the nearby roads and dirt tracks. Whole families, in their Sunday best, would pile out to stand and gaze at heaps of rubble or just flat fields, where once they lived and worked. When we passed on a tractor or in the jeep, they would nod and greet us, but in their eyes burned a resentment that they couldn't, or didn't want to hide. Then, having seen the reality, they got quietly into their vehicles and headed back to Gaza. The Egyptian army invasion of '48 and the war had changed their lives forever. And there was no way the clock could be turned back. For ourselves, we always maintained that when peace came, they would have to be compensated. And with Ibrahim's words, I thought about all their stories again.

A few weeks before, Abu Jassar, a floor tiler, had told me about his two-storied house and orange grove at Berbera, now a ruined village some four miles away.

'*Insh'allah*,' he sighed. 'We shall go back there one day'.

'Who knows?' I said. 'If there hadn't been that war in '48, things would have been different.' I looked into his eyes and added. 'We didn't start that war, Abu Jassar. And your village fired on Jewish lorries going to kibbutz Yad Mordekhai in '47, even before it started.' He picked up a floor tile and ran his finger along the edge.

'Maybe. Maybe one or two hotheads. I didn't. Most of us just wanted to work our lands. But when the Egyptians retreated, they told us to come with them and said that the Jews would slaughter us. So I took my family and followed. What would you have done?'

'Look,' I began, 'the area couldn't stay empty and desolate as it was. Israel had to secure its borders. Your villages are no longer here and others have settled the whole area. Their children have been born here and it's their home.' Abu Jassar looked back at me, his eyes sad.

'And my children? . . My home?' There was not a lot I could say, except mumble something about war and survival. Israel had survived, but surrounded by a sea of hatred and squalor. The Six Day War had provided an opportunity for barriers to come down in an air of optimism that at last something could be done.

'When there's a real peace,' I said, 'there will be a solution.'

'*Insh'allah*,' nodded Abu Jassar. 'May there be peace.'

Yes. We had high hopes immediately after the war. But the more nothing happened on the political front, the more inertia set in. And instead of resettlement and rehabilitation, the refugees in Gaza began to depend more and more upon travelling into Israel, greedily soaked up by the burgeoning post war economy as a supply of cheap labour. And every day, the once deserted junction at Ashkelon was swamped with hundreds of Arab workers, waiting for a bus or a builder's van to take them onwards to Tel Aviv.

And Abu Salaam? He left us in 1970 and I never saw him again, not even at the junction. But the memory of the proud, smartly-dressed *mukhtar*, transformed into a stubby, bald, baggy-trousered old bricklayer smiling '*Ana aaraf*', has remained with me.

Old enemies — sudden friends

Subkhi was a giant — six foot four, or more. But it was more than just his height. With massive square shoulders and biceps the girth of your average thigh, one sensed that with one blow of his fist, he could plant you into the ground — right up to your neck.

He didn't talk much. Just looked with hard, grey eyes, nodding when he understood, or gesturing if he wanted to know more. Most of the Arab building workers from Gaza had picked up a smattering of Hebrew words and expressions. Not Subkhi. He strained to explain himself, the tendons on his neck standing out like hawsers, his short cropped hair standing erect and stiff as a brush. Fais joked that by the time Allah, blessed be He, had finished making his body, there was nothing left for the head. Subkhi didn't seem to mind the joke — he was no one's fool, his watchful grey eyes following every movement of the lips, every twitch of an eyebrow, missing nothing.

Subkhi got to do the heavy jobs: demolishing old walls, digging foundation trenches in the sandstone, swinging his pick

slowly and methodically, every blow counting, striking the right
spot every time. Pausing now and again, he would look around
and as you walked by, his eyes followed, beetle-browed, just a
flicker of the eyelids acknowledging before he carried on.

His taciturn nature didn't endear him to most of the kibbutz,
especially to those who had no direct contact with the Arab building workers. A short time before, any of them could have been
stealing our irrigation pipes, planting mines on the dirt tracks
through our fields or screaming '*Itbakh Al Yahud!*' with the mob in
Gaza's Liberation Square. Now, just a few months after the Six
Day War, here they were, inside our kibbutz. And perhaps Subkhi
personified all those suspicions generated by years of border war-
fare, his eyes appearing to radiate resentment and hatred for all
the misfortunes his people had suffered. But we who worked with
him, had no such apprehensions, knowing that he just wanted to
get stuck into his work and receive the first regular pay he had
had in twenty years. Yet his very size, and silence, made you
sometimes wonder what might happen if he really did get angry.
Which was why I felt distinctly uneasy when he became annoyed
over a mistake in his pay slip.

The cowmen had wanted to break out a cill under the entrance
doorway to the deep litter shed — a six-foot-long, three-foot-deep
solid reinforced concrete beam.

'Cost a bomb,' I muttered to the cowman. 'We'll need to hire a
compressor from town.' With constant new improvements, the
cowsheds were a permanent building site.

'The cows are lacerating their udders getting into the yards,'
said Elisha. 'It's gotta be done, and before the winter rains make
them sink in even further!'

By chance, Abu Salaam, another of the workers from Gaza, was
laying blocks about ten yards away, one eye, as always, to what
was going on. As Elisha walked away, he hopped across the
muddy yard, finding the dry spots like Jesus walking on water.

'Give it to Subkhi,' he muttered. 'He'll do it.'

'It's not a manual job,' I said. 'Needs a compressor.'

'You ask him.' He winked, characteristically touching the side of his nose, '*Ana aaraf.*' I know.

I brought Subkhi to look at the cill. He pushed the dung aside with his enormous boot then leaned down to take a closer look. Even bent double, he was still the height of a cow's back. Straightening up, he grunted and nodded at Abu Salaam, and they conversed quietly; delicate negotiations were in progress. I was sure that Abu Salaam would take a cut, but that was their business. After a few short exchanges between them in Arabic, Abu Salaam turned to me.

'Needs a big sledgehammer,' he said. I nodded. 'And a full day's money, plus bonus hour.' On Friday, their Sabbath, they stopped work an hour early but received the full pay, which they called bonus. I considered it for a moment. It would certainly take Subkhi all of a day, if not more to knock that out. Didn't seem a fair price to me. I glanced from Abu Salaam to Subkhi and back again.

'You sure?' I asked. Subkhi nodded. What he wanted to understand, he understood. '*Fadal!*' I said: Agreed. Subkhi raised the faintest trace of a smile.

'*Quais*,' he murmured: Good. And we shook on it. My hand didn't recover until the next day.

The following morning, Subkhi shouldered the fourteen pound sledgehammer as though it were an umbrella, and strode down to the cowsheds. For the next few hours, the whole kibbutz shook to the thud, thud, thud coming from below. God knows what it did to the milk yields. I consoled the cowmen that a compressor would have been worse. Each time I passed by him on my rounds, he stood astride the beam, swinging the hammer with slow, regular strokes. I felt guilty. Wasn't that how the folk song hero 'John Henry' died?

Just before lunch, Abu Salaam appeared at my site hut.

'Bolt croppers,' he muttered. 'Reinforcement steel.' I sent him up to Rahamim, the steelfixer. An hour later, everything fell strangely still. Quite suddenly, I could hear birds singing, the thump of the washing machine in the laundry, a tractor climbing the hill. Everyone crossing the courtyard seemed to pause, as though something was missing. The thudding had ceased completely. I tensed. Perhaps he had collapsed. At that moment, Subkhi's huge frame blocked the doorway. He crossed his hands than cut them apart.

'*Khalas*,' he grunted: Finished. '*Khalasna!*'

'*Al Kull?*' The Lot? My voice must have betrayed disbelief. He narrowed his eyes and swept his hands apart again.

'*Ken*,' he muttered, in Hebrew, '*Hakol*.' Again, what he wanted to understand, Subkhi understood. I stood up and went to him.

'*Akhsan. Quais!*' Tremendous. Great! His eyes softened a little, just a little. Then he nodded, turned and made his way down to the casuarina trees where the others were just finishing their lunch.

I waited, then went round to the cowshed. All that remained of the massive beam was a smattering of concrete chips on the dung, and six gleaming, cut ends of reinforcement. By the fence, stood a neat pile of rubble. A compressor and rock drill couldn't have done it much quicker, or neater. The cows, watching and quietly chewing cud, seemed as stunned as I was.

When the cowmen came down from the dining hall, they too were amazed.

'What?' asked Elisha. 'Done already?' He scratched his head, 'Bloody hell!'

'How much does he get for that?' asked Motti, our home-grown chauvinist, who only ever saw the Palestinian problem through the sights of a rifle.

'A full day's pay,' I said.

'But he finished by lunchtime. Why?' I didn't bother to answer. Elisha slapped his shoulder.

'How much would you have done it for eh, fighter?' The cowmen laughed, then went in for the milking.

As I walked up to the road, Subkhi was backfilling a pipe trench by the boiler house. I hurried over to Abu Salaam.

'Look. Subkhi's done his day. He'll still get the money. He can go.' Abu Salaam took off his white woollen hat then jammed it back on his bald head again.

'Subkhi does what Subkhi wants.' He smiled and carried on laying blocks.

There and then I decided to add on two hours, but the week's sheets had already been collected early that morning. So I went up to telephone the wages office in Tel Aviv. Could they make sure he got the extra piece-work money and the bonus, all for next Thursday's payday? Moishe wasn't there. Avremeleh asked what all the fuss was about for one bloody Arab. Ignoring him, I asked to be transferred to Frieda in accounts. Sixty if a day, Frieda had the energy of a teenager. She liked the story and said she would do her best to hold up the wages run and tick-tack it in. And I forgot about it.

The following Thursday, shortly after Moishe's van had gone, Subkhi's huge frame blocked the doorway again. I thought he'd come to thank me, not that I needed him to. He'd deserved all he got. He had received the extra money and insisted on shaking my hand again, almost wrenching it off in the process. But there was something else. Thrusting the long pay slip in front of me, he pointed to one of the columns, then wrote the same figure in the air with his finger. I looked. The office had paid him correctly, but had deducted a few lira too much for National Insurance.

'A tiny sum,' I shrugged and smiled. Subkhi's brow furrowed — deep-ploughing, furrows.

'But . . it's my money,' he muttered, the tendons knotting in his neck as his eyes stared at me. Severely testing my rudimentary Arabic, I explained that it was a mistake at head office in Tel Aviv and I would deal with it. Suddenly, he stepped close, laid a surprisingly gentle hand on my shoulder and in halting Hebrew said:

'Ata. Ata, azor li!' You. You will help me! More like a statement of faith — or even a command. And I knew I had to resolve it. With Subkhi, as Abu Salaam said later, it was a matter of principle.

I telephoned later that day. Thankfully Moishe was there. Yes, he would sort it out for next payday. But when the wages van had gone, Subkhi caught me and pointed to the pay slip. Still there was no credit. Again I promised. But the following week, the mistake still hadn't been corrected. And with Subkhi's eyes glaring after me, I went to phone Moishe yet again.

'What's all the fuss over a couple of lira, for god's sake?' he snapped. 'He wouldn't get that back in Gaza.'

'Not the point,' I repeated. 'It's the principle. 'And,' I added, half joking, 'my physical wellbeing, friend.' But to no avail, and the following Thursday, Subkhi glared at me again. So on my next visit to Tel Aviv, I went into the office. Frieda had a day off so I left a note under her typewriter in giant red felt pen letters. Begging.

I waited anxiously the following Thursday, and when Moishe's van whisked through the gate with the pay slips, I decided I had an urgent appointment with the head of the poultry to discuss the new deep litter shed. Creeping back, I had almost reached the safety of the site hut, when Subkhi appeared out of the shadow of the trees and strode towards me. It was eighty in the shade but I started shivering. God. No. Not that damn refund again. I stopped and started to frame my apologies — how I'd gone to the wages office especially and how next week it would be done for certain. On my life! Subkhi lurched forward and laid his huge hands on my shoulders, eyes wide, yellow teeth glinting. I expected to be projected skywards like a ballistic missile. Instead, every muscle in his face worked as he fought to find the right Hebrew words.

'Ata . . Ata Ish tov,' You; A good man. 'Ish . . Yashar. . .' An . . honest man, he muttered.

He released his hold but my body continued trembling. I started to explain again; I had phoned, been to the office, etc. etc. Suddenly, the huge teeth broke into a mile-wide smile and, holding up his slip, waved it in front of my eyes.

'Shuf!' Look. 'Masari!' The money! And there it was. Hand-written in Frieda's, Czech-style figures. Three lira and forty grush. Peanuts to what he had earned from the piecework. But, like I said, Subkhi was a man of principles.

He strode over to where the others were having lunch, going from one to the other, pointing out the figures like a kid with a new toy. I never imagined he could smile so often. Finally, he went over to Abu Salaam and, towering over him like a giant, pushed a few crumpled notes into the old man's hand. Abu Salaam noticed me looking. He touched the side of his nose and winked, and I imagined him saying: '*Ana aaraf.*'

A year later, we had to cut down on investments. Subkhi left us to work in Tel Aviv, joining the crowd of workers from Gaza waiting by Ashkelon junction every morning for a contractor's van to pick them up. And one day, returning home from a meeting in town, I noticed the thick neck and bristling grey hair, towering above the throng at the crossroads. It was Subkhi.

The deep, grey eyes stared as we sped past. I waved. He looked, then nodded as the recognition came. We drove on and I never saw him again, but whenever I remember those times, I wonder whether this gentle giant still gets his National Insurance stamps on time?

Shimshon and the staircase

It was a matter of our work ethic — or rather Shimshon's lack of it, that was so exasperating. We had come to conquer manual labour; to live by the sweat of our brow. You could have a brilliant mind — and what Jew hasn't — or be wonderfully talented — ditto; but on the kibbutz, it was physical work that counted. Being 'a good worker', was the ultimate accolade and in our 'religion of work', being a shirker, a slakker or having a lackadaisical attitude to work, was the nearest thing to a cardinal sin. Shimshon had no such principles. He wasn't a kibutznik, and considered himself an artist. Gadi thought him more an *'artiste'* — a common epithet for a skiver. Either way, for a short period, Shimshon became absolutely indispensable.

After years of waiting and saving, of endless discussions, and of negotiating loans, we had at last built our new cultural centre and library: a modern concrete building on two levels, neatly set into the hillside. Everything was ready, walls decorated, floors tiled, furniture ordered. Everything, that was, except the staircase.

The architect in his wisdom, had decided on an in-situ terrazzo finish to the stairs and it required a specialist, a *mosaichik*. For the sake of a damn staircase, everyone complained, the whole building was standing empty and unused. But in the post Six Day War boom, with new buildings going up everywhere, good craftsmen were scarce and cost the earth. ..

I tried to explain this to the general meeting, 'What decent craftsman would traipse down to the desert for two flights of stairs, when there were whole blocks of flats going up in Jerusalem?' Eventually, after begging and pleading, Moishe, our building company supervisor, found a *mosaichik* in Ashkelon. But he wanted payment in cash.

Offrah, our treasurer flatly refused. The price was too high and anyway, the auditors would have her guts at the end of the year for paying cash on the nail. What about the porters in the Tnuva warehouse? I asked. Didn't she pay cash to load up the lorry after hours? That was different, she replied; they were emergencies. I reminded her of the next general meeting — the cultural committee, the librarians and the teachers were on the warpath. That too would be an emergency. The general meeting however, became more concerned with employing 'cowboy', non-union labour, than with the original problem. I explained that there was no option, but the discussions dragged on and the meeting broke up without a decision.

Moishe drove in on the Sunday. Either we took his man now, he said, or he would start him on a set of verandahs in Ashdod.

'We haven't decided yet.' I shrugged. 'You know . . cash . . . he's not in the union . .and. . .'

'Kibbutz!' Moishe grunted. 'Bloody collective decisions.' Then he winked. 'Tell me, did they vote against?'

'Well, no. Not exactly.' He grabbed my sleeve.

'Then what are you waiting for? The meeting didn't say you couldn't, did it?' Moishe had little time for ideologies. After managing to escape from Poland in 1940, he'd spent the early war years in Russia in a kholkoz. Later, he joined the Red Army and ended up in Berlin, where his commanding officer had turned a blind eye as he deserted. Joining a group of illegal immigrants to

Palestine in 1946, he'd spent his first years as a building worker on some kibbutz, but never wanted to join. 'Had enough of *collectiviut*,' he would smile.

'Okay,' I said, 'You've talked me into it.'

'Listen.' Moishe jabbed a finger at my chest, 'I don't want trouble with the kibbutz. It's your decision. Okay?'

'Okay. My decision. When does he start?'

'Next week.' We shook hands and as he turned away, he winked again. 'Cash-money, remember!'

'Sure. Sure,' I nodded. I wished I was.

On Sunday, I waited for the morning bus from Ashkelon. No one. The midday bus. Nothing. At about two o'clock, I was called out from checking some steelwork in the new garage. 'Someone to see you,' said Motele. A burly figure with cropped fair hair and a reddish face stood in the yard, hands on hip, legs astride, looking as though at any moment, he'd reach for his six-gun. My first reaction was that he was one of Moishe's Polish friends, but his 'Shalom' and first few words, told me that he was from Morocco. I wondered how and when some soldier of fortune from the far north must have passed through that desert kingdom long ago leaving his blond genes.

'You, David?' he grunted, 'Moishe told me to look for you.' Gently, I extricated my hand from his powerful handshake as he continued in a "I'm your man take it or leave it", tone. 'You want a *mosaichik*?'

'Sure.' I pointed to the new building, standing pristine and cream coloured in the green lawn. 'Want to see the job?' He ambled alongside with a John Wayne walk, which only reinforced the cowboy image. Terrazzo work could only be done once. After it set hard, that was it. I prayed that Moishe's judgement wouldn't fail me.

'What's your name?' I asked as we approached the library.

'Shimshon,' he replied, taking out a packet of cigarettes to offer me one. They were *Marlboro*. American. Expensive.

I handed him the drawings. He drew deeply on the cigarette, then blew smoke from his nostrils as he glanced up and down the rough concrete stairs.

'Not a simple job,' he muttered. 'All those rising bits and covings. Looks easy on paper.' I concurred. Waited. He folded the drawings and handed them back, blowing out a cloud of smoke, 'Have to be done on daywork.' My heart sank. First, I had agreed to cash on the nail, without authorisation. Now, it would be like an open cheque — he could take as long as he liked.

Shimshon sensed my apprehension.

'Listen,' he looked me straight in the eye, 'I don't mess about. You'll see. You only record the hours I'm on the job. Okay?' Later I realised why he'd added that and was glad. He lit another cigarette as I hesitated. It was take it or leave it time. I thought of the librarian, of Barukh and his cultural committee, the teachers, everyone, all waiting to use the building. I weakened.

'Okay.'

He turned to go, then stopped and swung back.

'Materials?'

'Over there,' I nodded. 'Under the staircase.'

'White cement?' he asked. 'How long?' Blue smoke drifted up the stairwell.

'About two months,' I said. It had been four, but I didn't want him to know how long we'd been waiting. It was also very expensive.

'White cement. Imported,' he muttered. 'Could have been months in the docks.' He spat into the dust, 'Must have a few fresh bags to mix with it.' I winced. More problems with Offrah. He turned and walked out into the sunlight. I touched his elbow.

'Er. When can you start?' He looked surprised.

'Why? Tomorrow.' Adding in Hollywood English: '*Okay*?' I nodded vigorously, too vigorously, I felt afterwards. 'And I have to have everything for the shuttering: plywood cut to size, battens, nails. Okay?' Again, I could only nod. We shook hands; said Shalom. And he was gone, strolling down the hill and out onto the road as though it was the middle of town, seemingly without a care whether he got a lift or not to the main road.

I rushed down to the carpenter's shop, but Shutzeh said he

Sorry. Not till I've finished the new wardrobes.

couldn't cut all that timber by tomorrow morning. There were cupboard doors to fix in the children's houses, shelves in the kitchen, etc. etc. I reminded him of the general meeting.

'Tell you what.' He glanced up at the holes in his corrugated sheet roof. 'You get that roof fixed. And I'll stay late and do it.' It was blackmail. Both of us.

The following day I waited for the early bus. No one got off. The builders' van came. Then the milk tanker. Still no Shimshon. Shutzeh passed me on his way up to breakfast.

'No *mosaichik*?' I shook my head. He grinned. 'Well. At least I got my roof repaired.' I gave up and went to work. After lunch, as I crossed the courtyard, a sound of hammering came from the library. I ran across. Who the hell was using up those special timbers? In the stairwell was Shimshon, fixing a piece of timber to the plywood.

'The battens were too broad,' he muttered. No reference to when he arrived or why he was late.

'I can get them planed down,' I said.

'No matter. I've sorted it out myself.' He drew on his cigarette and pointed, 'Look at those sharp steps and angles. Bloody architect; I'd like to nail him to the soffite.' I stood and watched as he cut and measured, nailing the battens to a broad strip of plywood to form the profiles to the sides of the stairs. When he had done, I helped him raise it alongside the concrete strings, then left him to it. Shimshon was definitely a loner.

After three days, the first moulds were in place. I popped in to see him. It was early afternoon. He asked the time. Didn't keep a watch, he said. That fitted. It was just gone two.

'I'll start casting tomorrow,' he said, then lit a cigarette and walked out. Suddenly he turned and came back towards me.

'I need a sub,' His blue eyes looked straight at me, 'haven't been paid a grush yet.'

'But you've only been here three days.'

'So what.' He nodded towards the stairs, 'Lot of work there.'

'I'll see what I can do,' I replied, more in hope than expectation.

'Good. Tomorrow then.' More a command than a request.

The next day he sifted the brown stone chips through his fingers.

'Hard stone this. Take a lot of grinding down. And if you want it to show, has to be in two layers. More work, you know.' Then, without a pause added, 'what about my sub?'

'Couldn't get it. I'll try the treasurer again tonight.'

'I need it . . ,' he grunted. He didn't have to say more. That evening, in the dining hall, I even got a smile from Matti, the librarian. The pressure was off, as I reminded Offrah when I asked for the money. She grudgingly counted out fifty lira. Made me sign for it. Like all treasurers, she hated parting with ready cash.

Shimshon took it with hardly an acknowledgement. I stayed and watched as he began to work, measuring out exact quantities of cement, quartz powder, stone chippings and white sand, like an artist mixing his palette. Tearing up the multi-layered cement bags, he took out the two middle, brown paper sheets, moistened them with clean water from a bucket and draped them over the vertical rising timbers to each step, gently smoothing the paper with his fingers.

'Makes sure they're even,' he said, lighting another cigarette, 'Less grinding down.' At this rate, I reckoned, most of his sub would go on the *Marlboros* — I didn't yet know about his other weakness.

First, he poured a thin creamy mix down the sides of the steps, gently tapping the ply with his hammer. Little by little, he formed the raised edges with the white mix, then the step fronts, centimetre by centimetre, before spreading a thin layer of ordinary cement mortar across the whole step.

'Save the white cement for the topping,' he murmured, as he laid it like icing on a cake and just as delicately. 'Saving you money, kibbutznik!' With the first step at the top finished, he lit another cigarette then stood back, thinking, before crouching down to repeat the whole operation. Two down. Twenty eight to go. No doubt about it — a real artist. I left him to it. When I came back around two that afternoon, five steps had been completed and Shimshon was cleaning out the buckets.

'That'll do for today,' he said, straightening up. I wanted to point out that the bus didn't go for another three hours. I didn't. Just made note of the time and wrote it in the day-book later.

The next day, no Shimshon. I panicked. Half a staircase was even worse. No one else would want to finish it. But he came on the following day and completed down to the first landing and on the next, laid the half landing.

'Can't work tomorrow,' he grunted. 'Landing has to go off solid. And anyway, it's Friday.' So what, I wanted to say, you're not a Moslem. But didn't.

On the Sabbath, people walked across to view progress, only to see rough timbers and a white mess all over the first flight. The rumbling started again; nearly two weeks and little to show for it. I laid low and kept quiet about the sub.

On Sunday, Shimshon turned up at noon. I'd given up about his timekeeping. But he stayed till six o'clock and completed the whole of the second flight in one go. But the last bus had long gone and he expected transport to Ashkelon. Just like that. I had to borrow the jeep. More mutterings.

'Drop me off here,' he said as we approached the centre of the town. I thought it was just a convenient point. But as I drove away, I saw him go straight into a bar. Not just the cigarettes, I thought. And I'd just managed to get him another sub.

On Monday, no Shimshon. So again, came the usual jokes in the dining room that evening about 'your invisible man'. Thankfully, on Tuesday he turned up, carrying a special electric grinder.

'My own,' he said. 'Won't charge you for the use. Cost you plenty if you had to buy one.' I just nodded. We had done him enough favours; he could do us one. A thin rubber tube siphoned water from a bucket hung overhead and trickled it through the centre spindle. Looked quite lethal, but with it, throughout the day, he polished the whole of the top flight one by one. They looked like marble, the brown stone standing out against the white background. Beautiful. He must have seen I was pleased; asked for another sub. I agreed. We had the grinder. And another day and he would be finished.

But the next day, again no Shimshon. Nor the next. Nor the whole week. In desperation, I almost decided to finish the grinding myself, but resisted. One slip of the wheel and a whole step could be ruined. To avoid the inquisition, I began eating later and later in the dining hall and taking the perimeter path round to my room. It didn't help.

'How's your vanishing *mosaichik*?' those standing by the work rota quipped. In adversity, he was all 'mine'.

'It'll be okay,' I replied. No one believed me. Nearly a month he'd been at it. I didn't believe it myself. Rahamim, the steel bender from Ashkelon, saved my life.

'No Shimshon?' he asked on his way down to the bus that afternoon.

'No,' I shook my head, 'I think I'll have to go round to his house.'

'No use going there,' Rahamim sighed. 'He only uses it to eat and sleep.' He sighed again. 'Three lovely kids. Nice wife.' He closed his eyes for a moment. 'You'll find him in the bar,' adding softly, 'if the money hasn't run out.' I couldn't get the jeep until late the next morning but just as I was hurrying down to the garage, a shout came from behind the dining hall.

'Hey, kibbutznik. I've been looking for you all over the place!' It was Shimshon.

'You,' I shouted back, furious, 'You. Looking for me?' He strolled towards me, a broad grin across his face.

'Here.' A brightly-coloured package dangled from his fingers. 'Some bon-bons for the children.' As he came up, he pulled another package from his pocket. 'Some perfume for the wife. Lovely wife you have.' He winked. 'Got to look after a woman like that you know.' Still angry, I hesitated. And all that must have cost him a bomb. He smiled again.

'Here. Take them. My pleasure. You work hard, you kibbutzniks.'

'Listen Shimshon. I appreciate it. But everyone is having my guts for garters because of those damn stairs. The best present you could give me would be to finish them off.'

'Not to worry. They'll be finished this week.' He slapped his chest, 'My life.' I wasn't sure that was sufficient guarantee.

'Look, Shimshon. The treasurer won't part with any more money till they are completely finished.' The smile vanished. His face suddenly clouded and he leaned towards me. I thought he was going to clock me one. Suddenly he relaxed.

'Sure. But I want the balance as soon as it's done. *Beseder?*' Okay? I breathed again and nodded.

Shimshon's was another world to ours. Not just the drinking, but a whole way of life, even though less than ten miles separated us. The inhabitants of Migdal-Ashkelon, like in many of the provincial towns, were new immigrants from North Africa, Iraq or Romania. In the kibbutz, we would have the occasional beer or glass of wine and drank mainly coffee. Their men used the local bar and often drank spirits. We danced Israeli dances, they rock-an'-rolled and did the 'Twist', we read Hebrew books and news-papers, they either couldn't read at all and were still grappling with the new language. Theirs was a macho culture, we strove for sex equality. When we were invited to one of their weddings, it was almost as foreign as when we went to an Arab Druze wed-ding in the mountains of Galilee. And in judging Shimshon, I had to keep these concepts at the front of my mind. But he didn't make it easy.

Anyway, after that last encounter, he came every day. Worked often until nightfall. And at the end of the week, he called me over and stood back as I looked.

'Well?' And he lit another cigarette.

'*Nehedar*.' Magnificent, I said, 'Great. Looks really great.' He pulled at my sleeve.

'Huh. What do you know.' He put his hand on my chest, 'You won't see another staircase polished like this. Anywhere. For you, I did it *speyshull* (special).' And I knew he had. We paid him in all about four hundred lira. In cash. Quite a sum in those days. But at last we had the staircase. And Barukh began to plan the opening ceremony for the centre.

A few weeks later, I happened to be driving through Ashkelon one afternoon. By the lights, I glanced sideways. Outside the bar, Shimshon was slumped at a table playing *Shesh-Besh*, a glass in one hand, an open packet of *Marlboro* cigarettes on the table beside him. As the lights changed, he happened to look up and, catching my eye, smiled sheepishly, as if to say: 'That's how I am, mate.' I drove off thinking how much a man like that could earn if he put his mind to it. *Mosaichiks* were in such demand, all over the country. In a few years, he could have made enough to retire for life. If he'd wanted, that is. . .

I saw him only once more after that, as I returned late from a meeting in Tel Aviv. Shimshon was sitting in the bar, alone, twirling an empty glass, a cigarette dangling in his other hand, his hair long and straggly. He didn't look up. And I hurried past, into the night.

Past and present

It looked just like any other black speck on the sand, part of the debris scattered over the shifting sand dunes through centuries of wind and rain. But the perfect circle and the dull glint made us look closer. No bigger than a finger nail, it was a tiny bronze coin and through the black patina, we could see the imperial Roman head. More exciting, around the perimeter was almost all of his name: 'Constantinus.' Soon, every stroll out on the dunes brought us more and more coins, the beginning of a sizeable collection which led us to create our own museum. Sadly, it was this very coin collection that led to its demise when the ancient past met the social problems of modern Israel.

Like most Israelis, we were fascinated by the ancient history of the country; part of getting back to our roots, we would call it today. And in a country where every pipeline trench or foundation pit unearths remains of one ancient civilisation or another, archaeology was a popular pastime and the coins were just a beginning. It didn't take us long to make further archaeological discoveries, ranging from Neolithic stone tools to mediaeval

Arabic pottery and glass, passing through Canaanite, Hellenistic, Roman, Byzantine and Mameluke remains — a span of more than six thousand years. Soon, for some of us, the hobby occupied much of our spare time.

The kibbutz sat astride the ancient route of the Via Maris, the biblical 'Way of the Sea', along which both peacetime traders and wartime armies travelled between the Fertile Crescent of Asia Minor and the Nile Valley. It also stood near the mouth of the *wadi*, with its spring of fresh water. Over the centuries, sand dunes thrown up by the sea had encroached on the land for several miles, forcing the road to run ever further inland and burying ancient settlements and harbours under many metres of fine, drifting sand. Yet it was these ever-shifting dunes that had provided our first finds and later, our more unique discoveries.

In the early days, before we had children, and spare time became just a wishful dream, *shabbat* really was a day of rest. We had time to wander over the dunes and down to the sea, and especially after a winter storm, made these finds of ancient coins. Later, when the kids were old enough to join us on the walkabouts, being closer to the ground, they far surpassed us in coin spotting.

Most of the coins were tiny and worn smooth. Quite a number though were distinct, preserved by a shiny black patina. Soon many of us had small collections of Roman, Byzantine and mediaeval Arabic coins. Most prized were those of the ancient semi-independent city of Ashkelon, with their characteristic head of the goddess Nike and Greek lettering. These were quite rare even in numismatic museums. And it was these particular coins — archaeologically quite valuable, that later caused the whole enterprise's undoing.

It wasn't long before more and more artefacts came to be scattered around the kibbutz: odd stone capitals on the dining hall patio, pieces of pottery and marble on people's verandas and of course the ever growing number of coins in odd drawers, which were easily mislaid. So we mooted the idea of setting up a museum. The final impetus came from an unexpected direction; it was when we nearly lost our Fordson tractor in the sea.

After every winter's gale, we would take a tractor and trailer down to the seashore to pick up driftwood. Many of the boats then plying the eastern Mediterranean were still traditional wooden craft and often their deckloads were less than secure. So throughout the winter, valuable driftwood baulks of teak and other exotic woods augmented the stocks in our carpenter's shop. Some, hardened in the salt water over too many seasons at sea, would blunt the teeth of our circular saw, but they were marvellous for climbing frames and posts in the children's playgrounds.

On one wet and windy March day, when work in the fields was impossible and the tractors were idle too, a few of us took the Fordson and a trailer down to the shore. Huge white waves rolled in from a grey sea, just the day for flotsam and jetsam. The trailer was about half loaded when a huge baulk tumbled out onto the sand. Rushing forward, we rolled it a metre or so up the slope before the next wave came, and so on, until it seemed well clear of the surf. We brought the tractor alongside and eventually managed to hump the timber onto the trailer. But it had taken longer than we anticipated and in the meantime, with the extra weight and the odd wave surging around the wheels, the trailer had become bogged down at the water line.

The wind was strengthening and soon, with ever larger waves breaking over the wheels, even the huge tractor tyres began to sink into the sand and the drawbar-pin became jammed. Our new, bright blue Fordson was in danger of becoming a shipwreck itself.

Panic set in and Motele ran off across the dunes to the kibbutz to fetch a caterpillar tractor, and we spent a fraught half-an-hour until he came back with the International TD6 and a cable. On his return, Motele told us that he'd noticed a row of large pots by the tamarisk trees, where the storm had ripped away the side of a sand dune.

Extricating the tractor and heavily-laden trailer took a another tense hour or more and we heaved a sigh of relief when the Fordson spluttered into life, apparently none the worse for its briny baptism. Shimon agreed to drive back alone with the loaded trailer, whilst Motele, Reuven and I clambered on the TD6 and clattered across the dunes to the tamarisks. And there they were; half a dozen reddish pottery jars, each about a metre long, upended on their mouths in a neat row and now half exposed. And it looked as though there were more.

'Roman or Byzantine,' we argued as we crouched down and started to scrape away more sand. Suddenly, without warning, half of one pot fell away and collapsed in pieces on the sand.

'Have to wait 'till it's dried out a bit,' I said. So we heaped the sand back against them and reluctantly drove away. There was still the trailer to unload. . .

The pots turned out to be late Roman, around third century AD, (or CE, Common Era, as we say in Israel). We conjectured that they must have been rinsed out and stood on end to dry, when the settlement was destroyed or abandoned. And they'd been standing there like that, for a millennium and a half!

Ancient maps showed a small town, Mayumas Ashkelon, near the mouth of the wadi. Could we have discovered it? But across the wadi, almost on the border — and it was still a very 'live' one at the time — was a small hill with stone foundations that could also have been that town. We didn't argue. More important was to salvage what we could and that spring, we managed to bring two whole pots back to the courtyard.

The following year, the government built an earth dam across the wadi to hold back the winter flood waters and replenish the underground water table. Whilst digging an associated pipeline through our fields to the dam, a cache of Canaanite pottery was uncovered, tightly embedded in the soil about three metres deep. It took hours of tough but delicate surgery to extricate two bowls and three small pitchers and many more hours of trembling fingers and glue to make them presentable.

Then, by chance a few weeks later, a Roman pillar — some ten foot of polished grey granite — was discovered under a heap of stones being cleared from the edge of one of the fields. It had probably come from the ancient ruins of Ashkelon, pilfered in the past by a local landowner wishing to impress the neighbours.

This, added to the pots and coins, gave us the impetus to actually set up the museum and we began badgering the members' committee to designate us a room somewhere — no simple problem with our permanent shortage of accommodation.

With delusions of grandeur, we made plans. The pillar would be a centrepiece of a paved courtyard in front of our museum. Here, we could exhibit the other large objects that our archaeology group had unearthed in the area. Apart from three huge storage pots, there were several capitals from the sand dunes, two ancient corn-grinding stones, dressed quoins and pieces of mosaic pavings. We saw the museum as an integral part of the proposed cultural and social centre being planned for the kibbutz. At the time however, the courtyard was a patch of bare sand, and the museum, one room in an old hut. But then you have to have dreams . . .

Uncovering the huge pillar was one thing; bringing back the two-and-a-half-ton chunk of granite was another. It was far too heavy to lift. After work one May evening, we coaxed it onto our hay-baler sledge and our little convoy hissed and screeched along the road, the two-inch pipes that served as runners, scoring red-hot grooves in the tarmac. God knows what the local council would have said. In front, clouds of blue smoke spewed from the exhaust as Motele, head bent over the Farmall steering wheel urged the aged tractor to top speed in second gear. Reuven and I followed in the jeep keeping sharp look-out to the rear. If someone had sped straight into the back of that stone hulk, there wouldn't have been much left of him to scrape away. Somehow, cylinders straining fit to burst, we managed to haul it up the hill, but by then the pillar decided that it had had enough and rolled off the sledge, just in front of the children's shelter. And remained there for a long time.

Apart from the Ashkelon coins, the most unique items in our collection, were the Neolithic flint tools. And here too, the discovery came by chance.

During the construction of the earth dam, the huge machines had scraped off some of the sand dune covering the high bluff overlooking the mouth of the wadi. At first, we thought they had left behind limestone chippings used in the construction, but it soon became apparent that the scattered stones were flint flakes that had been worked into tiny tools.

From then on, in every spare moment after work and at weekends, we combed the area. Soon, we had hundreds of tiny scrapers, arrowheads, saw blades and, most puzzling, long pointed flakes that we couldn't find in any of the literature. We contacted Jerusalem University but they couldn't shed more light either; archaeology in Israel was mainly centred around Biblical discoveries; prehistory was still the poor relative. We were lucky to find Tamar Yezreeli, who was working hard to give it status, and we became amongst the founder members of the 'Israel Prehistoric Society'. Through her we contacted two 'stone-age' enthusiasts from Ramat Gan who had surveyed most of the coastal dunes, and together, we pieced together a history of the finds.

The settlement would have been a Neolithic encampment overlooking the fresh water spring, about 5,000 BC. The tiny arrowheads would have been used for birding or fishing and the saw blades, about an inch long, would have been slotted into a wooden haft and used for cutting grain or more likely, the reeds that grew in the spring, the silica in the stems giving shiny edges to the saw teeth. And still no one could tell us the function of the delicate, elongated points, some nearly an inch long and so painstakingly worked from flakes of flint. Were they for winkling out sea food? Making holes for sewing leather? Either way, in such a high proportion, they were the most distinctive and unique characteristic of our finds. We could only marvel at the sophisticated talent of these so-called 'primitive' people, who could fashion brittle flint with such delicacy and aesthetic sensibility.

On a calm summer's shabbat, I would sit overlooking the mouth of the wadi, trying to imagine the scene all those thousands of years ago: no sand dunes, a settlement of rush-roofed huts and open hearths, men fishing and birding in the reed beds, some using the high bluff as a vantage point to keep lookout, others making new flint tools, women sewing leather garments and

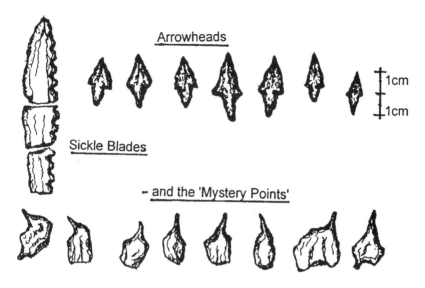

Flint tools.

cooking, children throwing pebbles into the water. A collective, egalitarian settlement, right here, some seven thousand years before us . . .

Once we obtained our museum room, we began to collect together as much as we could. Many coins were sent to an expert up north, who for a small charge, made out a card with date and history. 'Take good care,' he wrote one day. 'You have one of the best collections of Ashkelon coins I've seen.' We did. Kept them under glass, and the museum door locked. In a kibbutz then, you didn't need more . . . or so we thought. Until the outside world intruded . . .

During the sixties, the mass immigration had ceased but there were now many new immigrants living in poverty in the towns, principally those from the Arabic-speaking countries and Romania. With large numbers of children and overstretched social services, there was a growing problem of youth delinquency and alienation. So the kibbutzim, as part of their 'Zionist task', were asked to take in groups of deprived youngsters, hoping that the environment and education would do the trick.

It was quite a culture shock — for both sides. To the young-sters, the kibbutz was 'middle class' and part of the 'old timer', European-origin regime which dominated Israeli life. To us, they were a wild bunch with little regard or respect for anything or anyone. But though we had few illusions that many of them would want to come back and join us after the army, we took it on as a challenge. We hoped that they would be influenced by our non-violent, egalitarian way of life and at the same time, in treat-ing them decently, enable them to acquire more self-esteem. We also hoped that on their return to the towns, they would cease to regard us as 'them' and be less susceptible to the vicious quasi-fascist propaganda being peddled by Menachem Begin and his followers.

The No'ar youth group as it was known, numbered around twenty-three, including five girls, with an average age of fourteen. Many were semi-illiterate and some of the boys would have soon been in trouble with the police had they remained in town. One of our members was trained to become their educator and he and their classroom were financed by Youth Immigration services. The no'ar group worked a few hours a day and studied for the rest, most of them requiring individual attention. Some of us with spe-cial interests also took part in varying their lessons. Beni arranged art sessions and, drawing upon my old medical studies, I took them for biology lessons twice a week, utilising eyes and kidneys from the butcher in Ashkelon to arouse interest.

It was tough-going for all concerned, but after two or three years, most had regular jobs in the kibbutz and had taken good advantage of their schooling. Some proved to be very bright and most began to lose the chips on their shoulders with which they had arrived. One or two even joined us in looking for coins and flints and contributed the finds to the museum.

Their four-year stint came to a close as military age approached. We held a 'graduation' party, offered them candida-ture in the kibbutz after the army and knew that several would keep contact with kibbutz members who had 'adopted' them.

Some indeed did return to become members aftewards. But with just one or two of the boys, old habits died hard.

I happened to be away the week they left. When I returned, the museum door had been forced — and most of the coins, including all the ancient Ashkelon ones, had gone. Some of the boys had broken in and taken them, believing them to be worth a lot of money. It was a terrible blow to years of hard work, both for us archaeologists — and perhaps even more so, for their teacher who had invested so much time and energy in them.

I secured the door again, feeling guilty at having persuaded all the individual collectors to hand their finds into the museum. Barukh, who had personally found many of the Ashkelon coins, never stopped reminding me of his sacrifice for nothing. Some of the finer flint specimens had gone too and we never quite recovered from the trauma of that violation.

Occasionally, we would bump into ex-*no'ar* boys in Midgal-Ashkelon. Most had sorted themselves out, though one or two had had brushes with the local police. And years later, at the bus station, I met one who had been a particularly difficult lad. I felt embarrassed, wondering whether he would prefer me to greet or ignore him. I didn't need to worry. He nodded, then walked right up to me.

'Listen,' he said. 'You know. We didn't realise how lucky we were in the kibbutz. How you treated us like human beings.' He glanced around and blew out a cloud of smoke. 'Not like out here . . . in this jungle. No. *Taamin li,*' — believe me, he continued, 'I didn't appreciate it, but they were the best years of my life!'

After an exchange of news about some of the other boys, I felt emboldened.

'Tell me,' I said. 'What did you do with those coins?'

'Me?' he started to protest, then grinned bashfully. 'Sold them,' he muttered. 'To a man in Migdal.' He looked down. 'I'm sorry.' Then as if in mitigation, added. 'Didn't get much though.' We shook hands and, as I went to catch my bus, I wondered where those Ashkelon coins had ended up.

A friendship

When Harold died, I lost my closest friend — an ideological soul-mate, and a real kibbutznik. His death stirred my conscience, painfully reminding me that unwittingly, despite our close friend-ship, I had once destroyed something so dear to him. And equally unwittingly, I'd aparently helped to part him from the first true love in his life.

We first met in '49, on the training farm in Bedford. He was already an experienced farm hand, while I was part of a group of lily-fingered harvest campers, pulling onions or weeding sugar beet. Later, when I came to the farm, we shared a room and late into the night discussed Marx and Engels, argued over Kropotkin and Borochov, read Jack London and Zola and Gorky and listened to Berlioz and Shostakovitch. And when exhausted by a hard day's slog, we lay in our beds listening to Ginette Neveau playing Sibelius, before dropping off to sleep, with the record going round and round in that last groove until we woke the next morning.

We were all young fanatics, some thirty of us; ardent Socialist-Zionists preparing to settle on a kibbutz in Israel. Life was so full, each of us playing a full part in our small community and waiting to realise our ideals. Like Gorky's young hero in *Mother*, 'the cause' was paramount. Everything else, including one's personal life, was subordinate. Which was why we became so concerned when Harold fell for Tami. Or rather she for him.

Tami was a Sabra, a native Israeli. Not that attractive but vivacious and quite sexy. Harold was tall and thin, with a wisp of straggly beard, his ascetic appearance camouflaging his quite normal urges. He would stand on his bed mooning, besotted with the beautiful young wife of the Israeli farm manager and shouting to the walls, 'Rachel, Rachel. I love you. Want to hold you . . ,' thumping his fists on his pigeon chest as we rolled over on the beds, helpless with laughter.

Harold came from a poverty-stricken Jewish family in Manchester with a childhood that left him thin and almost emaciated — like some primitive evocation of Christ descending from the cross. But he was proud of his pigeon chest.

'I'm a unique biological specimen,' he would cackle, thumping his chest, his muscles like knots on a length of binder twine. He was tough and wiry. And my God, he could work! Outlasted all of us in a day's work in the fields, with an even rhythm that enabled him to finish the day at the same pace as he'd started.

Harold was the only real farmer in our group. Gershon played at keeping chickens, Gene and I worked outside in building and others in various factories in the town. Our ethos was work — the conquest of manual labour — but we were conscious that we were working outside, for others. Harold though, was already a 'kibbutznik', working OUR land, our own ten acres of Bedfordshire, harnessing Krupskaya, the old mare named after Lenin's wife and leading her out to harrow or to plough the fields. At times, when the share stuck in the heavy waterlogged clay, the mare would rear up on her hind legs like a cavalry charger, enormous hooves pawing the air, instilling panic into all of us — except Harold.

'Whoa. Whoa, Krupskaya,' he would call. 'Good girl. Good girl, Krupskaya.' Slowly the huge beast would come down on all-fours, pawing the ground with her foreleg, whilst Harold came close, his mouth by her bridle, murmuring sweetness as he backed her a few paces to free the plough, before starting all over again.

'She's bloody crazy, that horse,' he would say at the end of the day. 'Bloody crazy.' Yet somehow, under his gentle care, the field was ploughed in time, the seeds sown and the crop cultivated and brought to harvest. The field is still there today, behind a row of horse chestnut trees. The red-brick Georgian manor we used as our training farm has long gone. All that remains is one wall of the old, enclosed garden.

Harold had little experience with girls, his shyness making him appear aloof and the girls wary as though they would be taking on a prophet of sorts. But with the charisma of being one of the leading lights on the farm, Tami made a bee-line for him and soon they were deeply involved. She was a definite town girl and in our arrogance, we were convinced that she was the wrong one for him, just going for Harold because he was a leading member of the group. Even more worrying for us, was that Tami had no intention of going to a kibbutz and she was certain to take him away from our chosen path. To lose such an ideological stalwart and a pivotal member of our group would be a disaster.

Fearing the worst, and thinking that the relationship hadn't really got going yet anyway, Harold's date for departure to Israel was brought forward. He readily accepted the decision; after all, it was what we were all waiting for and wanted anyway. But Tami was studying in London and her parents were in England. She couldn't follow. So Harold left and they broke up. And we sincerely thought we were doing him a favour. Years later, I discovered that Harold never really recovered from that. She had been the first and perhaps his only real love. Right till the end of his life, he never forgot her; a saddened man forever. And though it had been our fault, we never felt any recrimination from him.

Tami might even have come out to join him later. But by that time, on the rebound, Harold had met Rina. Rina and Tami were similar in a way, both from German parents, strong-willed and determined. Perhaps that had something to do with it. But whereas Tami had been born in Palestine, as it was then, Rina was a child refugee from Germany, her family slaughtered without trace. The whole trauma had left Rina resentful with rarely a good word for anyone, yet intelligent and artistically talented and, like all the Germans, a marvellous worker. Rina was already in the kibbutz when Harold arrived. He was glad to be in Israel at last and got on with adapting to the new life and the heat and learning Hebrew. But he was still sad from the break-up and probably lonely; many of his friends were still behind in England. And Rina doted on him. She put a bright cloth on his rough wooden table and tidied his room each day. He was such a 'shlumper', his room always like a tip. In spite of being so fully aware in most spheres of life, Harold had always allowed his personal life to lead him wherever it would and they soon became involved.

Despite an indifferent education, Harold had an unquenchable thirst for knowledge. He read everything and loved all kinds of music, his deep nasal bass fitting so well into our choir. But he hated writing. Despite strong views on practically everything, he never wrote for our magazines, his lack of confidence a legacy of his poor childhood schooling. He also hated public speaking. In a small, friendly circle, he always came out with the most original concepts and ideas, as well as strongly-held personal opinions. But at the general meeting, much as we prodded, he nearly always sat shtum. Afterwards, as we strolled back to the rooms, infuriatingly he would let us know quite clearly and succinctly what he thought: 'Why the hell didn't you say so at the meeting?' we would moan. Harold would shrug and carry on walking. On the rare occasion when he felt so strongly that he did speak out, you could hear the proverbial pin drop. For if Harold had decided to speak at the general meeting, everyone listened. And his soft, halting and often humorous comments, usually swayed the outcome.

Harold and Rina moved in together and eventually married. Was it just on the rebound? There must have been something more, but all we could see as the years passed was that, despite their two lovely boys, she was becoming more and more neurotic

and shrewish and socially more difficult in the kibbutz. And
Harold, ever the stoic, would bend to her crises and mood swings
like a sapling in the wind, then straighten up to take the next one.
The years passed. The children grew up and went to school.
The constant struggle between those in the kibbutz who wanted to
remain close to its ideals, and those who saw it primarily as a successful modern farm, grew more acute. Harold knew which side
he was on and although he rarely spoke out, his very presence
gave moral strength and encouragement to all of us. And when he
did speak, everyone stopped muttering or knitting and listened.
He had to be right. But it was at work, in quiet discussions, in his
humorous ribbing of the 'Economists' as we called them, that he
had most effect, persuasively making people realise where the
neglect of ideals and principles would lead.

Despite his wiry frame, Harold had an immense appetite; we
always wondered where he put it all and he insisted on taking his
time eating. To the annoyance of the dining hall workers waiting
to clear away his table for the next sitting, he would sit and finish
his meal leisurely, often the only one left in a whole row of tables.
'Part of civilised living,' he would say.

The years passed. His hair grew thinner, his face more lined,
the slim body even more wiry. And he remained the conscience,
the critic, commenting from the sidelines and always with
humour. He coped with Yoram's wild schemes in the orchards
and with Eliyahu's tantrums in the cowshed, passing penetrating
and occasionally sarcastic comments about the farm manager or
the head of some committee or other; a sideways swiping that was
never malicious. Yet at times it was infuriating that he remained
on the sidelines instead of joining battle on the committees and in
the general meetings. But because it was Harold — and because of
Rina — we forgave him. For Rina's neuroses and increasing para-
noia were more than any of us felt we could handle and sadly, in
avoiding her, we restricted our social contact with Harold as well.

Rina cultivated her wonderful garden. She made lavish teas
and baked cakes when the boys came home each day from the
children's house and kept the room spotlessly clean. At work in

the clothes store, she sometimes produced beautifully knitted garments or sewn dresses — she had such talents and if only she had devoted more of her energies to them. But as her mood swings and ever-complaining tones wafted out from their window, we knew that he would be sitting there, taking it, with his infinite patience. The ultimate stoic.

Rina always had a dog. Each one was more gangly and vicious than the first and all were called Dobbie. Everyone hated the latest horror who growled whenever anyone approached their room. Harold would curse it occasionally too. But Rina seemed to dote on it, forever cadging scraps in the kitchen and off the dining room tables. And the dog ate well. So, for Harold, we suffered it. One day it snapped at Rachel as she walked by and bit her arm. There was an outcry. It should be put down, everyone said, and with jackals out in the dunes, rabies was an ever-present hazard. But Rachel's husband, Gadi, was the ultimate humanist. 'It would upset Rina too much,' he thought. So gradually it was forgotten.

It might have all remained like that. But then, one afternoon, my wife went to call a mother in the room adjacent to Rina, to come and feed her baby. Without warning, Dobbie leapt up at her from the shade of a nearby tree. She barely managed to turn away, then screamed as the dog landed on her back, leaving two long, teeth marks and deep scratches. I shudder to think what it might have done had she not shielded her face. Well, we'd all had enough of bloody Dobbie anyway by then and I didn't think twice. Running down to where the Druze night guards lived, I asked Kassim if I could borrow his Uzi, saying I was going for a stroll along the sand dunes by the border. We often went there to look for archaeological finds, so he didn't think twice.

It was mid-afternoon. All the field-workers were away and the children's nurses and cooks, showered and resting in their rooms. With the first breaths of afternoon breeze sighing through the trees, everything was still and quiet. Dobbie was lying quietly in the shade of a tree, together with Mo's alsatian, another mangey cur called Lucy. I slid the magazine into the automatic and crept up carefully. They turned to watch. If they both went for me, I'd only get Dobbie and the other might get me, but with my blood up, I didn't care.

Dobbie seemed to sense something. He rose slowly and, with a look of guilt, began to slink away, with Lucy following. The closer I came, the more they tried to distance themselves. I cocked the gun. Dobbie must have heard it and started to run. I aimed from the hip and pulled the trigger. The burst of gunfire echoed around the kibbutz like thunder in the silent afternoon. Lucy shot away almost as fast as the bullets. But in my blind anger, I appeared to have missed both of them despite emptying most of the magazine. Dobbie yelped and continued to run for a while. I followed wanting to fire again, furious that I had only winged it. How could I have missed? That's what happens when you fire in anger.

As he reached the back of Rina's house, the dog began to limp, but before I could close up on him, the courtyard was buzzing. Half-dressed and half-asleep, people had run out of their rooms, rubbing their eyes in disbelief, wondering whether the army had chased an infiltrator into the kibbutz or one of the guards had run amok. Quickly, a small group collected around me and I lowered the gun, explaining what I had done and why.

'Bloody good job too,' yelled Rachel. 'Wait till I see my coward, Gadi. Pity you didn't kill the stinking hound.' Suddenly Harold appeared, with Dobbie limping after him. His face flushed with fury, his eyes wide. No one had ever seen him like that. He flung out his arm at me.

'You wouldn't like it if I put a bullet through one of your kids, would you?' he shouted.

'A kid wouldn't have done this,' I snapped and turning my wife's back towards him, I pulled up her shirt and carefully peeled off the antiseptic dressing the nurse had put on in the meantime. 'There,' I yelled. 'That's what your darling Dobbie has done!'

'Dobbie would never do that,' he said, shaking his fist.

'Then who do you think did?' I screamed, waving my arms, 'God almighty?' In another moment, with both of us in such a temper, we would have gone for each other. We didn't. Instead, we just stood about two yards apart, glaring into each other's eyes, the long, long friendship somehow keeping the distance between us.

Suddenly, I looked down. The Uzi was still loaded and, like any automatic weapon, cocked from the last shot. And the safety catch was still off! I broke out in a cold sweat. If I'd accidentally squeezed the trigger, if someone had knocked my arm. . ? My God! And in that crowd. Slowly, I lowered my hands, slipped out the magazine and eased the bolt. Then, as everyone began to disperse in small groups, discussing the rights and wrongs, Rachel came over and patted me on the back, but I didn't feel at all like a hero. I'd just wanted rid of Rina's lousy cur, whether she threw a fit or not. Now Harold would have to face her.

My wife went with the nurse to get the wound dressed again. I sat on the edge of the children's sand-pit, the gun on my knees, staring at the ground. Suddenly Harold walked slowly towards me.

'Dobbie needs to be put out of its misery,' he said, matter-of-factly. How quickly we'd both cooled down. All that had passed between us over the years, the freezing winters in Bedford, the heat and the hard times when we first came out here to the desert, the empathy I felt for him in his trials with Rina, our shared ideas and sentiments about the kibbutz and about life, had all left a sediment that could not be washed away — whatever either of us did.

I looked up and stared, trembling. There were real tears in Harold's eyes. And suddenly, at that moment, it hit me: The king had no clothes! What presumptuous idiots we had been, just like all those years ago with Tami. Dobbie hadn't been for Rina. She just looked after its material comforts, but all along, the dog had been his. He had been the one who resisted getting rid of it, secretly cherishing a warm, undemanding creature to show affection. And now I, Harold's closest friend, had killed something so dear to him. I turned my head away, feeling so utterly wretched. For the first time ever, I couldn't look him in the face. After a few moments, I stood up, my anger having rapidly given way to a deep sorrow.

'Okay,' I murmured. 'Come, I'll do it. If you hold him.' Harold tied a string on the dog's collar and slowly, the three of us walked at the animal's limping pace, down into the eucalyptus grove. And there, by the perimeter fence, I put the barrel against its head and pulled the trigger. Just one round.

Dobbie convulsed, then slumped onto the sand. Harold stared at the dog.

'You sure it's dead?'

'Yes,' I said, 'I'm sure.' But he waited for about twenty minutes, which seemed like an eternity as I waited with him, still unable to look into his eyes, the two of us, alone, by the barbed wire fence, with the wind rustling the eucalyptus leaves. Eventually I managed to look up and our eyes met.

'Look. I'm really sorry Harold. I lost my temper.' He didn't react and I continued, 'If it had got at her face, Harold, she'd have been scarred for life'.

'Dobbie wouldn't have done that,' he murmured. 'I don't believe he would.' I just stood there. Nothing I could say.

The dog hadn't moved. Harold felt its stomach, then inside its ear. It was cold. He had brought a spade with him and without a word, he dug a deep hole in the sandy soil. Together we eased the body down. Harold covered the head with a handkerchief and whilst he looked on, I took the spade and covered it up. Then without a word, Harold took the spade and walked away towards his room. It was nearly four o'clock; the children would be coming home. They would be pretty upset too.

I let him go on up, then went to my room; we lived quite close by. On the path, Rachel came up to me holding her new baby.

'Well done, my friend. Pity it wasn't done sooner.' I nodded, then went down to hand the Uzi back to Kassim, head down and eyes misted over.

They got another dog, smaller but still a scraggy looking thing. This time we all knew it was for Harold, knowing it was something he needed and to which he could return affection. And Harold and I re-established our normal relationship.

The years passed. Our kids grew up and went into the army. People came and left the kibbutz. Then some of the children started to leave. His left too and he was alone with Rina but still working with the dairy herd, reliable and conscientious as only Harold could be. He continued to bemoan the kibbutz abandoning its principles; the rise of the careerists to form a hierarchy and the demise of the community spirit. Yet he never lost his wry sense of humour.

A few years later, Harold contracted cancer. It came from nowhere. Perhaps his soul, as well as his body, was ready for it. One day, we sat in his room, eating slices of one of Rina's cream and fruit cakes, talking about old times and where the kibbutz was heading. Already, the disease was having its effect. His face was dark and drawn. Even his pigeon chest no longer pouted. But still the old flashes of humour and the pointed observations.

My wife took a photograph of us together, Harold one leg crossed over the other in his easy chair, the beard even more straggly, the wry smile tinged with pain as he talked. But there was still the firm handshake as we parted. Two months later, he was dead. He'd bent with the breeze as usual, but this time, it had been too strong for him to spring back.

Strangely, the photograph came out blurred, the only one to do so in the whole roll of film. Perhaps it wasn't meant to be clear, so that I should remember him not as he was then, but as he always had been: eyes deep and sharp, chin jutting out, speaking his mind in a deep, soft Mancunian drawl. Like he always said: 'No justice in this life, mate.' No, there isn't.

Felafel in Gaza

I wrote this during the *Intafada* uprising in the occupied teritories.

My son came back from Gaza, weary and despondent. He'd spent a month in the Reserves, dodging the stones. As we talked, I remembered how, some time in the sixties, when he was about five years old, we'd sat one day on the hilltop together with his older sister. Below, were the crumbling slit trenches from the Suez Crisis of '56 and at the foot of the hill, behind the poultry houses, lay the blackened fence-post blown up by the *Fedayeen* three days before.

We stared past the barbed wire of the perimeter fence. Over the sun baked bed of the *wadi* and the dazzling white sand dunes, and across the unmarked border to the village of Beit Lehiya. In the distance, rose the hazy outline of the water tower outside Gaza with the distinctive clump of ancient pine trees. And the kids questioned me: Who blew up the post? Why did they shoot from the darkness? Who stole our irrigation pipes from the fields at

night? And I tried to explain, so that they would understand and
have hope for the future. Explain that the Egyptian army had
invaded in '48 to try to destroy our homeland. That they were driven back and that in the fierce fighting, the Arabs who lived
around here had fled, hoping to return. But there had been no
peace. And now they were kept in refugee camps near Gaza.
Miserable and desperate.

So they came across to steal; because they were hungry. And
the Egyptians gave them weapons, to shoot and plant mines. But
they were ordinary people, just like us, with children who wanted
to play and laugh. And when peace came, some would be able to
return. Others would get new homes and work. They would have
their own country and we would live as neighbours. In peace and
in friendship.

The kids listened and, as the sun dipped towards the west, we
watched the Arab fishing boats come out from Gaza strand to
spread their nets on a silvered sea.

'And one day,' I said, hugging them close, 'we'll all go to Gaza
and eat real *felafel*!' We stood up, brushed the sand from our shorts
and I took their hands to walk back to the children's house for
supper.

In '67 came the Six Day War. We cleared out and deepened the
slit trenches. Drew weapons from the armoury. Dug in and waited
as explosions and gunfire came from the Gaza Strip. Our well was
blown up, as well as two tractors left out in the fields. The kids felt
the ground tremble and were afraid. Mercifully, the brief night-
mare passed and the war ended swiftly. With relief and rejoicing,
the children came up from the deep shelters, blinking at the bright
sunlight. We returned our weapons to the armoury, cleaning them
on the lawn outside. I still have that black-and-white photograph:
my son, clean white shirt, buck teeth grinning, flicking out the
bullets from a Besa machine-gun belt. We were all smiling. Now
there would be peace. We wouldn't need the weapons any more, I
said. And, a week later, I took them to Gaza.

We hitched a lift in a car from Tel Aviv, along the once deserted
dead-end main road past Erez. Israelis were flocking down as

tourists to the once forbidden places. Staring at the felaheen in their dusty cloaks and buying up cheap Hong Kong watches and pens previously smuggled in by Egyptian army racketeers. And in the Square of the Palestinian Martyr, I bought them each a felafel! We strolled the three miles to the seashore. Bare footed fishermen, whose lantern lights we'd seen so many nights, sold their meagre catch in a concrete shed, whilst women in white keffiehs haggled over the prices. On the dunes behind us, ragged children ran amongst the white tin huts and tents of Shaati refugee camp, whilst old men stared from the shade, expressionless and silent. My daughter, now ten, clutched at my hand and looked away. Despite all my explanations, they were still, for her, the enemy — the ones who shot at night and who laid mines on the tracks in our fields.

By now, it was midday. The sun was almost overhead and everywhere, hot and dusty. The kids were weary and it was a long walk back to Gaza town. I pointed to an orange bus that was filling up. My son, now seven, nodded, but his sister absolutely refused. We stood and argued. Eventually she relented, but in the meantime the bus had gone. Just then, a small, blue taxi stopped beside us. My daughter tensed as the driver jumped out, short, moustached and smiling with blackened teeth. He looked at her then at me, soft, sad eyes, as if understanding. She must have noticed and reluctantly agreed to get in, yet clung to me in the back seat all the way. My son, sitting up front with the driver, enjoyed the experience.

We shook hands as I got out.

'Perhaps we shall soon all have peace,' I stammered in my rudimentary Arabic. He glanced skywards and spread his hands.

'Insh'allah.'

'Ma Salameh,' I smiled.

'Ma Salameh,' he replied. And we parted.

'See,' I said to the kids, gripping their hands, 'ordinary people. Just like us!' And we hitched back to the junction of our branch road, in a car full of Taiwan Rolex's and fake Parker pens.

They were euphoric times, those last months of '67. Suddenly, peace seemed to have broken out. We took trips to the West Bank and dipped our toes in the Jordan. Drove down in jeeps to Suez and deep into desolate Sinai to St. Catherine's monastery. And everywhere, there were smiles. The Palestinians hadn't had much joy from the Egyptian army or the Jordanian Legion either; the Israelis seemed no worse. And soon, the Israelis would be gone too, wouldn't they?

For us, it was a great chance. At last we could talk face to face with the Palestinians, destroy the monstrous images we had built up of each other, over the twenty years since '48. Israel had absorbed over two million Jewish refugees. Surely, together with the oil-rich Arab states, we could resolve their refugee problem? Live side by side, Israel and a Palestinian state? A unique opportunity was there, just waiting. Surely our leaders — and theirs, would grasp it.

It was not to be. The days of hope turned to inertia and despair. Attitudes hardened. The occupation continued. Jewish religious zealots drifted in from Brooklyn to settle on expropriated Arab land on the West Bank. Hideous concrete housing estates encircled the Old City of Jerusalem. And the refugees remained in their camps, more and more desperate.

So, yet another war later, I returned to the hilltop. Alone. I stood and gazed across the sand dunes. The trenches had fallen in. The kibbutz plastics factory had replaced the poultry houses and tall trees had grown along the wadi. Was it over twenty years since the three of us had sat there, talking about the future? When there would be peace, I told them. And they wouldn't have to fight. For sure. Didn't I promise them?

Both have now been through the army. Whilst her husband was on reserves duty up in the Golan, my daughter watched television news of yet more confrontations. And my son has been in Gaza. But no felafel this time. No leisurely stroll down to the seashore. Instead, by barricades of burning tyres, he faced a barrage of stones from youths who were not even born then, whilst arguing with hot-headed fellow conscripts to hold fire; that those kids just want to be free and run their own lives. That they too, are just ordinary human beings. That much, at least, he must have imbibed from our hilltop conversations. Some of his peers had even gone to gaol rather than serve in the occupied territories. It didn't make his agonising any easier.

In the distance, the water tower still shimmers. The border, still unmarked, is still there. And real peace seems just as far away. And I wonder: Will we ever go again to buy a felafel in Gaza?

Looking back

One November day, I returned to where it all began. For me, for Issy, Yehuda, Mikhal, for Dan and all the others. To the place where we had our training farm, in Bedfordshire.

Only the weather hadn't changed. Grey cloud, the odd spot of rain threatening, waiting for the wind to drop — a biting wind, stripping the last yellow leaves from bare branches and driving rustling brown waves against the high brick wall.

I looked around. All that had remained of the old Manor House was a short stretch of red brick wall abutting a new, yellow brick Community Centre; aluminium window frames and plastic guttering. Two lone trees stood in neat squares in the concrete pavings: a stunted plum and an apple tree, forlorn survivors of the old walled garden. A giant quince tree once stood in the centre, golden fruit veiled in dusty gossamer and succulent white flesh with the taste of pineapple. Around it hung cascades of red Victoria plums and apples of every hue. And from the dark green shade, brown eyes had beckoned, taunting. A taste of forbidden fruit.

At the old main entrance, the solid white gateposts still leaned askew, smitten by the last trailer loads of hay in that balmy summer of '52. The gates had long gone, progressively demolished by a succession of aspiring tractor drivers. Inside the gateway, the long gravel drive had now been cut short and beside it, the old Lodge was converted into a desirable country residence.

Old Arthur had lived there. Polished gaiters and brown check waistcoat, a feudal fixture and fitting that came with the Manor. The last squire had promised him all the windfall timber. We didn't know and used it for our weekend bonfires. He forgave us that, but never the destruction of his immaculate lawns that became our chicken runs. Now they too have gone, under the council playing fields that have also devoured the village green.

The Manor House itself survived the ravages of our training farm, only to fall to the local town planners and their tower block. Gone were the Georgian gables and soft red brick, along with the cow byres and tractor sheds. They now lay buried under two rows of purple-brick garages and tarmac. Above the cringing oak trees that remained, fourteen stories of glass and concrete now rose into the sky.

The avenue of horse chestnut trees though, had survived and still ran down to the ditch by the main road. Problem Row, we called it as we strolled in twos and threes on summer evenings after work. Back and forth under the green canopy, solving the world's problems — and agonising over our personal ones. And at weekends, as the moon rose, it was our lovers' lane, romances sprouting like mushrooms after rain with the girls visiting from London. Walking. Talking. Holding hands. Before the swinging sixties made that all old hat. I walked there with Marie. One problem never resolved . . .

Across the rough track behind the new garages, the knapped flint church still sat tight in its graveyard — the Lord of the Manor never walked far on Sundays. Sanctified, it had resisted the developers. Not so the old Church Lane, along which we'd cycled for miles between high hawthorn hedges, seeking work down rutted farm tracks where muddy-pawed mongrels snapped at our bicycle clips. A full-width road has evened out the rolling drunk-ard's bends and the concrete streets of sixties' overspill estates now carried names of the obliterated farms.

Along the windy pavements that have covered the hedgerows, mums in blue anoraks and drab head scarves trundled prams with Jason and Tracey, to the shops and laundrettes. Where bulge-eyed cows once chewed cud, unemployed lads lay under cus-tomised, clapped out Cortinas and young saplings that had sur-vived the east wind on the roundabout, had been snapped off by bored vandals. And at night, an orange streetlight glare must hide the stars and sky from the wondering eyes of childhood.

I walked back and stood by the gateposts. Across the main road from the Green were once marshes where we strolled down to the river. We sat by yellow flag rushes, dodging giant blue dragonflies and watching snipe drumming in the spring sky. Giant hypermarkets now covered the sedge and tall masts swayed in a newly dredged marina. And beyond, smoke belched from the power-station chimneys.

Behind the Lodge, two mighty cedars still arched their boughs and between them, the patch of grass where we played volleyball. Where Rachel's tightly coiled plaits broke loose to reveal the pre-Raphaelite glory of her hair. Where I fell in love with the unattain-able — and suffered the agonies. She was married. Happily. Two cedar trees, a summer splashed lawn, golden hair in the evening sunlight. That survives; the beauty — and the pain.

By the tower block, a gigantic holm oak now reached as far as the seventh floor — the old oak in whose shelter we once sawed logs for the winter fires. Beside it had been the outside loo where Marcus painted the seat bright blue, and Anita sat on it in the dark. And beyond was once the old laundry shed, where we sat late into the night by the warmth of a simmering copper, talking and argu-ing. Everything was black and white — or red. Discussing Engels, reading the gardener's tale from Boccaccio, listening to Prokofiev and Shostakovitch and reciting excerpts from Gorky's *Mother*, where the young revolutionary swears never to become encum-bered in marriage. We would never marry — ever!

With the early dusk, it was time to go. I walked down between the chestnut trees for the last time and out onto the sports field that has swallowed the village green, where every month we played the village eleven, and every month we lost. Who cared? We played to play then — a whole new world to play for after the horrors of the war.

I turned to look back to the tower block and, closing my eyes, saw the timber huts against the sand dunes, and wondered. Did we ever make it?

Glossary of Hebrew, Arabic and 'adopted' colloquial words

kh is pronouced as ch in scots loch

beseder	okay, fine!
davai!	Gee-up!, let's go!
dunam	4 dunams = 1 acre
dughri	straight out, no bullshit
falkha	arable crops
Fedayeen	Palestinian fighters
felakh	peasant, field-worker
finjan	Arab coffee pot
giyus, giyusim	mobilisation(s)
gizbar	treasurer
globus	ball-point pen
goy, goyim	gentile(s)
hagashah	dining-hall service
horra	frenetic round-dance
Kabalah	Jewish mysticism
kaf-kaf	wooden shower-sandal
keffieh	Arab headscarf
khamsin	hot desert wind
khaver	friend, comrade
kibbutz	collective setlement
kulak	'gentleman farmer'
kum-kum	coffee pot, kettle
kumsitz	coffee evening

lehitra'ot	goodbye, see you
maskir	general secretary
metapelet	children's nurse
meshek	farm, economy
no'ar	youth
Sabra	Israeli born
Seder	first night of Passover
shabbat	sabbath, day-off
shalom	hello, peace
shituf	sharing
shmira	guard duty
toranut	additional-work rota
Tnuva	marketing organisation
Tzahal	Israeli defence forces
vatikim	'old-timers'
wadi	dry river-bed